A Bibliography
of the Writings of
WASHINGTON IRVING

A Bibliography
of the Writings of
WASHINGTON IRVING
A Check List

COMPILED BY

STANLEY T. WILLIAMS

AND

MARY ALLEN EDGE

NEW YORK
OXFORD UNIVERSITY PRESS
1936

CONTENTS

The basis of arrangement of the bibliography is chronological although titles to which no specific date can be assigned have been arranged alphabetically by place of publication and publisher. American and English editions precede those in other languages. Languages other than English are arranged alphabetically; extracts follow the complete works.

v

INTRODUCTION

BIOGRAPHY and bibliography go hand in hand. The present bibliography has developed inevitably out of *The Life of Washington Irving;* it aspires to become both a supplement and a guide to the larger work; and its evolution into the dignity of a separate volume is natural. In its earliest form it was a brief, practical record of Irving's most important published books as they appeared during his lifetime. A study of his contemporary reputation, through the reviews of these, led logically to numerous other titles and editions printed before 1859; then to collected works; next to posthumous issues; and hence to the almost myriad editions, selections, and extracts which were released after the author's death. This substantial body of titles revealed the existence of European versions; urged an examination of Irving's associations with magazines; hinted at interesting composites, adaptations, special printings; and sent the biographer off upon bibliographical adventures more exciting than important. Nevertheless, it is agreeable to recall the eager search for a Spanish "Rip Van Winkle" in obscure libraries in the Peninsula; the acquisition of a Russian edition of *Astoria;* the tracking down of texts in Italian and Swedish. After all, such quests were not futile; they have enriched the bibliographical story of Irving as a whole. Gradually, then, the scope of this bibliography widened. The original plan of a long bibliographical note at the end of the biography proved inadequate. Instead there has resulted an individual volume designed for the student of Washington Irving, containing a check list of all his writings, a check list from its very nature imperfect and incomplete, but thorough, and extending from the year of Irving's first publication (1802) until the present time. Here exists in outline the literary career of our first man of letters.

Such a volume seemed even more practicable after the appearance in 1933 of the first detailed bibliography of Irving.[1] This book, whose genesis was in Mr. Langfeld's distinguished library of Irvingiana, will remain indispensable to the collector and useful to the literary historian. It includes analytical studies of first and second editions, unravelling

---

[1] *Washington Irving. A Bibliography*, compiled by William R. Langfeld and Philip C. Blackburn (New York, 1933). A few brief bibliographies antedated this book, *e.g.*, that in G. H. Putnam, *Washington Irving; His Life and Work* (New York, 1903), but until the publication of Mr. Langfeld's volume, the standard bibliography for the student of Irving was that compiled by Shirley V. Long in *The Cambridge History of American Literature*, I, 510–517. See also the *Critic* (New York), March 31, 1883.

skilfully, for example, the tangled skein of the separate numbers of *The Sketch Book*, and thus permitting conclusive identification of its variant copies. In the cases of other items similar complex problems are ingeniously reasoned, and the entire section called "Chronological List of Works" is of the utmost importance both to the Irving collector and to the bibliography of American literature. In other divisions of this work, Irving's posthumous pieces are described; his connections with magazines are defined; translations of his writings are listed, besides illustrated editions and editions in shorthand. In brief, this bibliography abounds in facts helpful to the biographer and the critic of Irving, as in its first detailed list of his contributions to magazines. What Mr. Langfeld and Mr. Blackburn omitted, quite properly from this descriptive bibliography, was an investigation of subsequent editions and also a record of biographical and critical literature concerning Irving. The present volume may, then, supplement the more technical work of its predecessor by sketching the later fortunes of Irving's books and by suggesting the nature of the related critical literature. Our debt to the earlier bibliography and its compilers we gratefully acknowledge. If studied together, the two volumes will be found to complement each other, and to offer, presumably, the most complete bibliographical record of any American literary figure.

Such a record makes possible deductions significant for literary history. First of all, it illumines indirectly conditions affecting the publication of books in nineteenth-century America; that is, it suggests the influence upon Irving, and so upon other writers, of the lack of international copyright law. The most enlightening study of this question in its relation to American literature occurs in a recent bibliography of James Fenimore Cooper.[1] In the recently published biography of Irving his conflicts with booksellers and publishers are frequently described,[2] but certain facts implicit in this bibliography of Irving may well be restated here. It will be observed, for instance, that Irving usually issued two editions of each work simultaneously, one in England, another in the United States. The reasons underlying this procedure Professor R. E. Spiller summarizes in his introduction to the bibliography of Cooper:

> The American copyright law of 1790 was explicit. An American author could copyright his book in the United States regardless of the date of publication elsewhere, but authors who were not citizens of the United States were allowed no protection whatever. The only determining factor was citizenship, although prompt copyright entry was a valuable protection against pirates. The English law was vague in its statement of its protection for the work of aliens. . . . Citizenship had nothing to do with the problem, for any author, whether English or not, could obtain protection in England by announcing his book there before its appearance in any other country.[3]

[1] *A Descriptive Bibliography of the Writings of James Fenimore Cooper*, by Robert E. Spiller and Philip Blackburn (New York, 1934).

[2] See *The Life of Washington Irving*, II, 20–23.   [3] *Op. cit.*, pp. 4–5.

Cooper's adjustment to these exigencies Professor Spiller discusses in his introduction, so effectively that it is likely to endure as a source for later historians of copyright.[1] Irving's management of the same problems should be described briefly here. From the days of his early apprenticeship in writing he was reluctantly trained in the warfare engendered by the absence of a just copyright system. As early as 1813 we hear of him striving to aid Thomas Campbell to obtain copyright for a work to be published at the same time in England and America.[2] Four years later, while forming a plan for the republication of selected English books in the United States, he commented on the fact that Moore's *Lalla Rookh* yielded no profits because of several rival editions in the United States.[3] Throughout his life Irving moved more easily than Cooper in the midst of these entanglements, for several reasons. One was such early experiences; another was his tact and his acceptance of conditions as they were; still another was that he wrote *The Sketch Book* under the stimulus of necessity. If writing were to be his trade, he must master the rules of the game. This knowledge he acquired with less friction than did Cooper. In 1819 he forwarded the manuscript of *The Sketch Book* to New York with explicit instructions to Henry Brevoort:

> I wish the copyright secured for me, and the work printed and then sold to one or more booksellers, who will take the whole impression at a fair discount, and give cash or good notes for it. This makes short work of it, and is more profitable to the author than selling the copyright.[4]

Yet even now he learned his next lesson, for English magazines instantly plotted to pirate the book.[5] To anticipate these, he was forced to issue an English edition with John Miller at his own expense.[6] Simultaneous printing in both countries was evidently the only resource of the American author against such practices.

From now on Irving lived alternately in Europe and America. But in whichever country he happened to be he kept in close communication with literary agents, who acted for him quickly and intelligently. Schemes for the precise timing of publication in both countries became integral parts of his battle for fame, with the victories not always on his side. To his grief, as one example, a spurious edition of *Salmagundi* was brought out in London in 1824, but *Bracebridge Hall* (1822) and *Tales of a Traveller* accomplished his international dating to a nicety, the latter appearing on August 25, 1824 in London, and exactly one day earlier in New York.[7] Even before he had written a line of the

---

[1] See S. T. Williams, "Authorship in Irving's Day," *Saturday Review of Literature*, December 29, 1934.

[2] P. M. Irving, *Life and Letters of Washington Irving* (New York, 1862–1864), I, 303.

[3] *Idem*, I, 374.

Irving to Henry Brevoort, London, March 3, 1819, *idem*, I, 415.

[5] *Idem*, I, 436.   [6] *Idem*, I, 445.

[7] Part I. See *idem*, II, 212.

Life and Voyages of Christopher Columbus (1828) Irving exhorted his
friend, C. R. Leslie, then his representative in England: *"Whichever
bookseller you make an arrangement with, get him to announce the work
at once as preparing for publication by me."* [1] The author's italics reflect
his anxiety. Of the English edition of this book he sent proof sheets
to America as fast as they came from the press. Such precautions, to
say nothing of his two years of intense toil in Madrid, might seem to
entitle Irving to the natural reward of his labors. Not so. The reader
of the biography may recall the unpleasant sequel. A few months
after the publication of the *Columbus* Irving learned that an anonymous
plagiarist was at work on an abridgment of his four volumes. Wearily
he sat down and after nineteen days' incessant work concluded the four
hundred pages of his own epitome of the book. Thus through the
vigilance of his friends and his own patience he was able to defeat this
"paltry poacher." [2] The careful synchronization of editions evident
in the bibliography was motivated by such merciless competition. Is
it strange that humble American authors without Irving's powerful
European connections and without his network of alert scouts should
hesitate before engaging in the vocation of writing?

Apart from such antics to preserve double copyrights, both Cooper
and Irving wasted days in haggling for terms of publication, in allotting
the author's share of the profits of his work, in arguing about matters
which to-day are usually settled, after brief discussion, with a stroke of
the pen. Let aggrieved authors of the twentieth century read Walter
Scott's frank letter to Irving on conditions in the trade, in which he
declares that, arrange it as you will, the bookseller "contrives to take
the lion's share of the booty." [3] Sometimes the copyright was sold
outright; in 1827 Irving offered that of the *Columbus* to John Murray
for three thousand guineas. A more usual method, however, was publication upon shares. "The mode of doing so . . . ," wrote Irving,

> is to agree about the number of copies in an edition, and the retail price to
> be placed upon them; to multiply the number of copies by the price of each,
> and divide the gross amount by six. For this sixth part, the publisher to
> give his notes to the author. [4]

Such was the contract for the English edition of the *Columbus;* for the
American version, the Carvills, then the most prominent booksellers
in New York, "agreed to give seven thousand dollars for the two thousand copies in sheets, one thousand dollars on delivery, the remainder
in four, six, and nine months." [5] At other times the copyright was
leased for a period of years; or the author managed the stereotyping;
or he bought the stereotype plates from the publishers; or he printed

[1] Irving to C. R. Leslie, Bordeaux, February 3, 1826, *idem*, II, 250.
[2] *Idem*, II, 352. See *The Life of Washington Irving*, I, 354-355.
[3] Walter Scott to Irving, Edinburgh, December 4, 1819, P. M. I., I, 443.
[4] Irving to John Murray, Madrid, July 29, 1827, *idem*, II, 263.
[5] Peter Irving to Irving, 1828, *idem*, II, 280.

at his own expense and received a premium. But whatever the method, "there is always," wrote Irving, "a chance for competition and piracy." [1]

Yet such confusion was more tolerable than the lack of international copyright. When nearly sixty years old, Irving still confronted the old obstacles, hampering his own writings and those of younger writers. "How much," he said in a public letter of 1840,

> this growing literature may be retarded by the present state of our copy-right law, I had recently an instance, in the cavalier treatment of a work of merit, written by an American, who had not yet established a commanding name in the literary market. I undertook, as a friend, to dispose of it for him, but found it impossible to get an offer from any of our principal pub-lishers. They even declined to publish it at the author's cost, alleging that it was not worth their while to trouble themselves about native works, of doubtful success, while they could pick and choose among the successful works daily poured out by the British press, *for which they had nothing to pay for copyright.* This simple fact spoke volumes to me, as I trust it will do to all who peruse these lines.[2]

Moreover, as the worth of American literature increased, in spite of these and other handicaps, piracy in England of American texts re-doubled, and the English law permitting copyright to foreigners was challenged. *"The poison chalice returned!"* remarked the *New-York Mirror*.[3] In 1851 Bentley planned suit against Bohn for alleged in-fringement of the copyright of Irving's works; and in the files of John Murray's Albemarle Street office is a curious autobiography of Wash-ington Irving, written to suggest that its author, by ancestry and by long sojourn abroad, was virtually an Englishman, and thus entitled to British copyright! [4]

With such facts in mind the titles and dates in this bibliography take on meaning. In addition, aside from the hints concerning the world of publishers, the reader will also find here other implications, concern-ing literary taste in America, concerning European attitudes toward books produced in the growing republic, concerning the relative vogue in America and Europe of particular works of Irving's, concerning, finally, Irving's general reputation during the span of approximately a century and a quarter.

Thus the bibliography shows that Irving during his lifetime was famous not merely as an essayist, but as a historian, a biographer, and a contributor to periodicals. For example, before the year of his death, there had appeared more than two score editions in English of both the *Life and Voyages of Christopher Columbus* and *The Conquest of Gra-nada*, besides eleven of the now forgotten *Biography of Margaret Miller*

---

[1] Irving to A. H. Everett, Bordeaux, January 31, 1826, *idem*, II, 248.

[2] Irving to the Editor of the *Knickerbocker*, January, 1840, *idem*, III, 150. See *The Life of Washington Irving*, II, 213–215.

[3] See *idem*, II, 213.

[4] See *idem*, II, 214.

Davidson. Again, although the first volume of his *Life of George Washington* was not printed until 1855, he himself lived to see during the four final years of his career ten editions of this biography. Not only did *The Sketch Book*, which was to outlive the changing literary fashions of an entire century, enjoy dozens of reprintings, but *Bracebridge Hall*, *Tales of a Traveller*, *The Alhambra*, and even lesser works, were repeatedly reissued. Before 1859 at least sixty different editions of *The Sketch Book* were available, and about one half this number of each of these three other books was also obtainable. Irving's hold upon his generation was not solely as the creator of Rip Van Winkle and Ichabod Crane. He was acclaimed as the versatile (so his contemporaries believed) delineator of English manor halls, Spanish palaces, and western forests, and as the gifted biographer of Columbus, Goldsmith, Mahomet, and George Washington.[1]

Through the bibliography we also see Irving as the most widely translated American writer of his generation, with the possible exception of Cooper. It should be remembered that translation of American books had not yet become the commonplace of to-day.[2] Irving's sway, within two decades of *The Sketch Book*, over substantial audiences in France, Germany, and Spain, is a notable part of his achievement as a pioneer in our literature. Prior to 1859 one or more of his books were translated into eleven European tongues (including Danish, Dutch, Greek, Icelandic, Polish, Russian, and Swedish), and after his death, besides further versions in these languages, into Czech, Welsh, and Esperanto.[3] French translations have been the most numerous and the most catholic in interest, but German versions have been hardly less comprehensive, despite their emphasis upon the tales and the Western books. Translations of the latter probably exerted an influence upon the German emigrations to America in the 'forties. Spanish translators stressed characteristically books dealing with Peninsula themes.[4] Versions in other languages have usually been evoked by special interests, such as the Italian in the *Columbus* or the Dutch in *A History of New York*. Greek, Czech, and Icelandic titles are, of course, inconsequential compared with the scores of translations in French and German, but all such add their mites of testimony concerning the sweep and vitality of Irving's contemporary fame.

The bibliography attests also Irving's influence, for good and ill, upon our flaccid commonplace culture of a century ago. This it does by demonstrating his insistent presence in the minds of the reading public. Episodes and characters from his stories, passages of description from his essays, anecdotes from his biographies appear and reappear

[1] See, in particular, pp. 88–93, under *The Life of Oliver Goldsmith*.

[2] See H. Lüdeke, "American Literature in Germany," *American Literature*, May, 1934, pp. 168–175; and Jean Simon, "French Studies in American Literature and Civilization," *idem*, pp. 176–190.   [3] See pp. 78, 93, 135.

[4] See pp. 33–35, under the Spanish translations of *The Alhambra*.

in endless reprintings in "selected works," gift books, annuals, magazines, illustrated collections, and school texts. So "Dame Irving," as
Laughton Osborn ruthlessly called him, helped to shape the literary
taste of his epoch.[1] In the numerous school texts for use in France
and Germany, adorned with many a learned annotation, young Euro-
peans first sampled the flavor of our mother tongue. Nowhere so clearly
as in these miscellaneous reprintings of Irving do we see him as a sentimental, vapid, but staple part of the mental diet of the epoch just preceding the Civil War.

Observe also, to complete the story, how in the wake of this en-
thusiastic if unwise acceptance of Irving as a classic, there followed
naturally the literature of criticism, or rather of adulation and eulogy.[2]
Note among these titles the less sentimental attitude of the last quarter
of the century, and, finally, in our own day, criticism based upon sounder
standards. Such recent evaluation studies Irving from the point of view
of the literary historian. It exhumes all that he has written in letters,
journals, and unpublished manuscripts.[3] It studies his greatest gift, his
style, and his place as a pioneer in a *bourgeois* culture. And always it
aims to place him in perspective. It observes that, though "Rip Van
Winkle" and "The Legend of Sleepy Hollow" are often reprinted, the
biographies and sentimental pieces seldom reappear in the modern age.
In fine, the bibliography shows that Irving survives for the literary historian as the exponent of a tradition, as an index to the culture of a
period; it reveals that he lives in *belles lettres* to-day primarily as a superb
technician in a few enduring sketches. Such facts, we believe, are patent
between the lines of this bibliography.

The Table of Contents lists the sections for this bibliography and
indicates the arrangement for each section. For particular titles, see the
Index to the bibliography, pp. 193–200. The last section (XI) deserves
perhaps further explanation; it attempts to list significant biographical
and critical writing concerning Irving. It should be noticed that this
part of the bibliography is selective. Since 1820 reviews of Irving's
books have been almost innumerable, and biographical and critical
estimates range from inconsequential diatribes and puffs to a few ex-
cellent analytical essays in recent criticism. The material collected for
this bibliography includes copies or notices of literally hundreds of
reviews or expositions of Irving's writings and character, many of
which are quoted or cited in the notes and in Appendix III of the biography. It would be confusing to record every ephemeral printed notice
apropos of Irving, and the last section pretends to no such encyclo-
pedic futility. Section XI does not record books and articles of a more
special nature, which have been uncovered by research; such also
receive attention in the notes of the biography. The titles listed are

---

[1] See *The Life of Washington Irving*, II, 102.
[2] See Section XI, pp. 181–192.
[3] See Sections IV and V, pp. 15–18.

representative and varied. They include specimens of criticism written at the outset of Irving's career and also evaluations published during the past year of 1935; among them are examples, throughout more than a century, of foreign criticism. It has seemed best in some cases, in order to suggest contemporary judgments of Irving, to refer to the original form of the review or notice in a magazine rather than to the reprinted version (*e.g.*, reviews of *The Alhambra*). The basic object of this section is, then, to present a discriminated catalogue of writings concerning Irving, biographical, critical, and broadly informational, which will prove serviceable in the future study of this author. Such a winnowing may seem somewhat arbitrary, but we hope that the completeness of the bibliography in other respects may condone these omissions, if omissions they can really be called.

The compilers of this bibliography have endeavored to examine personally as many titles as possible. Such titles are designated by an asterisk (*), and incompleteness in such entries is indicated by three dots (. . .). Other titles have been taken from printed sources. These sources have, whenever possible, been tested for accuracy, but undoubtedly their entries include condensations, alterations, variations of titles, and errors. The object, in the use of such material, has not been completeness, which from the nature of the bibliography is impossible, but the acceptance of only reliable data and the exclusion of all doubtful statements.[1] A few items, therefore, are fragmentary. We shall be grateful to readers who will supply corrections or supplementary information. Acknowledgments for aid in compilation are included under the general acknowledgments in the preface of *The Life of Washington Irving*. The chief sources of this bibliography are as follows:

SOURCES

Bibliographies and Catalogues

Årskatalog för svenska bokhandeln, 1856–1932. Stockholm, Svenska bokförläggareföreningen, 1856–[1933]

Aarskatalog over norsk litteratur, 1902–1933 . . . Oslo, Cammermeyer, 1903–34.

Allibone, S. A. A critical dictionary of English literature and British and American authors . . . Philadelphia, Lippincott, 1871. 3 v.

—— Supplement . . . by J. F. Kirk. Philadelphia, Lippincott, 1891. 2 v.

American catalogue of books . . . 1876–1900. New York, Publishers' weekly, 1881–1901.

Annual American catalogue, 1886–1910. New York, Publishers' weekly, 1887–1911.

---

[1] One source, for example, which remains inaccessible is the records, packed in bales, of G. P. Putnam's Sons, publishers of many of Irving's writings during his lifetime.

Astor library. Catalogue . . . New York, 1857–61. 4 v.

—— Supplement . . . New York, 1866.

— Catalogue. Cambridge [Mass.] 1886–88. 4 v.

Bibliografía española; revista general de la imprenta, de la librería y de las industrias que concurren á la fabricación del libro. Madrid, Cámara oficial del libro, 1901–22.

Bibliografía general española e hispano-americana. Madrid, Cámaras oficiales del libro, 1923–34.

Bibliographie de Belgique . . . Bruxelles, Bibliothèque royale, 1876–1933.

Boston Athenæum library. Catalogue . . . Boston, 1874–82. 5 v.

Bradford, T. L. Bibliographer's manual of American history . . . edited and revised by S. V. Henkels. Philadelphia, Henkels, 1907–10. 5 v.

British museum. Library. Catalogue of printed books . . . London, Printed by Clowes, 1881–1900.

—— Supplement. London, Printed by Clowes, 1900–01.

Brown university. John Carter Brown library. Bibliotheca americana . . . Providence, 1919–31. 3 v.

Brunet, J. C. Manuel du libraire et de l'amateur de livres . . . 5. édition . . . Paris, Didot, 1860–65. 6 v.

Catalogue Valdras 1929–1933 . . . Paris, Vald. Rasmussen, 1930–34.

Church, E. D. Catalogue of books relating to the discovery and early history of North and South America . . . compiled and annotated by George Watson Cole. New York, Dodd, 1907. 5 v.

The Critic. New York, 1883. No. 3, v. 65.

Cumulative book index . . . New York, Wilson, 1898–1934.

Dansk bogfortegnelse . . . København, Gad, 1861–1933.

Dansk boghandlertidende . . . København, Gad, 1855–1933.

Detroit. Public library. General catalogue [and supplements 1–3]. Detroit, 1889–1904. 5 v.

Deutscher Literatur-Katalog, 1904–1931. Leipzig, Kochler & Volckmar A. G. [1904–31?]

Deutsches Bücherverzeichnis der Jahre 1911–1930 . . . Leipzig, Verlag des Börsenvereins der deutschen Buchhändler, 1915–33.

Edinburgh. University. Catalogue of the printed books in the library of the University of Edinburgh. [Edinburgh] Printed by T. and A. Constable, ltd., at the University press, 1918–23. 3 v.

English catalogue of books . . . 1801=1836 . . . London, The Publishers' circular, limited, 1914.

English catalogue of books published . . . 1835–1933. London, The Publishers' circular, limited, 1864–1934.

Evans, Charles. American bibliography . . . Chicago, Blakely press, 1903–34. 12 v.

Faculty of advocates. Library. Catalogue of the printed books . . . Edinburgh and London, William Blackwood and sons, 1863–78. 6 v.

— Supplementary volume. Edinburgh and London, William Blackwood and sons, 1879.

Fletcher, W. I. The "A.L.A." index; an index to general literature . . . Second edition . . . Boston, Houghton Mifflin co., 1901.

Florence. R. Biblioteca nazionale centrale. Bolletino delle pubblicazioni italiane ricevute per diritto di stampa, 1886–1932. Firenze, 1886–1933.

Foley, P. K. American authors, 1795–1895; a bibliography of first and notable editions. Boston, 1897.

Georg, Karl. Schlagwort Katalog; Verzeichnis der Bücher und Landkarten in sachlicher Anordnung. Hannover, L. Lemmermann, 1889–1913.

Halbjahrsverzeichnis der Neuerscheinungen des deutschen Buchhandels . . . Leipzig, Verlag des Börsenvereins der deutschen Buchhändler, 1798–1934.

Heinsius, Wilhelm. Allgemeines Bücher-Lexikon, 1700–1892. Leipzig, Brockhaus, 1812–94.

Heredia y Livermore, Ricardo, *conde de Benahavis*. Catalogue de la bibliothèque de M. Ricardo Heredia . . . Paris, É. Paul, L. Huard et Guillemin, 1891–94. 4 v.

Hidalgo, Dionisio. Diccionario general de bibliografía española. Madrid, Impr. de las Escuelas pías, 1862–81. 7 v.

Hinrichs, J. C. Fünfjahrs-Katalog der im deutschen Buchhandel erschienenen Bücher, Zeitschriften, Landkarten, etc. . . . 1851–1912. Leipzig, Hinrichs, 1851–1912.

Islandica, an annual relating to Iceland and the Fiske Icelandic collection in Cornell university library . . . Ithaca, N. Y., Cornell university library, 1908–33.

John Rylands library, Manchester. Catalogue . . . Manchester, J. E. Cornish, 1899. 3 v.

Kayser, C. G. . . . Vollständiges Bücher-lexikon . . . 1750–1910. Leipzig, C. H. Tauchnitz, 1834–1912.

Kelly, James. American catalogue of books published in the United States from Jan. 1861 to Jan. 1871. New York, Wiley, 1866–71. 2 v.

Kief. Universitet . . . Catalogus librorum bibliothecae Caesareae universitatis S. Vladimiri . . . Kief, 1854–58. 5 v.

Langfeld, W. R. Washington Irving. A bibliography compiled by William R. Langfeld with the bibliographic assistance of Philip C. Blackburn. New York, The New York public library, 1933.

Leningrad. Universitet. [Catalogue of books in the University Library.] St. Petersburg, 1896–98. 2v.

Le Soudier, Henri. Bibliographie française . . . 2. édition . . . Paris, Le Soudier, 1900.

La librairie française. Catalogue général des ouvrages en vente au 1er janvier 1930 . . . Paris, au cercle de la librairie, 1931. 2 v.

—— Supplément au 1er janvier 1933 . . . Paris, au cercle de la librairie, 1933.

London catalogue of books published in Great Britain . . . from 1814 to 1846. Oxford, Hodgson, 1846.

London library. Catalogue . . . by C. T. Hagberg Wright . . . and C. J. Purnell . . . London, 1913–14. 2 v.

—— Supplement, 1913–1920 . . . London, 1920.

—— Supplement, 1920–1928 . . . London, 1929.

Lorenz, Otto. Catalogue général de la librairie française. 1840–1890. Paris, H. Champion, 1867–1932.

Lowndes, W. T. The bibliographer's manual of English literature . . . London, Bell & Daldy, 1865. 6 v.

Norsk bogfortegnelse, 1814–[1900]. Kristiania, 1848–1912.

Norsk bogfortegnelse, 1883–1933. Udgiven af Universitets-bibliotheket. Christiania, Cammermeyer, 1884–1934.

Pagliaini, Attilio. Catalogo generale della libreria italiana, 1847–1899. Milano, Assoc. tipografico-libraria italiana, 1901–05. 3 v.

Palau y Dulcet, Antonio. Manual del librero hispano-americano . . . Barcelona, Libreria anticuaria, 1923–27. 7 v.

Paris. Bibliothèque nationale. Catalogue général des livres imprimés. Auteurs. Paris, Imprimerie nationale, 1900–34.

Peabody institute of the city of Baltimore. Catalogue of the library . . . Baltimore, 1883–92. 5 v.

—— Second catalogue . . . including the additions made since 1882. Baltimore, 1896–1905. 8 v.

Pittsburgh. Carnegie library. Classified catalogue . . . Pittsburgh, Carnegie library, 1907–16. 10 v.

Poole, W. F. and Fletcher, W. I. Index to periodical literature . . . 1802–1881. Revised edition. Boston, Houghton Mifflin co., 1891. 2 v.

— — Supplements, Jan. 1882–Dec. 1901. Boston, Houghton Mifflin co. [c 1887–1902] 4 v.

Price, L. M. English > German literary influences. Bibliography and survey . . . Berkeley, University of California press, 1919. (University of California publications in modern philology, v. 9)

Publishers' trade list annual, 1873–1934. New York, Publishers' weekly, 1873–1934.

Quaritch, Bernard. General catalogue of books offered to the public [and supplements] . . . London, 1887–97. 17 v.

Quérard, J. M. La France littéraire; ou, Dictionnaire bibliographique des savants, historiens, et gens de lettres de la France. Paris, 1827–64. 12 v.

— La littérature française contemporaine, 1827–1849. Paris, 1842–57. 6 v.

Reader's guide to periodical literature . . . New York, Wilson, 1915–32.

Rich, Obadiah. Bibliotheca Americana nova . . . London, Rich and sons, 1846. 2 v.

Roorbach, O. A. Bibliotheca Americana . . . 1820–1861 . . . New York, Roorbach, 1852–61. 4 v.

Royal empire society, London. Catalogue of the library . . . [London] 1930–32. 3 v.

Sabin, Joseph. Bibliotheca Americana. A dictionary of books relating to America, from its discovery to the present time . . . New York, Bibliographical society of New York, 1868–1933. 24 v.

Salvá y Pérez, Vicente. Catálogo de la biblioteca de Salvá escrito por D. Pedro Salvá y Mallén . . . Valencia, Impr. de Ferrer de Orga, 1872. 2 v.

Schapiro, I. Bibliography of Hebrew translations of English works. New York, 1929.
Reprinted from the A. S. Freidus memorial volume.

Svensk bokförteckning, 1913–1931. Stockholm, Svenska bokhandlareföreningen, 1913–31.

Svensk bok-katalog för åren 1866–1925. Stockholm, Svenska bokförläggareföreningen [1878–1929]

United States catalog . . . Third edition. White Plains, N. Y., Wilson, 1912.

— — Supplement, 1912–1917. New York, Wilson, 1918.

— — Supplement, Jan. 1918–June 1921. New York, Wilson, 1921.

— — Books in print Jan. 1, 1928. New York, Wilson, 1928.

Whitaker's cumulative book list . . . 1924–1934. London, Whitaker, 1924–34.

Libraries

Birmingham, England. Free libraries.
British museum, London.
Granada. Universidad. Biblioteca.
Hispanic society of America, New York city. Library.
Historical society of Pennsylvania, Philadelphia. Library.
Library of Congress, Washington, D. C.
Madrid. Biblioteca nacional.
Mount Holyoke College, South Hadley, Mass. Library.
New York historical society. Library.
New York public library.
Paris. Bibliothèque nationale.
Seville. Biblioteca municipal.
Yale university library, New Haven.

Private Collections

Dr. Frank K. Hallock, Cromwell, Connecticut.
Mrs. Louis Dupont Irving, Tarrytown, New York.
William R. Langfeld, Philadelphia, Pennsylvania.
Luis Seco de Lucena, Granada, Spain.
Dr. Roderick Terry, Newport, Rhode Island.
Stanley T. Williams, New Haven, Connecticut.

STANLEY T. WILLIAMS and MARY ALLEN EDGE

New Haven, Connecticut, January 1, 1936

A Bibliography
of the Writings of
WASHINGTON IRVING

I. COMPLETE WORKS

Volumes of selected works published with the title: Works, have been included in this section.

The works of Washington Irving. Paris, Baudry and Galignani, 1824–29. 16 v.

The works of Washington Irving. Paris, Galignani, 1825. 10 v.
  First collected edition.
  Known as the large-type Galignani edition.
  Contents. — Salmagundi. A history of New York. The sketch book. Bracebridge Hall. Tales of a traveller.

Washington Irving's works . . . Zwickau, Schumann, 1828. (Pocket-edition of English classics)

The complete works of Washington Irving. With a memoir of the author. Paris, Galignani, 1834.

* The complete works of Washington Irving in one volume, with a memoir of the author. Paris, Baudry's European library [etc., etc.] 1834.
  Engraved portrait by Blanchard.
  Contents. — Memoir of Washington Irving. — Salmagundi. — A history of New York. — The sketch book. — Bracebridge Hall. — Tales of a traveller. — Life and voyages of Christopher Columbus. — Voyages and discoveries of the companions of Columbus. — A chronicle of the conquest of Granada. — The Alhambra.

* The complete works of Washington Irving in one volume, with a memoir of the author. Francfort o. M., Schmerber, 1834.
  Published in 6 pts.

* — — Francfort o. M., Schmerber, 1834.
  Pocket-edition.

* — — Francfort on the Main, Schmerber, 1835. 2 v.

* [The works of Washington Irving.] Philadelphia, Carey, Lea, & Blanchard, 1836.

* The works of Washington Irving . . . Philadelphia, Lea and Blanchard, 1840. 2 v.
  Contents. — v. 1. The sketch book. Knickerbocker's History of New York. Bracebridge Hall. — v. 2. Tales of a traveller. A chronicle of the conquest of Granada. The Alhambra.

The works of Washington Irving. Author's revised edition. New-York, G. P. Putnam, 1848–50.   15 v.

Published under Irving's supervision.

The volumes were issued in the following order:

A history of New York		September 1848
The sketch book		October 1848
Life and voyages of Christopher Columbus	Vol. I	November 1848
Bracebridge Hall		December 1848
Life and voyages of Christopher Columbus	Vol. II	January 1849
Life and voyages of Christopher Columbus	Vol. III	February 1849
Tales of a traveller		March 1849
Astoria		April 1849
The Crayon miscellany		May 1849
The adventures of Captain Bonneville		June [?] 1849
The life of Oliver Goldsmith		August [?] 1849
Mahomet and his successors	Vol. I	December 1849
Mahomet and his successors	Vol. II	April 1850
The Alhambra		May 1850
The conquest of Granada		August [?] 1850

* The works of Washington Irving . . . New-York, G. P. Putnam, 1849–55.   16 v.

New edition, revised.

The works of Washington Irving. Stuyvesant large-type edition. New York, G. P. Putnam, 1849–57.   12 v. in 10.

The works of Washington Irving. London, H. Bohn, 1850.   10 v.

The works of Washington Irving. London, Routledge, 1850.   8 v.

* . . . The works of Washington Irving . . . New York, G. P. Putnam's sons [c 1850–80]   28 v. in 14.

At head of title: The Kinderhook edition.

— — New York, G. P. Putnam's sons [c 1850–80]   10 v.

Each volume contains the text of two works, paged separately.

The complete works of Washington Irving. Now first collected. London, Bohn, 1851.   10 v.

* The works of Washington Irving. London, G. Routledge [1851?]   8 v.   12mo.

— — London, G. Routledge [1851?]   12 v.   post 12mo.

* The works of Washington Irving. New edition, revised. New York, G. P. Putnam, 1851–52.   15 v.

The works of Washington Irving. Riverside edition. New York, G. P. Putnam, 1851–60.   21 v.

The works of Washington Irving. London, H. G. Bohn, 1851–62.

Uniform with The Standard library.

The works of Washington Irving. Illustrated. London, H. G. Bohn, 1853. 10 v.

The works of Washington Irving. New edition, revised. New York, G. P. Putnam, 1853–54. 23 v.

* The works of Washington Irving. New edition, revised. London, Bohn, 1854. 10 v.

* The complete works of Washington Irving. In one volume. With a memoir of the author. Paris, Baudry's European library, 1854.

* The works of Washington Irving. New edition, revised. New York, G. P. Putnam & co., 1856–57. 10 v.
   A reissue of the 1849–51 editions.
   Vol. 2, 1856.
   Each volume has also special t.-p.

The works of Washington Irving. New edition, revised . . . New York, G. P. Putnam & co., 1857. 15 v.
   A reissue of the 1849–51 editions.

The works of Washington Irving. New edition, revised. New York, 1859–61. 22 v.

The works of Washington Irving. London, 1859–76. 14 v.

The works of Washington Irving. Sunnyside edition. New York, G. P. Putnam, 1860. 28 v.

— — New York, G. P. Putnam, 1860. 21 v.

The works of Washington Irving. National edition. New York, Putnam [1860?] 21 v.

The works of Washington Irving. New edition, revised. New York, 1860–61. 21 v.

The works of Washington Irving. New edition, revised. New York, G. P. Putnam, 1860–67. 28 v.
   100 copies printed on tinted paper.

* The works of Washington Irving. New edition, revised. New York, G. P. Putnam, 1861–64. 22 v.
   Vol. 1, 1864.
   Vol. 2, 12, 22 have engraved title-pages.

* The works of Washington Irving. New edition, revised. New York, G. P. Putnam, 1864. 26 v.

The complete works of Washington Irving. Geoffrey Crayon edition. With an introduction by Charles Dudley Warner. New York, G. P. Putnam [1865?] 27 v.

The works of Washington Irving. Library edition. London, Bell & Daldy, 1866. 10 v.

* . . . The works of Washington Irving. Knickerbocker edition. New York, G. P. Putnam, 1867.
   Specimen pages of the works.

The works of Washington Irving. Knickerbocker edition. New York, G. P. Putnam, 1869. 27 v.

* The works of Washington Irving. Knickerbocker edition. Phila-
     delphia, J. B. Lippincott, 1870–71.   27 v.
     Vol. 1–8, 10, 13, 15–17 are also "Author's revised edition."
[The works of Washington Irving] Author's revised edition. Phila-
     delphia, J. B. Lippincott & co., 1872.   28 v.
The works of Washington Irving. London, 1872–77.
The works of Washington Irving. New York, Pollard & Moss, 1874.
     A one-volume edition containing fragmentary texts of Irving's works.
* The works of Washington Irving. London, H. G. Bohn, 1876.   11 v.
     (Bohn's standard library)
* . . . Life and works of Washington Irving . . . with an original
     biographical sketch prepared expressly for this edition by R. H.
     Stoddard. Complete and unabridged. New York, Pollard & Moss,
     1880.
     At head of title: The Kaaterskill edition.
Irving's works. Geoffrey Crayon edition . . . [New York, G. P.
     Putnam's sons, 1880–83]   27 v.
* [The works of Washington Irving.] New York, G. P. Putnam's sons,
     1881.   8 v.
     People's edition.
     Vol. 1–3, 5–8 have added engraved title-pages.
The works of Washington Irving. Spuyten Duyvil edition. New
     York, G. P. Putnam [1881?]   12 v.
     Does not include P. M. Irving's Life and letters of Washington Irving.
* The works of Washington Irving. Hudson edition. New York, G. P.
     Putnam's sons, 1882.   27 v.
The works of Washington Irving. New York, R. Worthington, 1884.
     6 v.
The works of Washington Irving. Stratford edition. New York,
     G. P. Putnam's sons [1884?]   7 v.
     Contents. — The sketch book. Knickerbocker's History of New
         York. The life of Christopher Columbus. The life of George
         Washington.
The works of Washington Irving. Stuyvesant edition. New York,
     G. P. Putnam's sons [1884?]   7 v.
     Contents. — The sketch book. Knickerbocker's History of New
         York. Life of Christopher Columbus. Life of George Washington.
The works of Washington Irving. Tappan-Zee edition. New York,
     G. P. Putnam's sons [1889?]   12 v.
     Sold in an oak case with a bronze bust of Irving by John Rogers.
     Contents. — The sketch book. Knickerbocker's History of New
         York. Bracebridge Hall. Tales of a traveller. The Alhambra.
         The Crayon miscellany. Wolfert's Roost.
The works of Washington Irving. Knickerbocker edition. New York,
     G. P. Putnam, 1891.   40 v.
     Illustrated from photographs.

The works of Washington Irving. Author's autograph edition. New York, Putnam, 1895. 40 v.
Edition of 500 sets, printed on Ruisdael paper.

The works of Washington Irving. Limited Holly edition. New York, Putnam, 1895. 40 v.

The works of Washington Irving. Complete edition. New York, Putnam, 1897. 15 v.
With a life of Irving by R. H. Stoddard.

The complete works of Washington Irving. Westchester edition. New York, 1899. 20 v.
Edition limited to 1000 sets.

The works of Washington Irving. New York, Putnam [1901?] 23 v.
People's edition.

The complete writings of Washington Irving, including his life. New York, The Collegiate society, 1905. 21 v.
National edition.
Bibliographical foot-notes.
500 copies printed.

The works of Washington Irving . . . New York, T. Y. Crowell & co., 1909–10. 10 v.

The works of Washington Irving. New handy volume edition. New York, Putnam [1922?] 12 v.

The works of Washington Irving. London, Routledge [18–?] 12 v.

The works of Washington Irving. New York, Bigelow, Brown & co. [192–?] 10 v.
Nottingham edition de luxe.

The works of Washington Irving. New York, A. L. Burt co., inc. [192–?] 10 v.
Illustrated.

The works of Washington Irving. New York, A. L. Burt co. [191–?] 8 v.
Illustrated.

* The works of Washington Irving. New York, P. F. Collier [188–?] 3 v.

[The works of Washington Irving.] New York, The Continental press [190–?] 8 v.

[The works of Washington Irving.] New York, The Cortlandt press [19–?] 8 v.

The works of Washington Irving. New York, T. Y. Crowell & co. [191–?] 10 v.
Kelmscott edition.

The works of Washington Irving . . . New York, De Fau & co. [19–?] 16 v.

The works of Washington Irving. New York, Putnam [191–?] 24 v.
Hudson edition.

The works of Washington Irving. Nepperhan edition. New York, Putnam [192–?]   40 v.
Illustrated.

The works of Washington Irving. New York, Putnam [19–?]   40 v.
The new Knickerbocker edition.

The works of Washington Irving. New York, Putnam [192–?]   20 v.
The new Stuyvesant edition.

The complete writings of Washington Irving. Illustrated . . . by F. S. Coburn, Arthur Rackham, F. O. C. Darley [et al.]   New York, Putnam [n.d.]   40 v.
The new Sunnyside edition.
600 signed and numbered sets.

The works of Washington Irving. New York, Putnam [19–?]   20 v.
Pocantico edition.

The complete works of Washington Irving. New York, Putnam [192–?]   40 v.
Pocantico edition.
Illustrated.
1000 sets printed.

The works of Washington Irving. Popular edition. New York, Putnam [n.d.]   28 v.

* The complete works of Washington Irving. New York, Putnam [186–?]   26 v.
Riverside edition.

The works of Washington Irving. New York, Putnam [191–?]   12 v.
Spuyten-Duyvil edition.

The works of Washington Irving. New York, Putnam [191–?]   10 v.
Stuyvesant edition.

The works of Washington Irving. New York, George D. Sproul [191–?]   24 v.

French

* Œuvres complètes de M. Washington Irving, traduites de l'anglais sous les yeux de l'auteur, par M. Lebègue d'Auteuil . . . Paris, Boulland, 1825.   4 v.
Lettered on shelf-back: Washington.

German

* Washington Irving's Såmmtliche Werke. Uebersetzt von Mehreren und hrsg. von C. A. Fischer. Frankfurt a. M., J. D. Sauerländer, 1826–37.   74 v.
Each volume has also individual t.-p.

In Literarisches Conversationsblatt, Leipzig, Brockhaus, 1825, No. 199, p. 795, is an announcement of an edition of Irving's Works to be published by Duncker and Humblot, under the editorship of S. H. Spiker. No record has been found of the publication of this book.

II. SELECTED WORKS

Volumes of selected works published with the title: Works, have been included under I. Complete Works.

* Essays and sketches. By Washington Irving . . . London, C. Tilt, 1837. (Tilt's miniature classical library)
— — Carlsruhe, Nöldeke, 1839. (Tilt's miniature classical library)
* Extracts from the complete works of Washington Irving, comprising selections from each of his writings, interspersed with explanatory notices, by Charles Olliffe. Paris, Baudry, 1843.
Selections . . . New York, Wiley and Putnam, 1847. (Library of American books)
The Crayon reading book; comprising selections from the various writings of Washington Irving. Prepared for the use of schools. New-York, G. P. Putnam, 1849.
* The Irving gift, being choice gems from the writings of Washington Irving . . . Buffalo, Phinney & co., 1853.
The Crayon reading book; comprising selections from the various writings of Washington Irving. Prepared for the use of schools. New-York, G. P. Putnam, 1855.
* Selections from the works of Washington Irving. Illustrated by Henry Ritter and William Camphausen. . . . Leipzig, F. A. Brockhaus, 1856.
With a portrait of Henry Ritter.
— — Leipzig, F. A. Brockhaus, 1857.
* The Irving gift, being choice gems from the writings of Washington Irving . . . Buffalo, Phinney & co., 1857.
Essays and sketches . . . London, Bogue, 1858.
Essays and sketches . . . London, Groombridge, 1858.
* Irving vignettes. Vignette illustrations of the writings of Washington Irving, engraved on steel by Smillie, Hall. [*sic*] and others. With a sketch of his life and works, from Allibone's forthcoming "Dictionary of authors," and passages from the works illustrated. New York, G. P. Putnam, 1858.
Added engr. t.-p.
Irving gems. Selected from the works of Washington Irving. By J. H. B. Buffalo, Breed, Butler & co., 1861.
Memoir of Washington Irving, and selections from his works, by C. Adams. New York, 1870.

The Crayon reader: comprising selections from the various writings of Washington Irving. For the use of schools. New York, Putnam, 1871.

* [Selections.] (*In* The Sunnyside book . . . New York, G. P. Putnam & sons, 1871)

Tales and sketches by Washington Irving, in the corresponding style of phonography. Bath, I. Pitman, 1884.

—— London, I. Pitman & sons, 1884.

* Readings from Washington Irving, selected for the Chautauqua literary and scientific circle. New York, The Chautauqua press [c 1887] ([Chautauqua literary and scientific circle. Chautauqua home reading series, 1887/88, v. 5])

* Tales from Irving, selected from "The sketch book," "Tales of a traveller," "Wolfert's Roost," "Bracebridge Hall." First series. New York and London, G. P. Putnam's sons [c 1887] (Knickerbocker nuggets)

Tales and sketches by Washington Irving, in the corresponding style of phonography. London, New York, I. Pitman & sons [etc., etc.] 1890.
Key at foot of page.

. . . Selections from Washington Irving. Selected and arranged by Isaac Thomas . . . Boston, New York [etc.] Leach, Shewell & Sanborn [c 1894] (The Students' series of English classics)

Stories and legends, from Washington Irving . . . New York & London, G. P. Putnam's sons [c 1896]

Reviews and miscellanies, by Washington Irving. New York, London, G. P. Putnam's sons, 1897.
Author's autograph edition.
Edition limited to 500 copies.
Contents. — Reviews and miscellanies. — Stories and legends.

. . . Reviews and miscellanies, by Washington Irving. New York and London, G. P. Putnam's sons [1897]
At head of title: Knickerbocker edition.

Washington Irving. New York, Doubleday & McClure co., 1897. (Little masterpieces of literature, edited by Bliss Perry, 1st series, v. 3)
Published in 1922 with title: Irving.

* —— New York, Doubleday & McClure co., 1898. (Little masterpieces of literature, edited by Bliss Perry, 1st series, v. 3)

Tales and sketches, by Washington Irving . . . with printed key. New York, Pitman [1903?]

* . . . Washington Irving . . . New York, Doubleday, Page & co., 1907. (Little masterpieces, edited by Bliss Perry [1st series])

* Prose essays. Edited by Bliss Perry . . . [New York] Published by Doubleday, Page & co. for the Review of reviews co., 1909. (Library of little masterpieces, v. 6)

Selections from Irving, by Isaac Thomas. Boston and Chicago, Sibley & co. [1912?]

Tales by Washington Irving. Selected and edited with an introduction by Carl Van Doren. New York, Oxford university press [1919] (Oxford standard authors)

Irving stories, edited by Ruth Lombard Holcomb . . . New York and Boston, F. M. Ambrose and co., 1921. (The Windsor English classics)

Irving stories, edited by R. H. Creble . . . New York and Boston, F. M. Ambrose & co. [1921?]

. . . Irving, edited by Bliss Perry. Garden City, N. Y., Published for Nelson Doubleday, inc., Oyster Bay, N. Y., by Doubleday, Page & co., 1922. (The Pocket university, v. III, pt. 2)
Published in 1897 with title: Washington Irving, in the series of Little masterpieces.

— — Garden City, N. Y., Published for Nelson Doubleday, inc., by Doubleday, Page & co., 1924. (The Pocket university, v. III, pt. 2)

* Tales by Washington Irving. Selected and edited by Carl Van Doren. New York, Oxford university press [1928] (The World's classics)

— — [London] H. Milford, Oxford university press [1928] (The World's classics, 320)

* The bold dragoon, and other ghostly tales by Washington Irving. Selected and edited by Anne Carroll Moore with decorative diversions by James Daugherty and pleasingly published by Alfred A. Knopf, New Amsterdam, 1930.

Three stories . . . New Rochelle, N. Y., Walpole printing office, Random house, 1930. 3 v.
Half-title; each volume has also separate t.-p. with title vignette. "750 copies printed at the Walpole printing office, New Rochelle."
Contents. — v. 1. Rip Van Winkle. — v. 2. The headless horseman. — v. 3. The great Mississippi bubble.

— — London, Rodker, 1930. 3 v.

* Representative selections . . . with introduction, bibliography, and notes by Henry A. Pochmann . . . New York, American book co., 1934. (American writers series)

* — — New York [etc.] American book co. [c 1934]

Tales and sketches, by Washington Irving, in the corresponding style of Pitman's shorthand. London, Sir I. Pitman & sons, ltd. [19–?] Twentieth century edition.

Belles-lettres works . . . New York, Putnam [191–?] 12 v.
Ariel edition.
Contents. — Knickerbocker's History of New York. — Bracebridge Hall. — Tales of a traveller. — The Alhambra. — The Crayon miscellany. — Wolfert's Roost.

The lighter works of Washington Irving. New York, Putnam [n.d.]
    8 v.
    People's edition.
The lighter works of Washington Irving. New York, Putnam [n.d.]
    8 v.
    Riverside edition.
Washington Irving. Selections from his writings. With biographical
    and critical essay by E. W. Morse. New York, U.S. publishers'
    association [19–?] (Warner's library of the world's best literature)
Select works . . . Philadelphia, Childs & Peterson [185–?] 6 v.
Selections from Irving and Hawthorne, edited by O. J. Stevenson.
    Toronto, Canada, The Copp Clark co., ltd. [192–?] (Literature
    series)
See also, The beauties of Washington Irving; A book of the Hudson;
    The Crayon papers; Spanish papers; Wolfert's Roost.

Shorthand (*English*)
See, above, 1884, 1890, [1903?], London [19–?]

French
Trois contes . . . Paris, Hatier, 1933.

German
Erzählungen aus dem Englischen von Washington Irving von Wilhelm
    Adolph Lindau. Dresden, Arnold, 1822.
Ausgewåhlte Schriften . . . Frankfort, Sauerlånder [1843?]
Washington Irvings Ausgewåhlte Schriften . . . Hrsg. von Dr. J. V.
    Adrian. Frankfurt a. M., Sauerlånder, 1846/47. 4 v.
    2., verb. Auflage.
Washington Irving. Auswahl aus seinen Schriften . . . Leipzig,
    F. A. Brockhaus, 1856.
    Illustrated by Henry Ritter and William Camphausen.
Vier Erzählungen . . . Für den Schulgebrauch hrsg. von Péronne.
    Leipzig, G. Freytag, 1901.
— — Wien, F. Tempsky, 1910.
Vier Erzählungen . . . Für den Schulgebrauch hrsg. von Péronne.
    2. Auflage. Leipzig, G. Freytag, 1921.

Italian
Nel regno fatato: racconti di fate, genî e folletti. Versione italiana di
    F. Verdinois. Napoli, Società editrice Partenopea (tip. Napole-
    tana, F. Ricciardi), 1909.
    Not identified; probably a volume of selections from Irving.

Polish

Nadzwyczajne przygody człowieka osłabionych nerwów z dzieł
P. Washington Irving . . . Wyjęte. Warsaw, 1826. 12mo.
"Unusual adventures of a man of weak nerves, selected from the
works of Washington Irving." Not identified; probably a
volume of selections from Irving.

Serbo-Croatian

Izabrane crtice. Preveo Franjo Marković. Zagreb, 1878–79.   2 v.
([Matica hrvatska. Zabavna knjižnica. Sv. 14, 42])

III. POEMS

* On Passaic falls. Written in the year 1806. (*In* The Atlantic souvenir; Christmas and New Year's offering. 1827. Philadelphia, H. C. Carey & I. Lea [c 1826] p. 146–148)
* — (*In* Kettell, Samuel. Specimens of American poetry. Boston, S. G. Goodrich and co., 1829. v. 2, p. 173–174)
  With title: The falls of the Passaic.
  "The subjoined extract is the only poetry to our knowledge, that has been published with his [Irving's] name."
* — (*In* The New-York book of poetry . . . New-York, George Dearborn, 1837. p. 105–106)
  With title: The falls of the Passaic.
  Omits stanzas 5, 6, 7, and 10, and makes changes in punctuation.
* — (*In* Irvingiana . . . New York, C. B. Richardson, 1860. p. lxiii)
  With title: The falls of the Passaic.
* — (*In* The poems of Washington Irving, brought together from various sources by William R. Langfeld. New York, The New York public library, 1931. p. 4–5)
* The dull lecture. (*In* The Atlantic souvenir; Christmas and New Year's offering. 1828. Philadelphia, Carey, Lea & Carey [c 1827] p. 294)
* — (*In* The Lady's cabinet album . . . New-York, Published for the booksellers [1839] p. 291)
* — (*In* Irvingiana . . . New York, C. B. Richardson, 1860. p. lxiii)
* — (*In* The poems of Washington Irving . . . New York, The New York public library, 1931. p. 5)
* [Verse in Stratford album.] (*In* New-York mirror . . . New-York, 1833. v. 11, p. 136)
  Without title.
  Begins: Of mighty Shakspeare's *birth*, the room we see . . .
  Written in October, 1821.
* — (*In* American literature, Durham, N. C., Duke university press, 1932. v. 4, p. 296)
  With title: New verses by Washington Irving. By J. H. Birss.
  Begins: Of Mighty Shakespeare's birth the room we see . . .
* Written in the Deepdene album. June 24, 1822. (*In* Historical magazine. New York, C. B. Richardson; London, Trübner & co., 1860. v. 4, p. 181)
  Begins: Thou record of the votive throng . . .

* — (*In* The Cornhill magazine . . . London, Smith, Elder & co., 1860.
v. 1, p. [582])

* — (*In* The life and letters of Washington Irving. Edited by his
nephew, Pierre M. Irving . . . New York, G. P. Putnam, 1862–
64. v. 2, p. 85–86)
With title: Written in the Deep Dene album.

* — (*In* The poems of Washington Irving . . . New York, The New
York public library, 1931. p. 9–10)
With title: Written in the Deep Dene album.

* [Verses on the re-opening of the Park theater, New York, September 9,
1807.] (*In* The life and letters of Washington Irving . . . New
York, G. P. Putnam, 1862–64. v. 1, p. 204–208)
Without title.

* — (*In* Opening addresses. Edited by Laurence Hutton. New-York,
The Dunlap society, 1887. p. 22–26)
Without title.
"Spoken by Thomas Abthorpe Cooper."

* — (*In* The poems of Washington Irving . . . New York, The New
York public library, 1931. p. 6–9)
With title: Rhymed address.

* To Miss Emily Foster on her birth-day. (*In* The life and letters of
Washington Irving . . . New York, G. P. Putnam, 1862–64.
v. 2, p. 152–153)
Written in May, 1823.

* — (*In* The poems of Washington Irving . . . New York, The New
York public library, 1931. p. 10–11)

* Echo and silence. (*In* The life and letters of Washington Irving . . .
New York, G. P. Putnam, 1862–64. v. 4, p. 406)
Written in 1832.

* — (*In* The poems of Washington Irving . . . New York, The New
York public library, 1931. p. 11)

* Song. (*In* Harrison, Gabriel. The life and writings of John Howard
Payne . . . Albany, N. Y., Joel Munsell, 1875. p. 397)
"New York, Oct. 1810."

* — (*In* The poems of Washington Irving . . . New York, The New
York public library, 1931. p. 11–12)

* Signs of the times. (*In* Harrison, Gabriel. The life and writings of
John Howard Payne . . . Albany, N. Y., Joel Munsell, 1875.
p. 398)

* — (*In* The poems of Washington Irving . . . New York, The New
York public library, 1931. p. 12–13)

* [Poem.] (*In his* Notes and journal of travel in Europe 1804–1805
. . . New York, The Grolier club, 1921. v. 3, p. 25)
Without title.
Begins: Oh liberty thou goddess heavenly bright . . .

* — (*In* The poems of Washington Irving . . .   New York, The New York public library, 1931.   p. 13)
    With title: Untitled poem.
* [Poem.]   (*In his* Notes and journal of travel in Europe 1804–1805 . . . New York, The Grolier club, 1921.   v. 3, p. 32)
    Without title.
    Begins: In solemn silence a majestic band . . .
* — (*In* The poems of Washington Irving . . .   New York, The New York public library, 1931.   p. 13)
    With title: Untitled poem.
* The lay of the Sunnyside ducks.   (*In* Harriman, *Mrs*. J. Borden. From pinafores to politics.   New York, Henry Holt and co., 1923. p. 22–23)
* — (*In* The poems of Washington Irving.   New York, The New York public library, 1931.   p. 14)
* [Poem.]   (*In* Hellman, George.   Washington Irving, esquire . . . New York, A. A. Knopf, 1925.   p. 45–46)
    Without title.
    Begins: Tho england's [*sic*] sons are kind . . .
* — (*In* Spiller, R. E.   The American in England . . .   New York, Henry Holt and co. [c 1926]   p. 278)
    Quoted in part.
* — (*In* The poems of Washington Irving.   New York, The New York public library, 1931.   p. 15)
    With title: Untitled poem.
* The poems of Washington Irving, brought together from various sources by William R. Langfeld.   (*In* New York public library. Bulletin.   New York, 1930.   v. 34, p. 763–779)
* — — New York, The New York public library, 1931.
    "Reprinted from the Bulletin of the New York public library of November, 1930."
    See also, VI.   Individual Works: Abu Hassan;   The wild huntsman.

IV. COLLECTIONS OF PRINTED LETTERS

For single letters see notes in *The Life of Washington Irving*.

* Irvingiana . . . New York, C. B. Richardson, 1860.
* Leslie, C. R. Autobiographical recollections. Boston, Ticknor and Fields, 1860.
* The life and letters of Washington Irving. By his nephew Pierre M. Irving. New York, G. P. Putnam, 1862–64. 4 v.
* Waldron, W. W. Washington Irving and cotemporaries, in thirty life sketches, edited by William Watson Waldron . . . Introduction by Rev. Theodore Irving, LL.D., nephew of Irving . . . New York, W. H. Kelley & co. [1867]
* Correspondence of Washington Irving and John Howard Payne ⟨1821–1828⟩, edited by Payne's grandnephew, Thatcher T. Payne Luquer. (*In* Scribner's magazine. New York, 1910. v. 48, p. 461–482, 597–616)
* Letters from Washington Irving to Mrs. William Renwick, and to her son, James Renwick . . . written between September 10th, 1811 and April 5th, 1816. [New York, Columbia university, 1910?] Cover-title.
  "Printed for private distribution."
* The letters of Washington Irving to Henry Brevoort. Edited, with an introduction, by George S. Hellman . . . New York, Privately printed, 1915. 2 v.
  Edition of 255 sets.
* Letters of Henry Brevoort to Washington Irving, together with other unpublished Brevoort papers. Edited, with an introduction, by George S. Hellman . . . New York, Privately printed, 1916. 2 v.
  Edition of 310 sets.
* The Kennedy papers. A sheaf of unpublished letters from Washington Irving. (*In* The Sewanee review. Sewanee, Tenn., University press, 1917. v. 25, p. 1–19)
  Edited by Killis Campbell.
* Letters of Washington Irving to Henry Brevoort. Edited, with an introduction, by George S. Hellman . . . New York, G. P. Putnam's sons, 1918.
* Letters of Henry Brevoort to Washington Irving, together with other unpublished Brevoort papers. Edited, with an introduction, by George S. Hellman . . . New York, G. P. Putnam's sons, 1918.

* Hellman, G. S. Washington Irving, esquire, ambassador at large from the New World to the Old. New York, Alfred A. Knopf, 1925.
* Unpublished letters of Washington Irving. Spanish fêtes and ceremonies. By Stanley T. Williams. (*In* Yale review. New Haven, Conn., Yale university press, 1927. v. 16, p. [459]-484)
  Reprinted in Letters from Sunnyside and Spain . . . 1928.
* Letters of Washington Irving. Sunnyside and New York chronicles. By Stanley T. Williams. (*In* Yale review. New Haven, Conn., Yale university press, 1927. v. 17, p. [99]-117)
  Reprinted in Letters from Sunnyside and Spain . . . 1928.
* Letters from Sunnyside and Spain. By Washington Irving. Edited by Stanley T. Williams. New Haven, Yale university press; London, H. Milford, Oxford university press, 1928.
* Washington Irving and the Storrows. Letters from England and the Continent, 1821-1828. Edited by Stanley T. Williams. Cambridge, Massachusetts, Harvard university press, 1933.
* Washington Irving's letters to Mary Kennedy. By Stanley T. Williams and Leonard B. Beach. (*In* American literature. Durham, N. C., Duke university press, 1934. v. 6, p. 185-195)

V. JOURNALS

* The journals of Washington Irving (from July, 1815 to July, 1842) edited by William P. Trent and George S. Hellman. Boston [The Bibliophile society] 1919. 3 v.

  A limited number of copies for private distribution, issued to George S. Hellman.

* The journals of Washington Irving (hitherto unpublished); edited by William P. Trent and George S. Hellman . . . Boston, The Bibliophile society, 1919. 3 v.

  430 copies printed for members of the Society.

* Notes and journal of travel in Europe 1804–1805 by Washington Irving. With an introduction by William P. Trent and title-page and illustrations in aquatint designed and engraved by Rudolph Ruzicka . . . New York, The Grolier club, 1921. 3 v.

  Added t.-p. in aquatint has title: Mr. Irving's Notes and journal of travel in Europe 1804–1805. New York, The Grolier club, 1920.

  "Of Irving's Notes and journal two hundred and fifty-seven sets on rag paper (seven of which are for presentation and copyright) and three sets on Japanese vellum were printed for the Grolier club by D. B. Updike, The Merrymount press, Boston, in the month of September, 1921."

* Washington Irving diary, Spain 1828–1829, edited from the manuscript in the library of the Society by Clara Louisa Penney . . . New York, The Hispanic society of America, 1926. (*Half-title:* Hispanic notes & monographs; essays, studies, and brief biographies issued by the Hispanic society of America. Catalogue series)

* Tour in Scotland, 1817, and other manuscript notes by Washington Irving. Edited with a critical introduction by Stanley T. Williams. New Haven, Yale university press, 1927. (Washington Irving diaries, I)

  Edition of 525 copies.

* —— London, Oxford university press, 1927. (Washington Irving diaries, I)

* Notes while preparing Sketch book, &c., 1817. By Washington Irving. Edited with a critical introduction by Stanley T. Williams. New Haven, Yale university press, 1927. (Washington Irving diaries, II)

  Edition of 525 copies.

* — — London, Oxford university press, 1927. (Washington Irving diaries, II)
* Washington Irving diary, Spain 1828–1829, edited from the manuscript in the library of the Society by Clara Louisa Penney . . . New York, The Hispanic society of America, 1930. (*Half-title:* Hispanic notes & monographs; essays, studies, and brief biographies issued by the Hispanic society of America. Catalogue series)
* Journal of Washington Irving (1823–1824) edited by Stanley T. Williams. Cambridge, Harvard university press, 1931.
  The recently discovered manuscript by Irving on William the Conqueror: p. [245–257]
* — — London, Oxford university press, 1931.
* Journal of Washington Irving, 1803. Edited by Stanley T. Williams. London, New York, Oxford university press, 1934.

VI. INDIVIDUAL WORKS

ABU HASSAN

* Abu Hassan, by Washington Irving (hitherto unpublished) with an
introduction by George S. Hellman. Boston, The Bibliophile
society, 1924.
Printed by the Torch press, Cedar Rapids, Iowa.
Edition of 455 copies.
An English dramatization of the libretto, by Franz K. Hiemer, of
Weber's opera Abu Hassan.
* Extracts from Abu Hassan. (*In* The poems of Washington Irving,
brought together from various sources by William R. Langfeld.
New York, The New York public library, 1931. p. 15–19)

ADVENTURES OF CAPTAIN BONNEVILLE

* The Rocky mountains: or, Scenes, incidents, and adventures in the
Far West; digested from the journal of Captain B. L. E. Bonne-
ville, of the Army of the United States, and illustrated from various
other sources, by Washington Irving . . . Philadelphia, Carey,
Lea, & Blanchard, 1837. 2 v.
First American edition.
* Adventures of Captain Bonneville, or, Scenes beyond the Rocky
mountains of the Far West. By Washington Irving . . . London,
Richard Bentley, 1837. 3 v.
First English edition.
* Captain Bonneville, or, Enterprise beyond the Rocky mountains.
A sequel to "Astoria." By Washington Irving . . . Second
edition . . . London, Richard Bentley, 1837. 3 v.
* Adventures of Captain Bonneville; or, Scenes beyond the Rocky
mountains of the Far West . . . Paris, Baudry, 1837. (Collec-
tion of ancient and modern British authors, t. 193)
First Continental edition.
* Adventures of Captain Bonneville, or, Scenes beyond the Rocky
mountains of the Far West; by Washington Irving . . . Paris,
A. and W. Galignani, 1837.
Adventures of Captain Bonneville; or, Scenes beyond the Rocky

mountains of the Far West . . . London, Richard Bentley, 1840. 3 v.

* . . . The Rocky mountains, or, Scenes, incidents and adventures in the Far West . . . By Washington Irving. Philadelphia, Lea & Blanchard, 1843.

Adventures of Captain Bonneville in the Rocky mountains and the Far West . . . New York, 1847. 2 v.

* The adventures of Captain Bonneville, U.S.A., in the Rocky mountains and the Far West. Digested from his journal and illustrated from various other sources. By Washington Irving. Author's revised edition . . . New-York, G. P. Putnam, 1849. (*Added t.-p.:* The works of Washington Irving. New edition, revised, v. 10)

* —— New-York, G. P. Putnam, 1850. (*Added t.-p.:* The works of Washington Irving. New edition, revised, v. 10)

Adventures of Captain Bonneville . . . London, H. G. Bohn, 1850.

* The adventures of Captain Bonneville, U.S.A., in the Rocky mountains and the Far West . . . New-York, G. P. Putnam, 1851. (*Added t.-p.:* The works of Washington Irving. New edition, revised, v. 10)

—— New-York, G. P. Putnam, 1852. (*Added t.-p.:* The works of Washington Irving. New edition, revised, v. 10)

Adventures of Captain Bonneville, or, Scenes beyond the Rocky mountains of the Far West. New edition. London, George Routledge, 1855.

Adventures of Captain Bonneville, U.S.A., in the Rocky mountains and the Far West . . . Author's revised edition . . . New-York, G. P. Putnam, 1867. (*Added t.-p.:* The works of Washington Irving. New edition, revised, v. 10)

The adventures of Captain Bonneville, U.S.A., in the Rocky mountains and the Far West . . . Author's revised edition . . . New York, G. P. Putnam and son, 1868. Knickerbocker edition.

* Adventures of Captain Bonneville, U.S.A., in the Rocky mountains and the Far West . . . Author's revised edition . . . New York, G. P. Putnam's sons [1868] Hudson edition.

* The adventures of Captain Bonneville, U.S.A., in the Rocky mountains of the Far West . . . Author's revised edition . . . [New York, G. P. Putnam's sons, c 1868] (The works of Washington Irving. The Kinderhook edition, v. 6)

Adventures of Captain Bonneville, U.S.A., in the Rocky mountains and the Far West . . . Author's revised edition . . . New-York, G. P. Putnam, 1869. (*Added t.-p.:* The works of Washington Irving. New edition, revised, v. 10)

Adventures of Captain Bonneville . . . [place? publisher?] 1873.

. . . The adventures of Captain Bonneville, U.S.A. . . . The author's revised edition . . . New York, G. P. Putnam's sons [1882]
Copyright date: 1868.
Vol. [3] of a uniform edition in cloth, having at head of title "Hudson edition" (first issued in 1882) and lettered: Irving's works.
The adventures of Captain Bonneville, by Washington Irving. New York, J. W. Lovell co. [1883] (*On cover:* Lovell's library, v. 6, no. 311)
Adventures of Captain Bonneville . . . London, J. & R. Maxwell [1885]
The adventures of Captain Bonneville, and Wolfert's Roost, by Washington Irving. New York, G. P. Putnam's sons [c 1895] 2 v. Holly edition.
Plates accompanied by guard sheets with descriptive letterpress. Edition of 1000 sets.
. . . Captain Bonneville, by Washington Irving . . . New York and London, G. P. Putnam's sons [1897] 2 v.
At head of title: Knickerbocker edition.
Half-title of Vol. II: The adventures of Captain Bonneville, to which are added . . . Wolfert's Roost, The birds of spring, The Creole village, Mountjoy, Recollections of the Alhambra.
The adventures of Captain Bonneville, U.S.A., in the Rocky mountains and the Far West. Digested from his journal and illustrated from various sources by Washington Irving. New York, G. P. Putnam's sons, 1898. 2 v.
Colorado edition.
Edition of 100 copies, on linen paper.
* The adventvres of Captain Bonneville, V.S.A., in the Rocky movntains and the Far West; digested from his jovrnal and illvstrated from variovs other sovrces. By Washington Irving. Pawnee edition . . . New York & London, G. P. Pvtnam's sons, 1898. 2 v.
* The adventures of Captain Bonneville. By Washington Irving. New York, T. Y. Crowell & co. [1900?]
. . . The adventures of Captain Bonneville, U.S.A., in the Rocky mountains and the Far West . . . The author's revised edition. New York, G. P. Putnam's sons [1902] (*Publisher's lettering:* Irving's works)
At head of title: Hudson edition.
The adventures of Captain Bonneville . . . [New York, Belford co., 188–?]
The adventures of Captain Bonneville . . . New York, G. P. Putnam [19–?]
Hudson edition.
The adventures of Captain Bonneville . . . New York, G. P. Putnam [19–?]
New handy volume edition.

The adventures of Captain Bonneville . . . New York, G. P. Putnam [19–?]
Student's edition.

Extracts

The fur traders. [Extracts from Astoria and The adventures of
Captain Bonneville] *see* Astoria.

TRANSLATIONS

Dutch

* Lotgevallen en ontmoetingen van Kapitein Bonneville, op zijne
avontuurlijke togten aan gene zijde van het Klipgebergte van
Noord-Amerika; beschreven door Washington Irving . . . Naar
het Engelsch. Haarlem, Bij de wed. A. Loosjes, pz., 1838. 2 v. in 1.

French

* Voyages et aventures du capitaine Bonneville, à l'ouest des États-
Unis d'Amérique, au-delà des Montagnes rocheuses, par Wash-
ington Irving . . . Traduits de l'anglais par Benjamin Laroche
. . . Paris, Charpentier, 1837. 2 v. in 1.

German

* Abentheuer des Capitäns Bonneville; oder, Scenen jenseits der Fels-
gebirge des Fernen Westens. Von Washington Irving. Aus dem
Englischen von F. L. Rhode. Frankfort am Main, J. D. Sauer-
länder, 1837. 2 v. in 1.
Abenteuer des Capitain Bonneville; oder, Scenen im Felsengebirge
Nordamerikas, von Washington Irving. Ins Deutsche übertragen
von Dr. Ed. Freisleben. Leipzig i. B., B. Tauchnitz, Jun., 1837. 3 v.
Abenteuer des Capitain Bonneville . . . Aus dem Englischen von
A. von Treskow. Quedlinburg, Basse, 1837. 2 v.

Extracts

* Washington Irving's „Capitain Bonneville." (*In* Magazin für die
Literatur des Auslandes. Berlin, Hayn, 1837. 11. Bd., p. [305]–
306, 311–312)

THE ALHAMBRA

* The Alhambra: a series of tales and sketches of the Moors and
Spaniards. By the author of The sketch book . . . Philadelphia,
Carey & Lea, 1832. 2 v.
First edition.

* The Alhambra, by Geoffrey Crayon . . . London, Henry Colburn and Richard Bentley, 1832. 2 v.
  First English edition.
  Advertisements, numbered I–XV.
* — — London, Henry Colburn and Richard Bentley, 1832. 2 v.
  Advertisements, numbered I–XVII.
* The Alhambra; or, The new sketch book. By Geoffrey Crayon, gent. . . . Paris, Baudry, 1832.
* — — Paris, Baudry, 1832. 2 v.
* The Alhambra; or, The new sketch book. By Washington Irving. Paris, A. & W. Galignani, 1832.
* The Alhambra; or, The new sketch book. By Washington Irving. Paris, Lyons, B. Cormon and Blanc, booksellers, 1834–35. 2 v. in 1.
  Vol. 2, 1834.
  Tales of the Alhambra . . . London, R. Bentley, 1835. (Standard novels, no. 49)
  The Alhambra. A series of tales and sketches of the Moors and Spaniards. Philadelphia, Carey, Lea and Blanchard, 1836. 2 v.
* Tales of the Alhambra, to which are added Legends of the conquest of Spain, by Washington Irving . . . Paris, Baudry, 1840. 8vo. (Collection of ancient and modern British authors, t. 68)
* Tales of the Alhambra, by Washington Irving. Paris, Baudry, 1840. 16mo.
  The Alhambra. Vollständig akzentuirt und erläutert, zum Schul- und Privatgebrauche von Joh. Christ. Nossek. Znaim, Fournier, 1842.
  Tales of the Alhambra. Accentuirt und mit einem vollständigen grammatikalischen Commentar und phraseologischen Noten zum Schul- und Privatgebrauche hrsg. von Frz. Bauer. Celle, Schulze, 1845.
  Tales of the Alhambra. With a copious vocabulary compiled by E. Amthor. Revised edition. Leipzig, Renger, 1846.
* Tales of the Alhambra by Washington Irving, esq. Accentuirt und mit einem vollständigen grammatischen Commentar und phrase-ologischen Noten zum Schul- und Privatgebrauch von Franz Bauer . . . Mit einem Wörterbuche. Celle, Schulze, 1847.
  Tales of the Alhambra. By Washington Irving . . . Rev. and cor. by the author. London, R. Bentley [etc.] 1850. 2 v. in 1. (*On cover:* Standard novels, no. 49)
  Paged continuously.
  Contents. — Tales of the Alhambra. By W. Irving. — The last of the Abencerages. Tr. from the French of Chateaubriand, by Isabel Hill. — The involuntary prophet, by the author of "Brambletye house", "Zillah", &c.
  The Alhambra . . . Revised edition. New York, Crowell & co. [1851] ([The Astor prose series])

* The Alhambra. By Washington Irving. Author's revised edition.
  With illustrations by Felix O. C. Darley, engraved by the most
  eminent artists. New-York, G. P. Putnam, 1851.

Tales of the Alhambra. With a copious vocabulary compiled by
  E. Amthor. Revised edition. Leipzig, Renger, 1851.

* The Alhambra. By Washington Irving. Author's revised edition.
  With illustrations by Felix O. C. Darley, engraved by the most
  eminent artists. New-York, G. P. Putnam & co., 1852.

Tales of the Alhambra. Accentuirt mit einem vollständigen grammatikalischen Commentar und phraseologischen Noten, unter steter
  Hinweisung auf Wagner's „Neue englische Sprachlehre" und einem
  gedrängten Wörterbuche zum Schul- und Privatgebrauche, hrsg.
  von F. Bauer. 2., revidirte Auflage. Celle, Schulze, 1853.

The Alhambra. By Washington Irving. Author's revised edition.
  New York, G. P. Putnam & co., 1857. (The works of Washington
  Irving, v. 15)

The Alhambra. By Washington Irving. Author's revised edition.
  New York, G. P. Putnam & co., 1860. (The works of Washington
  Irving, v. 4)

— — New York, G. P. Putnam, 1863. (The works of Washington
  Irving, v. 15)

Tales of the Alhambra; or, The new sketch-book. Zum Schul- und
  Privatgebrauch mit grammatikalischen und phraseologischen
  Noten, Bezeichnung der Tonsilben und einem Wörterbuche ver-
  sehen von Franz Bauer. 3. Auflage. Celle, Schulze, 1863.

* . . . The Alhambra. By Washington Irving. Author's revised edition.
  New York, G. P. Putnam's sons [c 1865]
  People's edition.
  Added engr. t.-p.

The Alhambra . . . New York, G. P. Putnam's sons, 1868.
  Riverside edition.

The Alhambra . . . Author's revised edition. New York, G. P.
  Putnam and son, 1868.
  Added engr. t.-p.

Tales of the Alhambra. Mit erläuternden Anmerkungen zum Schul-
  und Privatunterricht, bearbeitet von P. Weeg. Münster, Brunn,
  1870. (Sammlung gediegener und interessanter Werke der englischen Literatur, 9)

The Alhambra . . . Author's revised edition. Philadelphia, J. B.
  Lippincott & co., 1871.
  Knickerbocker edition.
  Added engr. t.-p.

The Alhambra . . . Author's revised edition. Philadelphia, J. B.
  Lippincott & co., 1872. (On cover: Irving's works)
  Half-title: . . . Riverside edition.
  Added engr. t.-p.; vignette.

The Alhambra . . . Author's revised edition. Philadelphia, J. B. Lippincott & co., 1873.
Half-title: Irving's Alhambra.
People's edition.
Added engr. t.-p.; vignette.

* Tales of the Alhambra; or, The new sketch-book. By Washington Irving, esq. 4th edition, with German notes and a vocabulary for the use of schools and private teachers by Franz Bauer. Celle, Schulze, 1873. (Collection of books for the amusement and instruction of youth)
— — Celle, Schulze, 1873. (Collection of books for the amusement and instruction of youth)
Fifth edition.

* — — Zum Schul- und Privatgebrauch mit grammatischem Commentar, phraseologischen Noten und einem Wörterbuche versehen von Franz Bauer. Vierte Aufl. Celle, Schulze, 1873.

The Alhambra. Knickerbocker edition. New York, Putnam [1873?]

* Tales of the Alhambra. By Washington Irving . . . Paris, Baudry, 1874.

* Tales of the Alhambra. London, Chatto & Windus, 1875. (The Golden library)

The Alhambra. Hrsg. von C. Th. Lion. Berlin, Weidmann, 1877.

The Alhambra. Hudson edition. New York, Putnam, 1882.
Author's revised edition.

Tales of the Alhambra. With a copious vocabulary, compiled by E. Amthor. 5th edition. Leipzig, Renger, 1882.

. . . The Alhambra . . . Author's revised edition. New York and London, G. P. Putnam's sons [1882?]
Vol. [1] of a uniform edition in cloth having at head of title "Hudson edition" (first issued in 1882) and lettered: Irving's works.

* The Alhambra. By Washington Irving. New York, J. B. Alden, 1883.
Caxton edition.

Tales of the Alhambra. Für den Schul- und Privatunterricht bearb. von P. Weeg. 2. Aufl., revid. und vielfach verb. von J. H. Schmick. Leipzig, Lenz, 1884. (Sammlung gediegener und interessanter Werke der englischen Litteratur, 9)

* . . . The Alhambra. By Washington Irving. Author's revised edition. New York, G. P. Putnam's sons, 1885.
At head of title: Hudson edition.
Added engr. t.-p.

Tales of the Alhambra. Ausgewählt, mit Anmerkungen und einem Wörterbuch versehen von Heinrich Loewe. Berlin, Friedberg und Mode, 1885. (English authors for the use of schools, no. 7)

Tales of the Alhambra . . . Mit Anmerkungen zum Schulgebrauch hrsg. von G. Wolpert. Bielefeld, Velhagen und Klasing, 1885. (English authors, 4)

The Alhambra . . . Chicago, New York, and San Francisco, Belford, Clarke & co. [1885?]

The Alhambra. A selection. Erläutert und mit Wörterbuch versehen von A. Matthias. Berlin, Simion, 1887. (Rauch's English readings, Hft. 32)

Erzählungen aus Tales of the Alhambra. Hrsg. von G. Wolpert. Bielefeld, Velhagen & Klasing, 1887. (English authors, Lfg. 29) Ausgabe A.

* Tales of the Alhambra. Ausgewählt und für den Schulgebrauch erklärt von Hugo Wernekke. Leipzig, Renger, 1887. (Französische und englische Schulbibliothek, hrsg. von Otto E. A. Dickmann, Bd. 38)

* The Alhambra. By Washington Irving . . . New York, G. P. Putnam's sons, 1888.
Revised edition.
Added engr. t.-p.

Tales of the Alhambra. With a copious vocabulary compiled by E. Amthor. 6th edition. Leipzig, Renger, 1888.

. . . The Alhambra. By Washington Irving. Author's revised edition. New York & London, G. P. Putnam's sons [1889] (*Publisher's lettering:* Irving's works)
At head of title: Hudson edition.

Erzählungen aus Tales of the Alhambra. Hrsg. von G. Wolpert. Bielefeld, Velhagen & Klasing, 1889. (English authors, 4) Ausgabe B.

The Alhambra . . . Edited for the use of schools by Alice H. White . . . Boston, Ginn & company, 1891. (*On cover:* Classics for children)

— — Boston, Ginn & co. [c 1891] (Home and school library)

* . . . The Alhambra. By Washington Irving . . . New York and London, G. P. Putnam's sons [c 1891] 2 v.
At head of title: Knickerbocker edition.

The Alhambra. By Washington Irving. New York, T. Y. Crowell & co. [c 1891]
Title within ornamental border.

* . . . The Alhambra. By Washington Irving. Author's revised edition . . . New York, G. P. Putnam's sons, 1892. 2 v.
At head of title: Darro edition.
"Note to the 'Darro' edition" signed: R. H. L. [R. H. Lawrence]

Tales of the Alhambra. Ausgewählt und für den Schulgebrauch erklärt von Hugo Wernekke. Leipzig, Renger, 1892. (Französische und englische Schulbibliothek, hrsg. von Otto E. A. Dickmann, Bd. 38)

. . . The Alhambra. Selected from the author's revised edition . . . With introduction and explanatory notes, by J. W. Abernethy . . . New York, Maynard, Merrill & co. [c 1893] (English classic series, no. 117)

Tales of the Alhambra. Ausgewählt und für den Schulgebrauch er-
klärt von Hugo Wernekke. 2. Auflage. Leipzig, Renger, 1894.
(Französische und englische Schulbibliothek, hrsg. von Otto E.
A. Dickmann, Bd. 38)

Erzählungen aus Tales of the Alhambra. Hrsg. von G. Wolpert.
Bielefeld, Velhagen & Klasing, 1894.
Ausgabe A.

The Alhambra, by Washington Irving. From the author's revised
edition . . . New York, Boston, T. Y. Crowell & co. [1894]

. . . The Alhambra . . . Author's revised text edited by A. Marvin
. . . Students' edition. New York, London, G. P. Putnam's
sons, 1895. (Half-title: Irving's works. (Students' edition))

* The Alhambra. With an introduction by Elizabeth Robins Pennell.
Illustrated . . . by Joseph Pennell. London [etc.] Macmillan
and co., 1896.

* . . . Tales of the Alhambra. By Washington Irving. Selected for use
in schools. With an introduction and explanatory notes. New
York and New Orleans, University publishing co., 1896. (Standard
literature series [no. 4])

The Alhambra . . . Boston, The Howe memorial press, 1897. 2 v.
In raised letters for the use of the blind.

* . . . The Alhambra. By Washington Irving. Author's revised edition
. . . New York and London, G. P. Putnam's sons, 1897. 2 v.
At head of title: Darro edition.

Erzählungen aus Tales of the Alhambra. Hrsg. von G. Wolpert.
Bielefeld, Velhagen & Klasing, 1897.
Ausgabe A.

Erzählungen aus Tales of the Alhambra. Hrsg. von G. Wolpert.
Bielefeld, Velhagen & Klasing, 1898.
Ausgabe B.

— — Bielefeld, Velhagen & Klasing, 1900.
Ausgabe B.

The Alhambra. By Washington Irving. Edited by Alfred M.
Hitchcock . . . New York, The Macmillan co. [etc., etc.] 1900.
(Macmillan's pocket classics)

. . . Tales of the Alhambra . . . (A selection.) Transcribed into
Gabelsberger-Richter-Phonography by Richard Preuss. Dres-
den, W. Reuter, 1900. (Reuter's Bibliothek für Gabelsberger-
Stenographen, Bd. 104)

The Alhambra . . . Berlin, Herbig, 1901. (Modern English authors,
ed. by H. Saure, 12)
Contains also Lytton's The last days of Pompeii, and Poe's The
bells, The raven, Annabel Lee, and To one in Paradise.

The Alhambra. Mit einer Einleitung und erklärenden Anmerkungen
in Auswahl hrsg. von Th. Lion. 2., gänzlich umgearbeitete Auflage.
Berlin, Weidmann, 1902.

* . . . The Alhambra. By Washington Irving. Author's revised edition. New York & London, G. P. Putnam's sons [1902] (*Publisher's lettering:* Irving's works)
At head of title: Hudson edition.

Erzählungen aus Tales of the Alhambra. Hrsg. von G. Wolpert. Bielefeld, Velhagen & Klasing, 1903.
Ausgabe B.

— — Bielefeld, Velhagen & Klasing, 1904.
Ausgabe B.

* The Alhambra. By Washington Irving. Edited by Alfred M. Hitchcock . . . New York, The Macmillan co.; London, Macmillan & co., 1905. (Macmillan's pocket American and English classics)

The Alhambra. The author's revised text, edited by Arthur Marvin . . . New York, London, G. P. Putnam's sons, 1905.
Illustrated.

Erzählungen aus Tales of the Alhambra. Hrsg. von G. Wolpert. Bielefeld, Velhagen & Klasing, 1905.
Ausgabe A.

Selections from The Alhambra. Miniature edition. New York, Crowell and co., 1905.

The Alhambra . . . With an introduction by Elizabeth Robins Pennell. Illustrated . . . by Joseph Pennell. London, Macmillan and co., 1906.

Erzählungen aus Tales of the Alhambra. Hrsg. von G. Wolpert. Bielefeld, Velhagen & Klasing, 1907.
Ausgabe B.

The Alhambra . . . With an introduction by Elizabeth Robins Pennell. Illustrated . . . by Joseph Pennell. London, Macmillan and co., limited, 1908. (Pocket classics)

Selections from The Alhambra . . . London and New York, Macmillan, 1908.

* Legends of the Alhambra. By Washington Irving. With illustrations . . . by George Hood and an introduction by Hamilton Wright Mabie. Philadelphia & London, J. B. Lippincott co., 1909.

* Tales from The Alhambra. By Washington Irving. Adapted by Josephine Brower. With illustrations in colour by C. E. Brock. Boston and New York, Houghton Mifflin co. [c 1910]

Stories and legends of the Alhambra . . . New York, McLaughlin, 1911.

Tales from The sketch book and The Alhambra . . . 1913, *see* The sketch book.

The Alhambra . . . edited by Edward K. Robinson. Illustrated by Norman Irving Black. New edition. Boston, New York, Ginn and co. [c 1915]

Tales of Washington Irving's Alhambra, simplified by Leila H. Cheney. With illustrations in color by George Hood. Philadelphia and London, J. B. Lippincott co. [c 1917] ([The Children's classics])

Tales from The sketch book and The Alhambra . . . 1917, *see* The sketch book.

Tales from The Alhambra, by Washington Irving. Adapted by Josephine V. Brower; with illustrations in colour by C. E. Brock. Boston and New York, Houghton Mifflin co. [c 1917] (Riverside literature series)

The Alhambra, by Washington Irving; edited by Alfred M. Hitchcock . . . New York, London, The Macmillan co., 1920. ([Macmillan's pocket American and English classics])

Erzählungen aus Tales of the Alhambra. Hrsg. von G. Wolpert. Bielefeld, Velhagen & Klasing, 1921.
Ausgabe B.

The Alhambra . . . with an introduction by Elizabeth Robins Pennell. Illustrated . . . by Joseph Pennell. New York, Macmillan, 1925. (Cranford series)

Erzählungen aus Tales of the Alhambra. Hrsg. von G. Wolpert. Bielefeld, Velhagen & Klasing, 1925.
Ausgabe B.

. . . The Alhambra, edited by Frederick Houk Law. New York, Allyn & Bacon, 1926. (Academy classics for junior high schools)

The Alhambra, palace of mystery and splendor . . . Tales selected and rearranged by Mabel Williams. Illustrated by Warwick Goble. New York, The Macmillan co., 1926. (Children's classics)

. . . The Alhambra, edited by Frederick Houk Law. Boston, New York [etc.] Allyn and Bacon [c 1926] (Academy classics for junior high schools)

. . . Tales of the Alhambra (selected and abridged), by Washington Irving. Illustrated by H. G. Theaker. Philadelphia, D. McKay co. [1926] (The Newbery classics)

* The Alhambra. By Washington Irving. New York, Belford co. [18–?]
Contents. — The Alhambra. — The conquest of Granada. — The conquest of Spain. — Spanish voyages of discovery.

The Alhambra. Edited by Frederick Houk Law. New York, Burt [n.d.] (Cornell series)

— — New York, Burt [n.d.] (The Home library)

— — New York, Burt [n.d.] (New pocket edition of standard classics)

* The Alhambra. New York, T. Y. Crowell [19–?] (Luxembourg illustrated library)

* The Alhambra. New York, Thomas Y. Crowell & co. [n.d.]

The Alhambra . . . Edited by Elizabeth R. Pennell . . . New York, Newson & co. [192–?] (Standard literature series)

The Alhambra . . . New York, Putnam [19–?]
Gift edition.

— — New York, Putnam [19–?]
Large paper edition.

— — New York, Putnam [19–?]
New handy volume edition.

The Alhambra. The conquest of Granada . . . Philadelphia, David
McKay [19–?] (American classics series)

The Alhambra . . . Illustrated by Arthur A. Dixon and H. M.
Brock. Philadelphia, David McKay [19–?] (Raphael house
library)
Edited by Eric Vredenburg.

Tales of the Alhambra. Illustrated by Harry G. Theaker and others.
Toronto, McClelland & Stewart [19–?] (Golden treasury library)

Shorthand (English)

See, above, Tales of the Alhambra . . . 1900.

Extracts

* Ahmed al Kamel; or, The pilgrim of love. The libretto, (founded on
a tale by Washington Irving,) by the late Henry J. Finn, esq.
The music by C. E. Horn . . . New-York, M. C. Martin, 1840.
Cf. Wilson, J. G. Memorial history of the city of New York . . .
[New York] New York history co. [1892–93] v. 4, p. 174.

* Legend of the rose of the Alhambra. (In The Independent. New
York, Independent corporation, 1917. v. 89, p. 407–408)

TRANSLATIONS

Danish

* Alhambra. Af Washington Irving. Oversat af Frederik Schaldemose
. . . Kjøbenhavn, H. G. Brill, 1833–34. 2 v. in 1.

* Alhambra, paa dansk ved R. Schmidt. Kjøbenhavn, 1860.

* . . . Fortællinger fra Alhambra. Oversatte af Charles Sveistrup.
København, P. Hauberg & comp. [1888] ([Dansk folkebibliothek.
Bd. 60])
At head of title: Washington Irving.

Dutch

De Alhambra; of, Nieuwe schetsen en portretten. Naar het Engelsch
. . . door H. Frijlink . . . Amsterdam, Hendrik Frijlink, 1833.
2 v. in 1.

French

* Les contes de l'Alhambra, précédés d'Un voyage dans la province de
Grenade, traduits de Washington Irving par Mlle A. Sobry . . .
Paris, H. Fournier, 1832. 2 v.

* Contes de l'Alhambra, traduits par Mlle A. Sobry. Paris, H. Fournier,
1833. 2 v.

Les contes de l'Alhambra, précédés d'Un voyage dans la province de
  Grenade, traduits de Washington Irving par Mlle A. Sobry . . .
  Bruxelles, Hochshausen et Fournes, 1837. 2 v.

* L'Alhambra, chroniques du pays de Grenade; traduit par P. Christian. Paris, Lavigne, 1843.

L'Alhambra, chroniques du pays de Grenade; traduit par P. Christian. Paris, Delahaye, 1849.

* Nouveaux contes de l'Alhambra; traduits de l'anglais par O. Squarr
  [Charles Flor]. Bruxelles, Kiessling, Schnée et cᵉ, 1855.

* Nouveaux contes de l'Alhambra; traduits de l'anglais par O. Squarr
  [Charles Flor]. Bruxelles, A. Cadot, 1855.

* L'Alhambra de Grenade, souvenirs et légendes, par W. Irving.
  Traduit de l'anglais par M. Richard Viot. Tours, A. Mame et
  fils, 1886.

* Washington Irving. Contes de l'Alhambra. Traduit de l'anglais, par
  Émile Godefroy. Paris, G. Crès, 1921.

Extracts

* L'héritage du more. Avec étude littéraire sur la vie et l'œuvre
  d'Irving. Paris, H. Gautier [1887] (Nouvelle bibliothèque populaire à 10 centimes. No. 36)
  Contents. — L'héritage du more. — Le gouverneur Manco. — La
  légende de l'astrologue arabe. — Le fiancé fantôme.

* L'héritage du more . . . Paris, Lecène, Oudin et cie, 1895. (Nouvelle
  bibliothèque illustrée de vulgarisation)
  Porteur d'eau espagnol; ou, Le trésor enchanté. Troyes [n.d.]
  (Bibliothèque bleue, v. 10)
  A translation of Legend of the Moor's legacy.

* Le souterrain de l'Alhambra. Conte par Washington Irving.
  Limoges, M. Barbou, 1890.

German

Das [sic] Alhambra. Aus dem Englischen übertragen von Theod.
  Hell. Berlin, Duncker und Humblot, 1832. 2 v.

Die Alhambra. Aus dem Englischen des Washington Irving, von Joh.
  Sporschil. Braunschweig, Vieweg, 1832. 2 v.

* Die Alhambra; oder, Das neue Skizzenbuch von Washington Irving.
  Aus dem Englischen. Frankfurt am Main, J. D. Sauerländer,
  1832.

Neueste Crayon-Skizzen. Skizzenbuch und Novellen von 1839.
  Nach dem nordamerikanischen Original von Carlo Brunetti. Ham-
  burg, Herold, 1840.
  This volume has not been identified. Possibly it is a translation of
  The Crayon miscellany. The date: 1839 in title is unexplained.

Alhambra; oder, Das neue Skizzenbuch. Abbotsford und Newstead-
Abtei, Eine Reise auf den Prairien. Frankfurt am Main, Sauer-
länder, 1847. (Ausgewählte Schriften, 4)
2., sorgfältig verbesserte Auflage.
Fünf Erzählungen von W. Irwing's [sic] Alhambra. Gotha, Schloess-
mann, 1880. (Englische Schüler-Bibliothek, 3)
— — Gotha, Schloessmann, 1881. (Englische Schüler-Bibliothek, 3)
2. Aufl.
* . . . Die Alhambra; oder, Das neue Skizzenbuch von Washington
Irving. Mit einer Einleitung von L. Pröscholdt. Stuttgart,
Spemann, 1882. (At head of title: Collection Spemann)
Deutsche Hand- & Haus-Bibliothek, Bd. 19.
Fünf Erzählungen aus W. Irvings Alhambra. Mit einem Verzeichnis
der Redensarten. 3. Auflage. Berlin, Wiegandt und Schotte, 1885.
(Englische Schüler-Bibliothek, Bdchn. 3)
* Tales of the Alhambra, by Washington Irving. Ausgewählt und für
den Schulgebrauch erklärt von Hugo Wernekke. Leipzig, Renger,
1887. (Französische und englische Schulbibliothek, hrsg. von Otto
E. A. Dickmann, Bd. 38)
* . . . Sagen von der Alhambra von Washington Irving. Übersetzt
von Adolf Strodtmann. Leipzig, Bibliographisches Institut [1887?]
(Meyers Volksbücher, Nr. 180)
Die Alhambra; oder, Das neue Skizzenbuch. Gesamt-Ausgabe.
Halle a.d.S., O. Hendel [1888?] (Bibliothek der Gesamt-Lit-
teratur des In- und Auslandes, Nr. 198–200)
Tales of the Alhambra, by Washington Irving. Ausgewählt und
für den Schulgebrauch erklärt von Hugo Wernekke. Leipzig,
Renger [1889?] (Französische und englische Schulbibliothek . . .
Bd. 38)
Die Alhambra; oder, Das neue Skizzenbuch. Wortgetreu nach
H. R. Mecklenburgs Grundsätzen aus dem Englischen übersetzt
von R. F. Berlin, H. R. Mecklenburg, 1889–91. 5 v.
Die Alhambra; oder, Das neue Skizzenbuch. Gesamtausgabe.
Berlin, D. Hendel, 1925. (Hendel-Bücher, 198/200)
Geschichte von der Alhambra. Hrsg. von der Vereinigung für Arbeits-
unterricht und Kunsterziehung. Wien, Österreich, Bundesverlag,
1925. (Bunte Jugendschriften. Rotes Bdchn. Nr. 46)
Alhambra. Übersetzt von F. Bürger. Leipzig, Ph. Reclam, Jun.
[188–?] (Universal-Bibliothek, 1571–1573)

Extracts

Die Legende von der Rose der Alhambra; oder, Der Page und der
Gerfalk. Engl. Bearbeitung und Uebertragung ins Deutsche von
E. Springer. Berlin, A. Scherl, 1914. (Sprachenpflege, System
August Scherl, Englisch, 53. Bd.)

Das Vermächtnis des Mauren. Aus dem Englischen. Donauwörth, L. Auer, 1915. (Deutsche Jugendhefte, Nr. 19)

Das Vermächtnis des Mauren und andere Alhambrasagen. Mit Bildern von A. Schmidhammer. Reutlingen, Ensslin & Laiblin, 1921. (Bunte Jugendbücher, 23)
Neue Auflage.

Icelandic

Sögur frá Alhambra. Reykjavík, Félagið "Baldur," 1906.

Extracts

* Pílagrímur ástarinnar; eða, Sagan af Ahmed al Kamel. Eptir W. Irwing. Kaupmannahöfn, 1860.
Útgefandi Páll Sveinsson.
Translated by Steingrímur Thorsteinsson.

Italian

L'Alhambra, ed. Giacomo Mosconi. Milano, Stella, 1834. 3 v.

L'Alhambra; ossiano, Nuovi abbozzi di Goffredo Crayon. Traduzione dall' inglese di Pietro Unia. Torino, Tipografia dei fratelli Favole, 1841. 2 v.

Nuovi racconti dell' Alhambra. Milano, Sesto S. Giovanni, Soc. ed. milanese, 1911. (Biblioteca per tutti, no. 59)

Spanish

* Cuentos de la Alhambra, de Washington Irving. Traducidos por D. L. L. Valencia, J. Ferrer de Orga, 1833.
Translation by D. Luis Lamarca.
Contains eight tales.
— — [Valencia, Mallén y Berard, 1833]
— — Paris, 1833.
Added engr. t.-p.: Valencia, 1833.

* Cuentos de la Alhambra, de Washington Irving . . . Madrid, Casa de la Unión commercial, 1844.
Translated by D. Manuel M. de Santa Ana from the French version of Mlle Sobry.

* Las cinco perlas de la Alhambra. Cuentos originales . . . Escritos en inglés por Washington Irving, y traducidos del francés por D. Manuel M. de Santa Ana. Madrid, 1844.
A revision of the preceding edition.
Contents. — Historia de tres príncesas. — Una visita a la Alhambra. — Historia del príncipe Ahmed al Kamel. — La herencia del Moro. — La rosa de la Alhambra; ó, El page y el halcon.

* Cuentos de la Alhambra, de Washinglon [sic] Irving. Granada, Zamora, 1859.
On cover: . . . Washington Irwing [sic]
Contains ten tales.

Cuentos de la Alhambra.   Madrid, Manuel Tello, 1882.
> No copy of this edition is known to exist; it is advertised as in preparation on the cover of Hawthorne's El tesoro escondido y los pigmeos, Madrid, 1882.

* Cuentos de la Alhambra.   Versión directa del inglés por el Doctor José Ventura Traveset . . . precedida de una nota biográfica del autor por D. A. González Garbín. Granada, P. V. Sabatel, 1888.

* Cuentos de la Alhambra, por el caballero Wáshington Irving. Versión completa del inglés por J. Ventura Traveset y noticia biográfica por A. G. Garbín.   Valencia, Prometeo sociedad editorial [1888?]

* Cuentos de la Alhambra, por el caballero Wáshington Irving. Versión directa del inglés por el Doctor José Ventura Traveset . . . precedida de una nota biográfica del autor por D. A. González Garbín . . . Segunda edición, corregida y aumentada . . . Granada, Viuda é hijos de P. V. Sabatel, 1893.

* Leyendas de la Alhambra . . .   Barcelona, O. Salvatella, 1906.

* . . . Cuentos de la Alhambra.   Versión española con una nota biográfica sobre el autor y sus obras por Pedro Umbert . . . Barcelona, Henrich y comp. [1910?]
> Contents. — El viaje. — Gobierno de la Alhambra. — Interior de la Alhambra. — Tradiciones locales. — La casa del caballo. — Leyenda del astrólogo árabe. — Historia del príncipe Ahmed al Kamel; ó, El peregrino de amor.

* Cuentos de la Alhambra . . .   Valencia [1926?]   (Nueva biblioteca de literatura)

* Leyendas de la Alhambra.   By Carlota Matienzo . . . and Laura B. Crandon . . . Illustrated by Willis S. Levis.   Boston, New York, Ginn and co. [c 1927]   (International modern language series)

Cuentos de la Alhambra, de Washington Irving, relatados a los niños por Manuel Vallvé.   Con ilustraciones de S. Tusell.   3. edición. Barcelona, Araluce [1929?]   (Half-title: Colección Araluce)

* Mas cuentos de la Alhambra de Washington Irving, relatados a la juventud por Manuel Vallvé.   Con ilustraciones de J. Segrelles. Barcelona, Araluce [1933]   (Half-title: Colección Araluce)

* Cuentos de la Alhambra . . .   Escritos en inglés por el caballero norte-americano Washington Irving, traducción española de Don Domingo Sicilia y San Juan.   Barcelona [n.d.] Abridged.

* Cuentos de la Alhambra, por el caballero Wáshington Irving. Versión completa del inglés por José Ventura Traveset y noticia biográfica por A. G. Garbín.   Valencia, Prometeo [191–?]   (Nueva biblioteca de literatura)
> Advertisement in the back mentions the World War, 1914.

* Leyendas de la Alhambra, por Washington Irving.   Barcelona [n.d.] (La Novela breve)

Spanish

Extracts

* El astrólogo árabe [and] La herencia del Moro. [n.p., n.d.]
Pamphlet, 12mo; place and date may have been on the paper cover, which is missing; nothing is known in the Biblioteca nacional concerning this little book.
Cuento de la Alhambra. El comandante Manco y el soldado. (*In* Semanario pintoresco español. Madrid, 1840. Oct. 18, 25)
* El legado del Moro. Leyenda de la Alhambra por Washington Irving. Versión castellana de Natalia Cossío de Jiménez. Madrid, Jiménez Fraud [n.d.] (Colección infantil Granada) Illustrations by F. Marco.
* Leyenda del astrólogo árabe. (*In* Biblioteca de la juventud. [n.p., n.d.] p. 35-49) Leyendas maravillosas.
* Leyenda del príncipe Ahmed al Kamel; ó, El peregrino de amor . . . Madrid, Jiménez Fraud [n.d.] (Colección infantil Granada) With many illustrations.
* El príncipe Ahmed al Kamel; ó, El peregrino de amor. (*In* Biblioteca de la juventud. [n.p., n.d.] p. 50-75) Leyendas maravillosas.
* La rosa de la Alhambra. (*In* Colección de novelas. Traducidas por Don Rafael García Tapia. Granada, 1849)
* La rosa de la Alhambra . . . Madrid, Jiménez Fraud [n.d.] (Colección infantil Granada)
* Las tres bellas infantas. Leyenda de la Alhambra. Por Washington Irving. Versión castellana de Natalia Cossío de Jiménez. Madrid [n.d.] (Colección infantil Granada)
* Las tres bellas princesas . . . Madrid, Jiménez Fraud [n.d.] (Colección infantil Granada)

Swedish

Alhambra; eller, Nya utkast af Geoffrey Crayon . . . Stockholm, Hjerta, 1833. (Läsebibliothek af den nyaste utländska litteraturen i svensk öfversättning, 1) Translation by Mattias Ziedner.
Alhambra; eller, Nya utkast af Geoffrey Crayon, författare till Utkasten, Berättelser af en resande, Granadas eröfring, Christofer Columbi lefnad och resor m. m. Komplett i en volum. Stockholm, Hjerta, 1834. (Läsebibliothek af den nyaste utländska litteraturen i svensk öfversättning, 1)
—— Stockholm, Hjerta, 1863. (Läsebibliothek af den nyaste utländska litteraturen i svensk öfversättning, 1)
Alhambra. Öfversättning af O. V. Ålund. Stockholm, Aktiebolaget Hiertas bokförlag, 1881. (Vitterlek. Tidskrift för skönliteratur, 2)

ASTORIA

* Astoria, or, Anecdotes of an enterprise beyond the Rocky mountains. By Washington Irving . . . Philadelphia, Carey, Lea, & Blanchard, 1836. 2 v.
First edition.

* Astoria; or, Enterprise beyond the Rocky mountains. By Washington Irving . . . London, Richard Bentley, 1836. 3 v.
First English edition.

* Astoria; or, Enterprise beyond the Rocky mountains, by Washington Irving. Paris, Baudry's European library, 1836. (Collection of ancient and modern British authors, 146)
Binder's title: The Rocky mountains.

* Astoria; or, Enterprise beyond the Rocky mountains. By Washington Irving . . . Paris, A. and W. Galignani, 1836.

* Astoria; or, Enterprise beyond the Rocky mountains . . . London, Richard Bentley, 1839. (Bentley's standard library of popular modern literature [v. 2])

Astoria; or, Enterprise beyond the Rocky mountains. Philadelphia, 1841.

Astoria, or, Enterprise beyond the Rocky mountains. By Washington Irving. Paris, Galignani & co., 1846.

* Astoria; or, Anecdotes of an enterprise beyond the Rocky mountains. By Washington Irving. Author's revised edition. Complete in one volume. New-York, George P. Putnam, 1849. (*Added t.-p.:* The works of Washington Irving. New edition, revised, v. 8)
First issue of revised edition.

* Astoria: or, Anecdotes of an enterprise beyond the Rocky mountains. By Washington Irving. Author's revised edition. Complete in one volume. London, Henry G. Bohn, 1850. (Bohn's shilling series, no. 24)
On cover: Two volumes in one.

Astoria; or, Anecdotes of an enterprise beyond the Rocky mountains. By Washington Irving. Author's revised edition. New York, G. P. Putnam, 1851. (*Added t.-p.:* The works of Washington Irving. New edition, revised, v. 8)

—— New York, G. P. Putnam, 1855. (*Added t.-p.:* The works of Washington Irving. New edition, revised, v. 8)

—— New York, G. P. Putnam, 1860. (*Added t.-p.:* The works of Washington Irving. New edition, revised, v. 8)

—— New York, G. P. Putnam, 1867. (*Added t.-p.:* The works of Washington Irving. New edition, revised, v. 8)

* Astoria; or, Anecdotes of an enterprise beyond the Rocky mountains. By Washington Irving. Author's revised edition . . . New York, G. P. Putnam and son, 1868.
Half-title: . . . Knickerbocker edition.

* — — New York, G. P. Putnam and son, 1868. (*Half-title:* . . .
People's edition)

* Astoria; or, Anecdotes of an enterprise beyond the Rocky mountains,
by Washington Irving. Author's revised edition . . . New York,
G. P. Putnam's sons, 1868. (*Publisher's lettering:* Irving's works)
At head of title: Hudson edition.

* Astoria; or, Anecdotes of an enterprise beyond the Rocky mountains,
by Washington Irving. Author's revised edition . . . [New York,
G. P. Putnam's sons, c 1868] (The works of Washington Irving.
The Kinderhook edition, v. 7)

Astoria; or, Enterprise beyond the Rocky mountains. Author's
revised edition. Knickerbocker edition. New York [1873?]

Astoria; or, Anecdotes of an enterprise beyond the Rocky mountains
. . . Author's revised edition . . . New York, G. P. Putnam's
sons [1874?] (*On cover:* Irving's works)
Half-title: Peoples [*sic*] edition.

* Astoria; or, Anecdotes of an enterprise beyond the Rocky mountains
. . . New York, G. P. Putnam's sons, 1881.
Author's revised edition.

. . . Astoria; or, Anecdotes of an enterprise beyond the Rocky mountains, by Washington Irving. Author's revised edition . . . New
York, G. P. Putnam's sons [1882?]
Vol. [2] of a uniform edition in cloth having at head of title "Hudson edition" (first issued in 1882) and lettered: Irving's works.

Astoria; or, Anecdotes of an enterprise beyond the Rocky mountains.
New York, G. P. Putnam's sons, 1885.
Hudson edition.

. . . Astoria; or, Anecdotes of an enterprise beyond the Rocky mountains, by Washington Irving. Author's revised edition . . . New
York, G. P. Putnam's sons, 1889. (*Publisher's lettering:* Irving's
works)
At head of title: Hudson edition.

* Astoria; or, Anecdotes of an enterprise beyond the Rocky mountains.
[By] Washington Irving. Tacoma edition. New York and London, G. P. Putnam's sons, 1897. 2 v.

. . . Astoria, by Washington Irving . . . New York and London,
G. P. Putnam's sons [1897] 2 v.
At head of title: Knickerbocker edition.
Half-title: Astoria; or, Anecdotes of an enterprise beyond the
Rocky mountains.

. . . Astoria; or, Anecdotes of an enterprise beyond the Rocky mountains, by Washington Irving. Author's revised edition . . . New
York, G. P. Putnam's sons [1902] (*Publisher's lettering:* Irving's
works)
At head of title: Hudson edition.

Astoria . . . New York, Belford co. [188–?]

Astoria . . . New York, G. P. Putnam's sons [19-?]
Gift edition.
Astoria . . . New York, G. P. Putnam's sons [19-?]
Large paper edition.
Astoria . . . New York, G. P. Putnam's sons [19-?]
New handy volume edition.
Astoria . . . New York, G. P. Putnam's sons [19-?]
New Knickerbocker edition.
Astoria . . . New York, G. P. Putnam's sons [19-?]
Student's edition.
Astoria . . . New York, G. P. Putnam's sons [n.d.]
Waldorf edition.
* Astoria, or, Anecdotes of an enterprise beyond the Rocky mountains.
By Washington Irving. New York, United States book co. [n.d.]
Contents. — Astoria. — Salmagundi. — Adventures of Captain
Bonneville.

Extracts

* [Advance excerpts.] (*In* New-York mirror. New-York, 1836. v. 14,
p. 198)
The fur traders of the Columbia River and the Rocky mountains as
described by Washington Irving in his account of "Astoria," and
the record of "The adventures of Captain Bonneville," with some
additions by the editor. New York and London, G. P. Putnam's
sons, 1903. ([The Knickerbocker literature series, 3])
Edited by Frank Lincoln Olmsted.
* . . . Travels in Missouri and the South . . . Notes by F. A. Sampson. Columbia, Mo., 1910.
Extracts from Astoria, and from Irving's letters.
Cover-title.
From The Missouri historical review. Columbia, Mo., October,
1910. p. [15]-33.

TRANSLATIONS

Dutch

* Astoria, of, Avontuurlyke reize naar en over het Klipgebergte van
Noord-Amerika, ondernomen in het belang der door den Heer
J. J. Astor opgerigte peltery compagnie en beschreven door Wash-
ington Irving . . . Haarlem, de wed. A. Loosjes, pz., 1837. 2 v.
Engr. t.-p.

French

* Voyages dans les contrées désertes de l'Amérique du nord, entrepris
pour la fondation du Comptoir d'Astoria sur la côte nord-ouest.
Par Washington Irving . . . Traduit de l'anglais par P. N.
Grolier . . . Paris, P. Dufart, 1839. 2 v.

* Astoria, voyages au delà des Montagnes Rocheuses, par Washington Irving. Traduit de l'anglais par P.-N. Grolier. 2. édition. Paris, A. Allouard, 1843. 2 v. in 1.

German

* Astoria . . . (*In* Magazin für die Literatur des Auslandes. Berlin, Hayn, 1836. 10. Bd., p. [561]–562, 566–568, 570–571, 575–576)

Astoria; oder, Die Unternehmung jenseits des Felsengebirges. Von Washington Irving. Aus dem Englischen von A. von Treskow. Quedlinburg und Leipzig, G. Basse, 1837. 2 v. in 1.

Astoria, oder, Abenteuer in den Gebirgen und Wåldern von Canada. Aus dem Englischen von Dr. E. Brinckmeier. Braunschweig, G. C. E. Meyer, Sen., 1837. 3 v.

* Astoria. Von Washington Irving. Aus dem Englischen. Frankfurt am Main, J. D. Sauerländer, 1837. 3 v. in 1.

* Astoria; oder, Geschichte einer Handelsexpedition jenseits der Rocky Mountains. Aus dem Englischen des Washington Irving. Stuttgart und Tübingen, J. G. Cotta, 1838. (Reisen und Länderbeschreibungen der älteren und neuesten Zeit, Lfg. 14)
Added series t.-p.

Astoria. Frei aus dem Englischen übertragen von E. von Kraatz. Braunschweig, G. Westermann, 1910. (Lebensbücher der Jugend. Hrsg. von Friedrich Düsel, Bd. 10)

Das Astoria-Abenteuer. Nach den zeitgenössischen Aufzeichnungen Washington Irvings erz. Ill. von L. Berwald. 7. Auflage. Stuttgart o. J., Union, 1919.

— — Stuttgart o. J., Union, 1920. 9. Auflage.

Extracts

* Eine Menschenjagd. (*In* Magazin für die Literatur des Auslandes. Berlin, Hayn, 1837. 11. Bd., p. 28)

Swedish

Astoria; eller, Kolonien bortom Klippbergen . . . Af Washington Irving . . . Öfversättning. Stockholm, L. J. Hjerta, 1837. 2 v. (*Added t.-p.:* I Nytt läse-bibliothek)
Translated by A. F. Dalin.
Issued in 7 pts.

THE BEAUTIES OF WASHINGTON IRVING

See also, II. Selected Works

* The beauties of Washington Irving . . . Illustrated with six etchings by William Heath. Glasgow, Richard Griffin & co., 1825.
Six colored plates, engraved.

* The beauties of Washington Irving, esq. . . . Illustrated with six etchings, by William Heath, esq. London, J. Bumpus, 1825.
* The beauties of Washington Irving . . . Illustrated with six etchings by William Heath. A new edition. Glasgow, R. Griffin & co., 1830.

The beauties of Washington Irving. With illustrations by George Cruikshank. London, Printed by C. Whittingham, 1835.

* The beauties of Washington Irving . . . Illustrated with wood cuts, engraved by Thompson; from drawings by George Cruikshank, esq. The fourth edition. London, T. Tegg and son [etc., etc.] 1835. Illustrated t.-p.
* The beauties of Washington Irving . . . Philadelphia, Carey, Lea, & Blanchard, 1835.
* The beauties of Washington Irving . . . Philadelphia, Carey, Lea & Blanchard, for G. W. Gorton, 1838.

The beauties of Washington Irving . . . Philadelphia, Lea and Blanchard, 1839.

* The gentleman in black, and Tales of other days. With illustrations by George Cruikshank and others. London, C. Daly, 1840.

A collection, identical with The beauties of Washington Irving.

* The illustrated beauties of Irving, with Life by S. Austin Allibone, and a notice of Sunnyside by H. T. Tuckerman. Philadelphia, Childs & Peterson, 1849.

The gentleman in black, and Tales of other days. With illustrations by George Cruikshank and others. St. Louis, Edwards & Bushell, 1857.

Illustrated beauties of Irving. Vignette illustrations of the writings of Washington Irving . . . Philadelphia, Childs & Peterson, 1858.

* The beauties of Washington Irving. Illustrated by George Cruikshank. London, William Tegg, 1866.

The beauties of Washington Irving . . . London, Sonnenschein & co., 1884.

The beauties of Washington Irving . . . Illustrated with wood cuts, engraved by Thompson from drawings by George Cruikshank, esq. . . . London, William Tegg [n.d.]

BIOGRAPHY AND POETICAL REMAINS OF THE LATE MARGARET MILLER DAVIDSON

See also, Spanish Papers

* Biography and poetical remains of the late Margaret Miller Davidson. By Washington Irving . . . Philadelphia, Lea and Blanchard, 1841. 8vo.
First edition.
* — — Another issue. 12mo.

* Biography and poetical remains of the late Margaret Miller Davidson. By Washington Irving . . . Third edition. Philadelphia, Lea and Blanchard, 1842.

* Life and poetical remains of Margaret M. Davidson. By Washington Irving . . . London, Tilt and Bogue, 1843. 8vo.

* Life and poetical remains of Margaret M. Davidson. By Washington Irving. London, David Bogue, 1843. 12mo.

* Biography and poetical remains of the late Margaret Miller Davidson. By Washington Irving . . . A new edition, revised. Philadelphia, Lea and Blanchard, 1843.
Cover-title.

Life and recollections of Margaret Davidson, and her poetical remains . . . London [1845?]
Engr. t.-p.: Recollections of M. and L. Davidson.

Biography and poetical remains of the late Margaret Miller Davidson. By Washington Irving . . . A new edition, revised. Philadelphia, Lea and Blanchard, 1846.

Biography and poetical remains of the late Margaret Miller Davidson. By Washington Irving . . . A new edition, revised. New York, Clark, Austin & co., 1852.

Biography and poetical remains of the late Margaret M. Davidson. London [1854]

Biography and poetical remains of the late Margaret Miller Davidson. By Washington Irving . . . A new ed., rev. Boston, P. Sampson and co., 1857.

Translations

German

Biographie der jungen amerikanischen Dichterin Margarethe Miller Davidson. Aus dem Englischen. Leipzig, F. A. Brockhaus, 1843.

Leben . . . der Lucretia Maria Davidson aus dem Englischen der Miss Sedgwick und Biographie der jungen amerikanischen Dichterin Margaretta Davidson. Aus dem Englischen des Washington Irving. Leipzig, Brockhaus, 1848.

BIOGRAPHY OF JAMES LAWRENCE, ESQ.

See also, Spanish Papers

* Biography of James Lawrence, esq., late a captain in the navy of the United States: together with a collection of the most interesting papers, relative to the action between the Chesapeake and Shannon, and the death of Captain Lawrence . . . New-Brunswick, Printed and published by L. Deare, 1813.
From the Analectic magazine, August, 1813.

—— (*In* An account of the funeral honours bestowed on the remains
of Capt. Lawrence and Lieut. Ludlow, with the eulogy pronounced
at Salem, on the occasion, by Hon. Joseph Story.   To which is
prefixed, an account of the engagement between the Chesapeake
and Shannon, with documents relative to the same, and biographical and poetical notices . . .   Boston, Joshua Belcher, 1813.
p. 17–32)

—— (*In* The Book hunter. [place?] Jan. 1932)

A BOOK OF THE HUDSON

See also, II.   Selected Works

* A book of the Hudson.   Collected from the various works of Diedrich
Knickerbocker.   Edited by Geoffrey Crayon.   New-York, G. P.
Putnam, 1849.
Printed by John F. Trow.
Binder's title: Tales of the Hudson.
Contains Putnam's advertisements dated November, 1848.
Contents. — Introduction [first part of Letter to the editor of
The Knickerbocker magazine, from The Knickerbocker, March,
1839; republished in Spanish papers]. — Communipaw [from
The Knickerbocker, September, 1839; republished in Spanish
papers]. — Guests from Gibbet island.   A legend of Communi-
paw [from The Knickerbocker, October, 1839; republished in
Wolfert's Roost]. — Peter Stuyvesant's voyage up the Hudson.
From The history of New York. — The chronicle of Bearn island.
Showing the rise of the great Van Rensellaer [*sic*] dynasty, and
the first seeds of the Helderberg war.   Compiled from Knickerbocker's History of New York. — The legend of Sleepy Hollow
[from The sketch book]. — Dolph Heyliger [from Bracebridge
Hall]. — Rip Van Winkle [from The sketch book]. — Wolfert
Webber, or, Golden dreams [from Tales of a traveller].

* —— New-York, G. P. Putnam, 1849.
Added t.-p. and plates done in lithography by Sarony & Major,
117 Fulton Street, New York.

* —— New York, G. P. Putnam, 1849.
Printed by R. Craighead.
Publisher's list dated March, 1849.

Stories of the Hudson, by Washington Irving; with illustrations by
Clifton Johnson.   New York, Dodge publishing co. [c 1912]
"This collection of stories is identical with a volume that Irving
himself published in the year 1849, except that the tale of
Wolfert's Roost has been added."

Extracts

* Guests from Gibbet-island. A legend of Communipaw . . . (*In* The Knickerbocker sketch-book . . . New-York, Burgess, Stringer and co., 1845. p. [115]–132)

BRACEBRIDGE HALL

* Bracebridge Hall, or, The humourists. A medley, by Geoffrey Crayon, gent. . . . New-York, Printed by C. S. Van Winkle, 1822. 2 v. 8vo.
First edition.
The first American edition was limited to 1000 copies. Irving made many alterations and additions as the work was in press, so that the first English edition differs considerably from the American. The two editions were published within two days of each other, the American appearing on the 21st of May and the English on the 23rd.
— — Another issue.
Printed in sixes.
* Bracebridge Hall; or, The humorists. By Geoffrey Crayon, gent. . . . London, John Murray, 1822. 2 v. 8vo.
First English edition.
— — Another issue. 2 v. 16mo.
* Bracebridge Hall; or, The humorists. By Geoffrey Crayon, gent. Paris, Baudry, 1823. 2 v.
Bracebridge Hall; or, The humorists. By Geoffrey Crayon, gent. . . . New edition. London, John Murray, 1824. 2 v.
* Bracebridge Hall; or, The humorists. By Geoffrey Crayon, gent. . . . A new edition . . . London, John Murray, 1825. 2 v.
* Bracebridge Hall, or, The humourists. A medley, by Geoffrey Crayon, gent. . . . Third American edition . . . New-York, Printed by C. S. Van Winkle, 1826. 2 v.
* Bracebridge Hall; or, The humorists. By Geoffrey Crayon, gent. Paris, A. & W. Galignani, 1827. 2 v.
* Bracebridge Hall: or, The humourists. A medley. By Geoffrey Crayon, gent. . . . Fourth American edition. Philadelphia, Carey & Lea, 1830. 2 v.
* — — Philadelphia, Carey & Lea, 1833. 2 v.
* Bracebridge Hall; or, The humorists. By Geoffrey Crayon. Paris, Baudry, 1834. 2 v.
Bracebridge Hall; or, The humorists. A medley. By Geoffrey Crayon, gent. Philadelphia, Carey & Lea, 1835. 2 v.
* Bracebridge Hall: or, The humourists. A medley. By Geoffrey Crayon, gent. . . . A new edition. Philadelphia, Carey, Lea & Blanchard, 1836. 2 v.

* Bracebridge Hall; or, The humourists. A medley. By Geoffrey Crayon, gent. . . . A new edition. Philadelphia, Carey, Lea & Blanchard, 1838. 2 v.

* Bracebridge Hall; or, The humorists. By Geoffrey Crayon, gent. . . . London, John Murray, 1845. (Murray's home and colonial library, v. 11)

Bracebridge Hall, by Washington Irving. New York, G. P. Putnam's sons, 1848. (Works of Washington Irving. Author's revised edition, v. 6)

Bracebridge Hall, by Washington Irving. New York, G. P. Putnam's sons [1848?] 2 v.
Pocket edition.

* Bracebridge Hall; or, The humorists. A medley by Geoffrey Crayon, gent^n . . . Author's revised edition. Complete in one volume. New York, George P. Putnam, 1849. (*Added t.-p.:* The works of Washington Irving. New edition, revised, v. 6)

* Bracebridge Hall; or, The humorists. A medley by Geoffrey Crayon . . . London, Henry G. Bohn, 1850.
Author's revised edition.

Bracebridge Hall . . . London, John Murray, 1850.

Bracebridge Hall; or, The humorists. A medley by Geoffrey Crayon, gent^n . . . Author's revised edition. Complete in one volume. New York, George P. Putnam & co., 1853. (*Added t.-p.:* The works of Washington Irving. New edition, revised, v. 6)

* Bracebridge Hall. By Washington Irving . . . Illustrated with fourteen original designs by Schmolze, engraved on steel by Greatbach and others. New York, G. P. Putnam, 1858.

Bracebridge Hall; or, The humorists. A medley. By Geoffrey Crayon, gent^n . . . Author's revised edition . . . New York, G. P. Putnam, 1860. (*Added t.-p.:* The works of Washington Irving. New edition, revised, v. 6)
Second added t.-p., engr.

Bracebridge Hall; or, The humorists. A medley. By Geoffrey Crayon, gent. . . . The author's revised edition. Complete in one volume. New York, G. P. Putnam's sons [c 1865]
Added illustrated t.-p.
People's edition.

Bracebridge Hall; or, The humorists. A medley. By Geoffrey Crayon, gent. New York, G. P. Putnam and son, 1867.
Author's revised edition.

Bracebridge Hall, or, The humorists. A medley. By Geoffrey Crayon, gent. . . . The author's revised edition . . . Philadelphia, J. B. Lippincott & co., 1870. (*On cover:* Irving's works)
Half-title: . . . Riverside edition.
Added engr. t.-p.; vignette.

Bracebridge Hall, or, The humorists. A medley. By Geoffrey Crayon, gent. . . . The author's revised edition . . . New York, G. P. Putnam's sons [1874?] (*On cover:* Irving's works)
Added t.-p., engr., with vignette.
Half-title: People's edition.

* Bracebridge Hall. By Washington Irving. Illustrated by R. Caldecott. London, Macmillan & co., 1877. 12mo.
First edition with these illustrations.
Illustrated t.-p.

* —— London, Macmillan & co., 1877. 8vo.
Second edition with Caldecott's illustrations.
Illustrated t.-p.

Bracebridge Hall; or, The humorists. A medley. Erklärt von C. Th. Lion . . . Berlin, Weidmann, 1878. 2 v.

. . . Bracebridge Hall; or, The humorists; a medley by Geoffrey Crayon, gent. . . . Author's revised edition . . . New York, G. P. Putnam's sons [c 1880] (*Half-title:* Irving's works. Geoffrey Crayon edition, v. 3)
Added engr. t.-p.

Bracebridge Hall; or, The humorists; a medley by Geoffrey Crayon, gent. . . . Author's revised edition . . . [New York, G. P. Putnam's sons, c 1880] (The works of Washington Irving. The Kinderhook edition, v. 1)

Bracebridge Hall. By Washington Irving. Illustrated by R. Caldecott. London, Macmillan & co., 1882. 12mo.

* —— London, Macmillan & co., 1882. 8vo.

* Bracebridge Hall, from Washington Irving's Sketch-book; with one hundred and twenty illustrations by R. Caldecott, engraved by James D. Cooper. London, Macmillan & co., 1882. 4to.
Cover-title.
Printed by R. & R. Clark, Edinburgh.

* . . . Bracebridge Hall; or, The humorists. By Geoffrey Crayon, gent. . . . Author's revised edition . . . New York, G. P. Putnam's sons, 1882.
Hudson edition.
Added engr. t.-p.

. . . Bracebridge Hall; or, The humorists, a medley, by Geoffrey Crayon, gent. . . . The author's revised edition . . . New York, G. P. Putnam's sons [1882]
Vol. [4] of a uniform edition in cloth having at head of title "Hudson edition" (first issued in 1882) and lettered: Irving's works.
Copyright date: 1880.

* Bracebridge Hall; or, The humorists. New York, J. B. Alden, 1883.

* . . . Bracebridge Hall; or, The humorists . . . London, F. Warne and co., 1886. (Warne's "Crown" library)

* Bracebridge Hall. By Washington Irving. Illustrated by R. Calde-
  cott. London, Macmillan & co., 1887.
  Illustrated t.-p.
  . . . Bracebridge Hall; or, The humorists; a medley, by Geoffrey
  Crayon, gent. . . . The author's revised edition . . . New York,
  G. P. Putnam's sons, 1889. (*Publisher's lettering:* Irving's works)
  At head of title: Hudson edition.
  Added engr. t.-p.
  Bracebridge Hall . . . London, Nelson, 1890. 2 v.
  Surrey edition.
  Bracebridge Hall. By Washington Irving. Illustrated by R. Calde-
  cott. London, Macmillan & co., 1892.
  Reprint of 1882 edition.
  —— London, Macmillan & co., 1895.
* Bracebridge Hall; or, The humourists. Washington Irving. Surrey
  edition . . . New York & London, G. P. Putnam's sons, 1896. 2 v.
  . . . Bracebridge Hall, by Washington Irving . . . New York and
  London, G. P. Putnam's sons [1897] 2 v.
  At head of title: Knickerbocker edition.
  Half-title: Bracebridge Hall; or, The humorists.
  Bracebridge Hall . . . Edited, with notes, introduction, and a
  glossary, by J. D. Colclough. Dublin, Brown & Nolan, 1898.
  (English texts)
  Bracebridge Hall, by Washington Irving. Chicago, W. B. Conkey co.
  [c 1900]
  Illuminated t.-p.
* Bracebridge Hall; or, The humorists. By Washington Irving . . .
  New York, T. Y. Crowell & co. [1900?]
  Bracebridge Hall; or, The humorists. Auswahl. Für den Schulge-
  brauch erklärt von G. Wolpert. Leipzig, Renger, 1902. (Franzö-
  sische und englische Schulbibliothek, hrsg. von Otto E. A. Dick-
  mann, Bd. 138)
  . . . Bracebridge Hall; or, The humorists; a medley, by Geoffrey
  Crayon, gent. . . . The author's revised edition . . . New York,
  G. P. Putnam's sons [1902] (*Publisher's lettering:* Irving's works)
  At head of title: Hudson edition.
  Added engr. t.-p.; vignette.
  Bracebridge Hall. By Washington Irving. Illustrated by R. Calde-
  cott. London, Macmillan, 1903. (Illustrated pocket classics)
  Bracebridge Hall. By Washington Irving. With numerous illustra-
  tions by R. Caldecott. London, 1904.
  . . . Selections from Bracebridge Hall . . . edited with notes and
  introduction by Samuel Thurber . . . Boston, New York [etc.]
  Houghton Mifflin co. [c 1910] (The Riverside literature series)
  Bracebridge Hall, by Washington Irving . . . London, Bell, 1914.
  (Bohn's popular library)

Bracebridge Hall. By Washington Irving. Illustrated by R. Caldecott. London, Macmillan, 1925. (Illustrated pocket classics)

Bracebridge Hall; a sequel to Old Christmas; illustrated by R. Caldecott. New York, Macmillan, 1928. (Dainty books)

Bracebridge Hall; or, The humorists . . . London, H. G. Bohn
[193-?] (Bohn's popular library, no. 73)

Bracebridge Hall; or, The humorists . . . [New York, Belford co.,
188-?]

* Bracebridge Hall; or, The humorists. By Washington Irving . . .
New York, T. Y. Crowell & co. [n.d.]

Bracebridge Hall . . . New York, Harcourt, Brace and co. [19-?]

Bracebridge Hall . . . New York, Harcourt, Brace and co. [193-?]
Pocket edition.

Bracebridge Hall . . . New York, Putnam [19-?] (Ariel booklets)

Bracebridge Hall . . . New York, Putnam [19-?]
Gift edition.

Bracebridge Hall . . . New York, Putnam [19-?]
Large paper edition.

Bracebridge Hall . . . New York, Putnam [19-?]
New handy volume edition.

Bracebridge Hall . . . New York, Putnam [19-?]
Student's edition.

Bracebridge Hall . . . Philadelphia, Henry Altemus [19-?] (Altemus'
new vademecum series)

Extracts

Bachelors and Bachelors' confessions, by Washington Irving. Pictures by Cecil Aldin. London, William Heinemann, 1909.

Dolph Heyliger . . . London, J. Chapman, 1851.

Dolph Heyliger; a story from Bracebridge Hall . . . edited by G. H.
Browne . . . Boston, D. C. Heath & co., 1901. (Heath's home
and school classics. The young reader's series)

Dolph Heyliger . . . Boston, D. C. Heath & co., 1904.

Illustrations of Washington Irving's Dolph Heyliger, designed and
etched by John W. Ehninger. New-York, G. P. Putnam, 1851.
Contains The haunted house.

* The widow. By Washington Irving. (*In* The perverse widow. By
Sir Richard Steele. The widow. By Washington Irving. Pictures
by Cecil Aldin. New York, E. P. Dutton and co., 1909. p. 21–31)

* Wives, by Washington Irving. The henpecked man, by Sir Richard
Steele. Pictures by Cecil Aldin. New York, Dutton, 1909.

* "Review, with selected extracts in illustration." (*In* The Bouquet
of popular literature. London, 1822. v. 1, p. 11–26)

TRANSLATIONS
Danish

Bracebridge-Hall, oversat af Wallich. København, Schubothe, 1829. 2 v.

Dutch

Mijn verblijf op het kasteel Bracebridge; naar het Engelsch, door Steenbergen van Goor. Amsterdam, C. L. Schleyer, 1828. 2 v.

French

* Le château de Bracebridge, par Geoffroy[*sic*]-Crayon, traduit de l'anglais par M. Jean Cohen . . . Paris, Hubert, 1822. 4 v.
* Les humoristes, ou, Le château de Bracebridge, par Washington Irving, traduit de l'anglais par Gustave Grandpré . . . Paris, Corbet, 1826. 2 v.

"Je dois prévenir le lecteur que je n'ai pas traduit en entier Les humoristes, ou *Le château de Bracebridge;* j'en ai retranché quelques chapitres qui offrent peu d'intérêt, et en cela je me suis conformé à l'opinion unanime des journalistes anglais qui ont rendu compte de cet ouvrage." — *Cf.* "Avertissement."

German

Bracebridge Hall . . . [Leipzig? 1822]
* Bracebridge-Hall; oder, Die Charaktere. Aus dem Englischen des Washington Irving übersetzt von S. H. Spiker . . . Berlin, Duncker und Humblot, 1823. 2 v.
* Bracebridge Hall; oder, Die Charaktere. Aus dem Englischen des Washington Irving übersetzt von S. H. Spiker . . . Zweite, verbesserte Auflage. Berlin, Duncker und Humblot, 1826. 2 v.
Bracebridge Hall; oder, Die Charaktere . . . Wien, 1826. 3 v.
Bracebridge Hall; übersetzt von Henriette Schubert. Zwickau, Schumann, 1826. 4 v. (Taschen-Bibliothek der auslåndischen Classiker)
* Bracebridge-Hall; oder, Die Charaktere . . . Frankfurt, Sauerlånder, 1827. 6 v. in 2. (*Added t.-p.:* Washington Irving's Såmmtliche Werke, 13. –18. Bd.)
* Bracebridge-Hall; oder, Die Charaktere. Aus dem Englischen des Washington Irving übersetzt von S. H. Spiker. Wien, Chr. Fr. Schade, 1828. 3 v.
Humorist. Frankfurt, 1829.
Bracebridge Hall. Aachen, 1839.
Bracebridge-Hall. Mit erklärenden Anmerkungen hrsg. von E. A. Toel . . . Lüneburg, Herold und Wahlstab, 1841.
Bracebridge-Hall; oder, Die Charaktere. Frankfurt-am-Main, Sauerländer, 1846. 2., sorgfältig verbesserte Auflage. (Ausgewählte Schriften . . . Th. 2)

Extracts

Die alten Sitten. (*In* Eos. München, Fleischmann, 1824. No. 152 ff)
Der dicke Herr. (*In* Eos. München, Fleischmann, 1824. No. 143 ff)
Dolph Heyliger, aus Bracebridge Hall. Hrsg. von A. Seedorf. Berlin, Simion, 1889. (Rauch's English readings, 40)

Duelle. (*In* Eos. München, Fleischmann, 1824. No. 154–155)
[Extracts.] (*In* Zeitung für die elegante Welt. Leipzig, Voss, 1822.
No. 206–208)

Italian

Extracts

Annetta Delarbre, racconto di Washington Irving; versione dall'
inglese di Ercole Rivolta. Milano, Francesco di Omobono Manini,
1839.
Dolph Heyliger, ovvero, La casa degli spiriti; racconto di Vashington-
Irving. Prima traduzione dall' inglese. Milano, G. Truffi e socii,
1835. (Romanzi e curiosità storiche di tutte le nazioni. Terza
serie, v. 39)

Polish

Galerya obrazów życia ludzkiego, czyli charaktery. Wilno, 1829. 2 v.
Translated by Józef Bychowiec.

Russian

Extracts

Аннета Деларбръ. (*In* Московскій Телеграфъ. Moscow, 1828.
v. 5, p. 28–49; v. 6, p. 159–171)
Annette Delarbre.
Баккалавръ Саламанкскій. (*In* Московскій Телеграфъ. Moscow,
1826. v. 12, p. 14–37, 66–83)
The student of Salamanca.
Заколдованный домъ. (*In* Московскій Телеграфъ. Moscow,
1827. v. 5, p. 14, 75, 125)
The haunted house.

Swedish

Bracebridge Hall; eller, En vår på landet i England. Stockholm,
Hæggström, 1828.
Translated by J. Ekelund.
Bracebridge Hall; eller, Minnen och intryck från en vår på landet i
England. Öfversättning. Stockholm [J. L. Törnqvist] 1865.
(Familjebibliotek, 6)

Byron. (*In* Galignani's messenger. Paris [1824?])

Charles the Second; or, The merry monarch . . . London, Longman,
Hurst, Rees, Orme, Brown, and Green, 1824.
By John Howard Payne and Washington Irving.

— — London, T. Dolby [1824]

— — Philadelphia [etc.] Neal & Mackenzie, 1829.

* Charles the Second. By John Howard Payne and Washington Irving.
    (*In* Quinn, A. H., *ed*. Representative American plays. New York,
    The Century co., 1917. p. 141–164)

A CHRONICLE OF THE CONQUEST OF GRANADA

* A chronicle of the conquest of Granada. By Fray Antonio Agapida
    . . . Philadelphia, Carey, Lea & Carey, 1829. 2 v.
    First edition.

* — — Another issue. 2 v. in 1.

* — — Philadelphia, Carey, Lea & Carey, 1829. 2 v.
    Large paper edition.

* A chronicle of the conquest of Granada. From the MSS. of Fray
    Antonio Agapida. By Washington Irving. In two volumes . . .
    London, John Murray, 1829. 2 v.
    First English edition.

* A chronicle of the conquest of Granada. From the MSS. of Fray
    Antonio Agapida. By Washington Irving . . . Paris, A. and W.
    Galignani, 1829. 2 v. 12mo.
    First Continental edition.

* — — Paris, A. &. W. Galignani, 1829. 2 v. 8vo.

* A chronicle of the conquest of Granada. From the MSS. of Fray
    Antonio Agapida, by Washington Irving. Paris, Baudry, 1829. 2 v.

* A chronicle of the conquest of Granada. By Fray Antonio Agapida.
    Philadelphia, Lea & Carey, 1833. 2 v. in 1.

— — Philadelphia, Lea & Carey, 1835. 2 v.

A chronicle of the conquest of Granada. By Fray Antonio Agapida.
    Philadelphia, Carey, Lea and Blanchard, 1836. 2 v.

A chronicle of the conquest of Granada. By Fray Antonio Agapida
    . . . Philadelphia, Carey, Lea, & Blanchard, 1838. 2 v.
    New edition.

* A chronicle of the conquest of Granada. By Washington Irving. Mit
    sprachwissenschaftlichen Noten und einem Wörterbuche. Leipzig,
    Baumgärtner, 1841.

* A chronicle of the conquest of Granada. From the MSS. of Fray
    Antonio Agapida. Paris, Baudry, 1842. 2 v. (Collection of an-
    cient and modern British authors, t. 350)

* History of the conquest of Granada. From the MSS. of Fray Antonio
    Agapida. London, George Routledge and co., 1850.

* Chronicle of the conquest of Granada. From the MSS. of Fray
    Antonio Agapida. New-York, G. P. Putnam; London, John Murray,
    1850. (*Added t.-p.*: The works of Washington Irving. New edition,
    revised, v. 14)

The conquest of Granada . . . London, H. G. Bohn, 1850.

A chronicle of the conquest of Granada, to which is added Legends of the conquest of Spain. [place?] 1850. 2 v. in 1.

Chronicle of the conquest of Granada. From the MSS. of Fray Antonio Agapida, by Washington Irving. Author's revised edition. [New York, G. P. Putnam, c 1850] (The works of Washington Irving. The Kinderhook edition, v. 3)

Chronicle of the conquest of Granada, from the MSS. of Fray Antonio Agapida, by Washington Irving. Author's revised edition. New York, G. P. Putnam's sons [c 1850]
Knickerbocker edition.
Added t.-p.: Conquest of Granada.

Chronicle of the conquest of Granada. From the MSS. of Fray Antonio Agapida. New-York, G. P. Putnam; London, J. Murray, 1851. (*Added t.-p.:* The works of Washington Irving. New edition, revised, v. 14)

—— New-York, G. P. Putnam; London, J. Murray, 1852. (*Added t.-p.:* The works of Washington Irving. New edition, revised, v. 14)

Chronicle of the conquest of Granada . . . London, H. G. Bohn, 1852. (Bohn's shilling series)

A chronicle of the conquest of Granada. London [1854]
Includes Legends of the conquest of Spain.

A chronicle of the conquest of Granada . . . [place?] 1866. 2 v. in 1.

Chronicle of the conquest of Granada. From the MSS. of Fray Antonio Agapida. By Washington Irving. Author's revised edition. New York, G. P. Putnam, 1867.

Chronicle of the conquest of Granada. From the MSS. of Fray Antonio Agapida, by Washington Irving. Author's revised edition. Philadelphia, J. B. Lippincott & co., 1870.
Added engr. t.-p.
Knickerbocker edition.

A chronicle of the conquest of Granada . . . [place?] 1873.

. . . Chronicle of the conquest of Granada, from the MSS. of Fray Antonio Agapida, by Washington Irving. Author's revised edition. New York, G. P. Putnam's sons, 1882.
At head of title: Hudson edition.

* A chronicle of the conquest of Granada, from the MSS. of Fray Antonio Agapida. To which is added Legends of the conquest of Spain. By Washington Irving. London, George Bell and sons, 1882. 2 v.
Paged continuously.
Legends of the conquest of Spain has half-title only.

. . . Chronicle of the conquest of Granada, from the MSS. of Fray Antonio Agapida, by Washington Irving. Author's revised edition. New York, G. P. Putnam's sons [1882?]

Vol. [10] of a uniform edition in cloth, having at head of title "Hudson edition" (first issued in 1882) and lettered: Irving's works.

The conquest of Granada . . . New York, J. B. Alden, 1883.

. . . Chronicle of the conquest of Granada, from the MSS. of Fray Antonio Agapida, by Washington Irving. Author's revised edition. New York, G. P. Putnam's sons [1889] (*Publisher's lettering:* Irving's works)
At head of title: Hudson edition.
Added engr. t.-p.

. . . Chronicle of the conquest of Granada, by Washington Irving. Author's revised edition . . . New York, London, G. P. Putnam's sons, 1893. 2 v.
At head of title: Agapida edition.

* Chronicle of the conquest of Granada. From the MSS. of Fray Antonio Agapida. By Washington Irving. Author's revised edition. Illustrated. Philadelphia, David McKay, 1894.

* A chronicle of the conquest of Granada . . . To which is added Legends of the conquest of Spain . . . London, George Bell & sons, 1894–96. 2 v. (Bohn's library of standard works)
Cover-title: Granada and Spain. Washington Irving.
Paged continuously.

The conquest of Granada . . . [place?] 1895. 2 v. in 1.

. . . The conquest of Granada, by Washington Irving . . . New York and London, G. P. Putnam's sons [1897] 2 v.
At head of title: Knickerbocker edition.
Half-title: Chronicle of the conquest of Granada.

. . . Chronicle of the conquest of Granada, from the MSS. of Fray Antonio Agapida, by Washington Irving. Author's revised edition. New York, G. P. Putnam's sons [1902] (*Publisher's lettering:* Irving's works)
At head of title: Hudson edition.

The conquest of Granada, by Washington Irving. London, J. M. Dent & sons, ltd.; New York, E. P. Dutton & co. [1910] (*Half-title:* Everyman's library)
Introduction signed: E. R.
Title within ornamental border.

The conquest of Granada . . . [New York, Belford co., 188–?]

The conquest of Granada. By Washington Irving . . . New York, Burt [19–?] (Cornell series)

The conquest of Granada. By Washington Irving . . . New York, Burt [19–?] (Home library)

The conquest of Granada . . . New York, F. F. Lovell & co. [187–?]

The conquest of Granada. By Washington Irving . . . New York, Oxford university press [19–?] (The World's classics)

The conquest of Granada. By Washington Irving . . . New York, G. P. Putnam's sons [19–?]
Gift edition.
— — New York, G. P. Putnam's sons [19–?]
Large paper edition.
— — New York, G. P. Putnam's sons [19–?]
New handy volume edition.
— — New York, G. P. Putnam's sons [19–?]
Student's edition.
The conquest of Granada. By Washington Irving . . . Philadelphia, David McKay [19–?]

Extracts

The conquest of Granada. [An article by Irving.] (*In* The Quarterly review. London, John Murray, 1830. v. 43, p. 55–80)
Incorporated in the introduction to the 1850 edition by Putnam; republished in Spanish papers.

TRANSLATIONS

Dutch

De verovering van Granada, beschreven van Washington Irving; uit het Engelsch. Haarlem, de wed. A. Loosjes, pz., 1830. 2 v.

French

* Histoire de la conquête de Grenade, tirée de la chronique manuscrite de Fray Antonio Agapida par Washington Irving. Traduite de l'anglais par J. Cohen . . . Paris, T. Dehay, 1829. 2 v.
* Histoire de la conquête de Grenade, tirée de la chronique manuscrite de Fray Antonio Agapida par Washington Irving. Traduite de l'anglais par J. Cohen . . . Louvain, F. Michel, 1830. 2 v. in 1.
* Conquête de Grenade, par Adrien Lemercier, d'après Washington Irving . . . Tours, A. Mame, 1840. (Bibliothèque de la jeunesse chrétienne)
* — — Tours, A. Mame, 1842. (Bibliothèque de la jeunesse chrétienne)
3. édition.
* — — Tours, A. Mame, 1845. (Bibliothèque de la jeunesse chrétienne)
4. édition.
* — — Tours, A. Mame, 1852. (Bibliothèque de la jeunesse chrétienne)
6. édition.
* — — Tours, A. Mame, 1856. (Bibliothèque de la jeunesse chrétienne)
7. édition.
* — — Tours, A. Mame, 1859. (Bibliothèque de la jeunesse chrétienne)
8. édition.
* — — Tours, A. Mame, 1862. (Bibliothèque de la jeunesse chrétienne)
9. édition.

* Histoire de la conquête de Grenade; traduite de l'anglais, et précédée
  d'une étude sur les ouvrages de Washington Irving, par Xavier
  Eyma. Bruxelles, Paris, Lacroix, Verboeckhoven et cie, 1864. 2 v.
  (Collection d'historiens contemporains)
* — — Bruxelles, Paris, Lacroix, Verboeckhoven et cie, 1865. 2 v.
  (Collection d'historiens contemporains)
* Conquête de Grenade, par Adrien Lemercier, d'après Washington
  Irving . . . Tours, A. Mame, 1865. (Bibliothèque de la jeunesse
  chrétienne)
  10. édition.
* — — Tours, A. Mame, 1868. (Bibliothèque de la jeunesse chrétienne)
  11. édition.
* — — Tours, A. Mame, 1873. (Bibliothèque de la jeunesse chrétienne)
  12. édition.
* — — Tours, A. Mame, 1877. (Bibliothèque de la jeunesse chrétienne)
  13. édition.
* — — Tours, A. Mame, 1882. (Bibliothèque de la jeunesse chrétienne)
  14. édition.

Extracts

* [A review, with extracts.] (*In* Revue encyclopédique. Paris, 1829.
  v. 43, p. 719)

German

* Die Eroberung Granada's, aus den Papieren Bruders Antonio Agapida
  von Washington Irving. Aus dem Englischen übersetzt von K.
  Meurer . . . Frankfort, Sauerländer, 1829. 2 v. (Sämmtliche
  Werke, Bdchn. 35–37)
  Die Eroberung von Granada. Von Washington Irving. Aus dem
  Englischen von Gustav Sellen. Leipzig, Wienbrack, 1830. 3 v.
  Translation by Karl Ludwig.
  — — Leipzig, Wienbrack, 1836. 3 v.

Spanish

* Crónica de la conquista de Granada. Escrita en inglés por Mr. Washington Irving. Traducida al castellano por Don Jorge W. Montgomery . . . Madrid, Imprenta de I. Sancha, Abril de 1831. 2 v.
  Crónica de la conquista de Granada. Sacada de los manuscritos de
  Fr. Antonio Agapido [*sic*] por Mr. Washington Irving, y traducida
  del inglés por Don Alfonso Escalante. [Granada? 1844?]
  Advertised in El Abencerraje, Granada, 1844. No copy is known
  to exist.
  Crónica de la conquista de Granada . . . Traducida al castellano
  por Don Jorge W. Montgomery . . . Madrid, 1858.
* La conquista de Granada. Por H. L. Bulwer. Precedida de una
  Introducción por Washington Irving, traducida libremente por la

Señorita Doña Margarita López de Haro . . . Madrid, Murcia y Marti, 1860.
A translation of Bulwer's history, preceded by condensed excerpts from Irving; an extremely rare item.
Crónica de la conquista de Granada. Estractada de la que escribió en francés Vashington [sic] Irving, por Adriano Lemercier, y vertida al castellano de la octava edición francesa, por J. R. Barcelona, Magrina y Subirana, 1861.
* Historia de la conquista de Granada, extractada de la que escribió en inglés Washington Irving por Adriano Lemercier, y vertida al castellano de la octava edición francesa por J. R. Barcelona, Librería de J. Subirana, 1861. (Biblioteca escogida de la juventud, 6)
Bound with this is: Historia de la conquista del Perú y de Pizarro, por Enrique Lebrun, traducida de la quinta edición francesa, por J. R. Barcelona, Librería de J. Subirana, 1862.

Swedish

Krönika öfver Granadas eröfring, (utdragen) ur munken Antonio Agapidas handskrifter. Öfversättning från engelska originalet af Lars Arnell. Åbo, 1830–31. 2 v.

THE CRAYON MISCELLANY

* The Crayon miscellany. By the author of The sketch book . . . Philadelphia, Carey, Lea, & Blanchard, 1835. 3 v.
Vol. 2: Philadelphia, Carey, Lea, and Blanchard, 1835.
Published in three parts.
No. 1: A tour on the prairies. — April, 1835.
No. 2: Abbotsford. Newstead Abbey. — May 30, 1835.
No. 3: Legends of the conquest of Spain. — October, 1835.
Each volume has also individual t.-p.
* Miscellanies. By the author of "The sketch-book." . . . London, John Murray, 1835. 3 v.
Published in three parts.
No. 1: A tour on the prairies. — March, 1835.
No. 2: Abbotsford. Newstead Abbey. — May 1, 1835.
No. 3: Legends of the conquest of Spain. — July or August, 1835.
Each volume has also individual t.-p.
* A tour on the prairies. By the author of The sketch book. London, John Murray, 1835. 12mo.
* — — London, John Murray, 1835. 8vo.
* A tour on the prairies. By Washington Irving. Paris, A. & W. Galignani, 1835. (Miscellanies, No. 1)
* A tour on the prairies. By Washington Irving. Paris, Baudry, 1835. 276 p.

* — — Paris, Baudry, 1835. 242 p.

* A tour on the prairies, over the hunting grounds of the Osage and Pawnee Indians, in the Far West, on the borders of Mexico. By Washington Irving. Second edition. Paris, A. and W. Galignani and c°., 1835. (*Added t.-p.:* Miscellanies, No. 1 . . .)

* Abbotsford and Newstead Abbey, by Washington Irving. Paris, A. and W. Galignani, 1835.

* Abbotsford, and Newstead Abbey. By Washington Irving . . . Paris, Baudry, 1835. 217 p.

* — — Paris, Baudry, 1835. 249 p.

Crayon miscellany . . . No. 1. A tour on the prairies. Philadelphia, Carey, Lea, & Blanchard, 1836.

* Legends of the conquest of Spain. By Washington Irving . . . Paris, Baudry's European library, 1836.

* — — Paris, A. and W. Galignani, 1836.

* Legends of the conquest of Spain . . . London, John Murray, 1836.

Crayon miscellany . . . [place?] 1848.
Does not include Legends of the conquest of Spain.

* The Crayon miscellany. Author's revised edition . . . New York, George P. Putnam, 1849. (Works . . . New edition, v. 9)
Contents. — A tour on the prairies. — Abbotsford and Newstead Abbey.

A tour on the prairies. By Washington Irving. London, H. G. Bohn, 1850.

Abbotsford and Newstead Abbey . . . With an appendix, peculiar to this edition. London, H. G. Bohn, 1850. (Bohn's shilling series)

A tour on the prairies. By Washington Irving. Author's revised edition. London, G. Routledge, 1850. (The Popular library)

Abbotsford and Newstead Abbey. By Washington Irving. Author's revised edition. London, G. Routledge, 1850. (The Popular library)

The Crayon miscellany. Author's revised edition . . . New-York, G. P. Putnam, 1851. (*Added t.-p.:* The works of Washington Irving. New edition, revised, v. 9)

A tour on the prairies . . . London, 1851.

Abbotsford and Newstead Abbey. By Washington Irving. With an appendix peculiar to the present edition. London, H. G. Bohn, 1853.

A tour on the prairies; and, Abbotsford and Newstead Abbey. By Washington Irving. New edition. London, G. Routledge & co., 1855.

Abbotsford and Newstead Abbey . . . London, Bell & Daldy, 1864.

The Crayon miscellany . . . The author's revised edition. Complete in one volume. New York, G. P. Putnam, Hurd and Houghton, 1865.
Half-title: . . . Riverside edition.
Added engr. t.-p.; vignette.

The Crayon miscellany, by Washington Irving . . . [New York, G. P. Putnam's sons, c 1865] (. . . Works, Kinderhook edition, v. 6) Author's revised edition.

* The Crayon miscellany, by Washington Irving. The author's revised edition. Complete in one volume. New York, G. P. Putnam's sons [c 1865] Added t.-p., with vignette. Riverside edition.

The Crayon miscellany . . . The author's revised edition . . . Philadelphia, J. B. Lippincott & co., 1871. (*On cover:* Irving's works) Half-title: . . . Riverside edition. Added engr. t.-p.; vignette.

The Crayon miscellany. By the author of "The sketch book." Knickerbocker edition. With illustrations. Philadelphia, 1874.

The Crayon miscellany . . . New York, G. P. Putnam's sons, 1882. Revised edition.

. . . The Crayon miscellany . . . The author's revised edition . . . New York, G. P. Putnam's sons [1882] Copyright date: 1865. Vol. [8] of a uniform edition, in cloth, having at head of title "Hudson edition" (first issued in 1882) and lettered: Irving's works.

* Abbotsford and Newstead Abbey . . . New York, J. B. Alden, 1883.

The conquest of Spain . . . New York, J. B. Alden, 1883.

Abbotsford and Newstead Abbey. By Washington Irving. New York, J. W. Lovell co., 1883. (Lovell's library, v. 5, no. 224)

A tour on the prairies . . . New York, J. W. Lovell co., 1883. (Lovell's library, v. 6, no. 305)

Abbotsford . . . Mit Anmerkungen zum Schulgebrauch hrsg. von E. Paetsch. Ausg. A. Mit Anmerkungen unter dem Text. Bielefeld, Velhagen und Klasing, 1886. (English authors, 15)

* The conquest of Spain . . . New York, United States book co. [1890] (Lovell's literature series, no. 112)

. . . The Crayon miscellany . . . New York and London, G. P. Putnam's sons [c 1895] 2 v. At head of title: Knickerbocker edition.

. . . The Crayon miscellany, by Washington Irving. The author's revised edition . . . New York, G. P. Putnam's sons [1902] (*Publisher's lettering:* Irving's works) At head of title: Hudson edition. Added engr. t.-p.; vignette.

. . . A tour on the prairies, by Washington Irving, edited for school use by George G. Wells . . . and Joseph B. Thoburn. Oklahoma city, Harlow publishing co., 1926. (The Western series of English and American classics)

— — Oklahoma city, Harlow publishing co., 1927.

* Abbotsford, and Newstead Abbey. By the author of "The sketch
  book." London, John Murray [n.d.] (*Half-title:* Miscellanies)
  Cover-title: Scott and Byron.

A tour on the prairies . . . [New York, Belford co., 188–?]

Abbotsford and Newstead Abbey . . . [New York, Belford co., n.d.]

The conquest of Spain . . . [New York, Belford co., n.d.]

The conquest of Spain . . . New York, F. F. Lovell & co. [187–?]

The Crayon miscellany . . . New York, G. P. Putnam's sons [192–?]
  New handy volume edition.

The Crayon miscellany . . . New York, G. P. Putnam's sons [19–?]
  New Knickerbocker edition.

The Crayon miscellany . . . New York, G. P. Putnam's sons [19–?]
  Student's edition.

Miscellanies . . . New York, G. P. Putnam's sons [19–?]
  New Knickerbocker edition.

Extracts

The bee hunt . . . Taylorville, Ill., Parker publishing co. [19–?]
  (Eight page classics)

[Extracts from Abbotsford.] (*In* The Casket. London, J. Murray,
  April, 1836)

* [Excerpts from A tour on the prairies: The honey camp, A bee
  hunt.] (*In* New-York mirror . . . New-York, Apr., 1835. v. 12,
  p. 318)

Translations

Dutch

Togt door de prairiën van Noord-Amerika. Naar het Engelsch van
  W. Irving. Amsterdam, H. Frijlink, 1835.
  Engr. t.-p.

French

* Voyage dans les prairies à l'ouest des États-Unis, par Washington
  Irving. Traduit par Mlle A. Sobry, traducteur des Contes de
  l'Alhambra. Paris, Fournier jeune, 1835. (*Half-title:* Mélanges,
  t. 1)

* Walter Scott et Lord Byron, ou, Voyages à Abbotsford et à Newstead,
  par Washington Irving. Traduit par Mlle A. Sobry . . . Paris,
  Fournier jeune, 1835. (*Half-title:* Mélanges, t. 2)

* Un tour dans les prairies, à l'ouest des États-Unis. Traduit de
  l'anglais de Washington Irwing [*sic*] par Ernest W * * * Tours,
  R. Pornin et cie, 1845. (Gymnase moral d'éducation)

* Un tour dans les prairies, à l'ouest des États-Unis. Traduit de
  l'anglais de Washington Irving par Ernest W * * * Nouvelle
  édition. Tours, A. Mame et fils, 1850. (Gymnase moral d'éducation)

* — — Tours, A. Mame, 1851. (Gymnase moral d'éducation)
* — — Tours, A. Mame, 1854. (Gymnase moral d'éducation)
* — — Tours, A. Mame, 1858. (Bibliothèque des écoles chrétiennes,
  1. série)
* — — Tours, A. Mame, 1862. (Bibliothèque des écoles chrétiennes,
  1. série)
* — — Tours, A. Mame, 1865. (Bibliothèque des écoles chrétiennes,
  1. série)
* — — Tours, A. Mame, 1866. (Bibliothèque de la jeunesse chrétienne,
  3. série)
* — — Tours, A. Mame, 1872. (Bibliothèque de la jeunesse chrétienne,
  3. série)
Voyage dans les prairies du Far West. 1832. Paris, Plon, 1933.

German

* Eine Reise auf den Prairien. Von Washington Irving. Aus dem
  Englischen. Mit dem Bildniss des Verfassers. Frankfurt am Main,
  J. D. Sauerländer, 1835.
Reise durch die Prairien. Aus dem Englischen . . . Berlin, Veit
  und Comp., 1835.
Miscellaneen. Von Washington Irving. Aus dem Englischen von
  H. Roberts. Braunschweig, Vieweg und Sohn, 1835. 2 v.
  Each volume has also individual t.-p.
  Contents. — Bd. 1. Abbotsford und Newstead-Abtei. — Bd. 2. Eine
  Wanderung in die Prairien.
* Washington Irvings Wanderbuch. Aus dem Englischen . . . Berlin,
  Veit und Comp., 1835. 2 v.
  Contents. — Th. 1. Reise durch die Prairien. — Th. 2. Abbotsford
  und Newstead; oder, Walter Scott und Byron.
* Ausflug auf die Prairien zwischen dem Arkansas und Red-River,
  von Washington Irving. Stuttgart und Tübingen, J. G. Cotta,
  1835. (Reisen und Länderbeschreibungen der älteren und neuesten
  Zeit, Lfg. 4)
  Half-title: Ein Ausflug in die Prairien von Washington Irving.
* Erzählungen von der Eroberung Spaniens. Frankfurt, 1836.
* Erzählungen von der Eroberung Spaniens. Von Washington Irving.
  Aus dem Englischen. Frankfurt a. M., 1836. (Washington Irving's
  Sämmtliche Werke, 54.–56. Bd.)
* Sagen von der Eroberung und Unterjochung Spaniens. Aus dem
  Englischen des Washington Irving, übersetzt von Lenardo.
  Aachen, Hensen und Comp., 1839.

Extracts

[Extracts from Abbotsford.] (*In* Europa. [place? date?] No. 1)
* Legenden aus der Zeit der Eroberung Spaniens. (*In* Magazin für
  die Literatur des Auslandes. Berlin, Hayn, 1836. 9. Bd., p. 19–20)

A tour on the prairies. [Extracts.] (*In* Magazin für die Literatur des Auslandes. Berlin, Hayn, 1835. 7. Bd., p. [141]–142)

Italian

Viaggio per le praterie occidentali degli Stati Uniti, di Washington Irving. Prima versione italiana. Milano, Tipografia e libreria Pirotta e c., 1837. 2 v. (*At head of title:* Amenità dei viaggi e memorie contemporanee. Terza serie, 12)

Russian

* Поѣздка въ луговыя степи. Сочиненіе Вашингтона Ирвинга. Moscow, 1837.

Исторія жизни, путешествій, открытій и приключеній въ Новомъ Свѣтѣ. St.-Petersburg, 1839. 2 v.

A tour on the prairies, translated by Dmitrïï Paskevich.

Spanish

Leyendas españolas. Versión castellana por José F. Godoy. Nueva York, D. Appleton y cia, 1919.

Extracts

El album de Waterloo. (*In* Museo de familias. Barcelona [1840] v. 4)

— (*In* Nuevo siglo ilustrado. Madrid, 1869. May 2, 9)

* Amores del rey Don Rodrigo con la princesa Eliata. (*In* La Crónica . . . Madrid, 1845, p. 206–207)

* Leyendas de la conquista de España. Por Washington Irving. (*In* La Crónica . . . Madrid, 1845, p. 219–222)

THE CRAYON PAPERS

See also, II. Selected Works

* The Crayon papers. By Washington Irving. New York, J. W. Lovell co. [1883] (*On cover:* Lovell's library, v. 5, no. 249)

Contents. — Mountjoy. — The great Mississippi bubble. — Don Juan. — Broek. — Sketches in Paris in 1825. — American researches in Italy. — The taking of the veil. — The charming Letorières. — The early experiences of Ralph Ringwood. — The Seminoles. — The conspiracy of Neamathla. — Letter from Granada. — Abderahman. — The widow's ordeal. — The Creole village. — A contented man.

The Crayon papers. By Washington Irving. Preceded by the Life of Washington Irving, by Richard Henry Stoddard. New York, J. B. Alden, 1883.

The Crayon papers. By Washington Irving . . . New York, T. Y. Crowell & co. [1900?]

The Crayon papers . . . [New York, Belford co., 188–?]

* The first locomotive again. (*In* The Knickerbocker sketch-book . . . Edited by Lewis Gaylord Clark . . . New-York, Burgess, Stringer and co., 1845. p. [25]-29)

* The haunted ship. A true story — as far as it goes. By the author of "The sketch-book." (*In* Heath's book of beauty. 1836 . . . Edited by the Countess of Blessington. London, Longman, Rees, Orme, Brown, Green, and Longman [etc., etc., 1836] p. [253]-257)
— (*In* The New-York mirror . . . New-York, 1836. v. 13, p. 218)
With title: A [*sic*] haunted ship . . .
* — (*In* Friendship's offering . . . Boston, Phillips & Sampson, 1849. p. [326]-330)
* — (*In* American literature. Durham, N. C., Duke university press, 1934. v. 5, no. 4, p. 364-367)
Title: An uncollected tale by Washington Irving. By Nelson F. Adkins.
* — — [n.p., 1934]

* Histoire des établissemens européens aux Indes orientales, par A. Chardin, suivie d'un extrait de l'article sur Marco Polo, de M. Walkenaer . . . d'un extrait de la vie de John Mandeville, par Washington Irving, et d'une notice sur le Camoens, par Mme de Stael [*sic*]. Paris, 1832. (Bibliothèque populaire, t. 22)

Historia de la conquista de México, por . . . Bernardino Sahagún . . . Publicala por separado de sus demás obras Carlos María de Bustamante . . . México, Imprenta de Galvan á cargo de Mariano Arévalo, 1829.
A translation of this was begun by Irving, but never finished.

A HISTORY OF NEW YORK

* A history of New York, from the beginning of the world to the end of the Dutch dynasty. Containing among many surprising and curious matters, the unutterable ponderings of Walter the Doubter, the disastrous projects of William the Testy, and the chivalric achievements of Peter the Headstrong, the three Dutch governors of New Amsterdam; being the only authentic history of the times that ever hath been, or ever will be published. By Diedrich Knickerbocker . . . New York, Inskeep & Bradford; Philadelphia, Bradford & Inskeep [etc., etc.] 1809. 2 v.
First edition.
Printed in Philadelphia.
* A history of New-York . . . The second edition with alterations . . . New York, Inskeep & Bradford; Philadelphia, Bradford & Inskeep [etc., etc.] 1812. 2 v.

* A history of New York . . . The third edition . . . Philadelphia, M. Thomas, 1819. 2 v.

A history of New York . . . Paris, Galignani & co., 1820.

* A humorous history of New York . . . A new edition . . . London, Printed for W. Wright, 1820.
First issue, with no half-title.

* —— Second issue, with half-title: A humorous history of New York.

A humorous history of New York . . . London, John Murray, 1820.
First English edition; follows text of second American edition.
Half-title: A history of New York.

* A history of New York . . . A new edition . . . London, John Murray, 1820.

* —— London, John Murray, 1821. 2 v.

* A history of New-York . . . A new edition. Glasgow, Printed for John Wylie & co. by Robert Chapman, 1821.

A humorous history of New York . . . London, W. Sharpe & son, 1821.

* A humorous history of New York . . . Second edition. London, Printed for W. Wright, 1821.

* A history of New-York . . . By Diedrich Knickerbocker . . . Paris, Printed by Jules Didot for A. and W. Galignani, 1824. 2 v.

* A history of New York . . . Paris, Baudry, 1824.

A history of New York . . . A new edition . . . London, J. Murray, 1824.
Illustrations by C. R. Leslie and W. Allston, engraved by C. Rolls, J. Romney, W. Finden, and A. W. Warren.

* A history of New-York . . . London, T. Tegg [etc., etc.] 1824.

* A history of New York . . . Fourth American edition. By Diedrich Knickerbocker. New York, Printed by C. S. Van Winkle, 1824. 2 v.

* A history of New-York . . . London, John Bumpus [etc., etc.] 1825.

A history of New York . . . London, W. C. Wright, 1825. (Charlton Wright's cabinet edition)

A history of New York . . . London, R. Thurston, 1828.

* A history of New-York . . . Philadelphia, Carey, Lea & Carey, 1829. 2 v. in 1.
Sixth American edition.

A history of New York . . . Philadelphia, Carey & Lea, 1830. 2 v.

A history of New-York . . . Philadelphia, Carey & Lea, 1831. 2 v.
Seventh American edition.

A history of New York . . . Seventh edition . . . London, 1832. 2 v.

* A history of New-York . . . Seventh American edition . . . Philadelphia, Carey & Lea, 1832. 2 v.

A history of New-York . . . 7th American edition . . . Philadelphia, Carey & Lea, 1832–34. 2 v.

A history of New York . . . London, T. T. & J. Tegg, 1833.

A history of New-York . . . Philadelphia, Carey & Lea, 1834. 2 v.

A history of New York . . . London, T. Tegg, 1834.
Frontispiece by William Heath.

A history of New York . . . By Diedrich Knickerbocker. London, T. T. & J. Tegg, 1835.

A history of New York . . . London, John Murray, 1835.
Plates by Cruikshank.

* A history of New York . . . Seventh American edition . . . Philadelphia, Carey & Lea, 1835. 2 v.

* A history of New-York . . . A new edition . . . Philadelphia, Carey, Lea, & Blanchard, 1836. 2 v.

* A history of New-York . . . London, Printed for Thomas Tegg and son, 1836. (Murray's family library, v. 55)
Drawings by Cruikshank.

A history of New York . . . A new edition . . . Philadelphia, Carey, Lea & Blanchard, 1837. 2 v. (*On cover:* . . . Works, 3–4)

A history of New York . . . Philadelphia, Carey & Lea, 1838. 2 v.

A history of New York . . . London, Thomas Tegg and son, 1838. (Murray's family library, v. 55)
Drawings by Cruikshank.

A history of New York . . . Philadelphia, Lea & Blanchard, 1839. 2 v.

* A history of New York . . . London, Thomas Tegg and son, 1839. (Murray's family library, v. 55)
Drawings by Cruikshank.

The history of New York . . . [London, W. Smith, 1839] ([Smith's standard library])

A history of New York . . . New edition . . . Philadelphia, Lea & Blanchard, 1842. 2 v.

A history of New York . . . New York, G. P. Putnam, 1843.

A history of New York . . . London, W. Smith, 1845.

Knickerbocker's History of New York . . . New York, Putnam's sons [1848?] 2 v.
Preface dated 1848.
Pocket edition.

* A history of New York . . . New York, G. P. Putnam, 1848.
New edition.

* A history of New-York . . . New-York, G. P. Putnam, 1849.

* A history of New-York . . . By Diedrich Knickerbocker . . . Philadelphia, Lea & Blanchard, 1849. 2 v.

A history of New York . . . Author's revised edition . . . New York & London, 1850. (Works . . . New edition, revised, v. 1)

A history of New York . . . Author's revised edition. London, H. G. Bohn, 1850. (Bohn's shilling series)

Knickerbocker's History of New York and Salmagundi . . . London, George Routledge and co., 1850.

* A history of New-York . . . New-York, G. P. Putnam, 1850.
    First issue of this edition. The same plates were used in the edition dated 1867.
    Added engr. t.-p.
    Illustrations by F. O. C. Darley.
    Fifty copies printed on large paper.
    On cover: Knickerbocker. Illustrated. Irving.

* A history of New York . . . The author's revised edition. Complete in one volume. New York & London, Putnam, 1851. (Works . . . New edition, revised, v. 1)

A history of New York, with illustrations by F. O. C. Darley. New York, Putnam, 1852.

— — New York, Putnam, 1853.

— — New York, Putnam, 1853. (The Universal library)

A history of New York . . . With illustrations by Felix O. C. Darley, engraved by eminent artists . . . New York, Putnam, 1854.

Knickerbocker's History of New York . . . London, W. S. Orr & co., 1854.

A history of New-York . . . New York, G. P. Putnam & co., 1856. (*Added t.-p.:* The works of Washington Irving. New edition, revised, v. 1)

A history of New York . . . The author's revised edition. Complete in one volume . . . New York, G. P. Putnam & co., 1857. (*Added t.-p.:* The works of Washington Irving. New edition, revised, v. 1)

— — New York, G. P. Putnam & co., 1859. (*Added t.-p.:* The works of Washington Irving. New edition, revised, v. 1)

Knickerbocker's History of New York. With portrait of the author and other steel engravings. [place?] 1860.

* A history of New York . . . Author's revised edition. New York, Putnam [c 1864]
    Half-title: Irving's Knickerbocker. Riverside edition. With designs by Darley.

* . . . Knickerbocker's History of New York. By Washington Irving. . . . New York and London, G. P. Putnam's sons [c 1865] 2 v.
    At head of title: Pocket edition.

* A history of New York . . . The author's revised edition. Complete in one volume. New York, G. P. Putnam and son, 1867.
    Half-title: Irving's Knickerbocker . . .
    Illustrations after Darley, Allston, *et al.*
    110 copies on large paper.

A history of New York . . . The author's revised edition. Complete in one volume. New York, G. P. Putnam and son, 1868.
    Half-title: Knickerbocker. Knickerbocker edition. With illustrations.

* Knickerbocker's History of New York. The author's revised edition. Complete in one volume. New York, G. P. Putnam and son, 1868.

A history of New York . . . [place? 1868] (Masterpieces of fiction)

A history of New York . . . The author's revised edition. Philadelphia, J. B. Lippincott & co., 1871.
Knickerbocker edition.
Includes two engr. t.-p.'s: the first with imprint, New York, G. P. Putnam; the second, New York, Putnam and son.

A history of New York, from the beginning of the world to the end of the Dutch dynasty . . . By Diedrich Knickerbocker. Author's revised edition. Philadelphia, J. B. Lippincott & co., 1873. (*On cover:* Irving's works)
Half-title: Irving's Knickerbocker. Riverside edition. With designs by Darley.
Added engr. t.-p.: Knickerbocker's New York.

A history of New York . . . Author's revised edition. New York, Putnam [1873?]
Knickerbocker edition, with illustrations.

. . . A history of New York . . . Author's revised edition . . . With an essay on Irving's life and work, by C. D. Warner. New York, G. P. Putnam's sons [1880] (*Half-title:* Irving's works. Geoffrey Crayon edition, v. 1)
Title-page and frontispiece follow p. lxix.
Added engr. t.-p.

A history of New York . . . The author's revised edition. New York, G. P. Putnam's sons [c 1880] (Works . . . Hudson edition)

A history of New York . . . Author's revised edition . . . [New York, G. P. Putnam's sons, c 1880] (The works of Washington Irving. The Kinderhook edition, v. 2)

A history of New-York . . . Author's revised edition . . . New York, G. P. Putnam's sons [c 1880]
On cover: The Stratford edition.

. . . A history of New York . . . The author's revised edition . . . New York and London, G. P. Putnam's sons [1882?]
Preface dated 1848.
Vol. [11] of a uniform edition in cloth, having at head of title "Hudson edition" (first issued in 1882) and lettered: Irving's works.

— — Another issue.
Without caption: Hudson edition.

A history of New York . . . New York, J. W. Lovell co., 1883. (*On cover:* Lovell's library, v. 5, no. 236)

A history of New York . . . Chicago, New York, and San Francisco, Belford, Clarke & co. [1885?] (*Lettered on cover:* Irving's works)

* A history of New-York . . . New edition, containing unpublished corrections of the author, with illustrations by Geo. H. Boughton,

Will H. Drake, and Howard Pyle, and etchings by Henry C. Eno
and F. Raubicheck . . . New-York, Printed for the Grolier club,
1886. 2 v.
Edition of 175 copies, on Holland paper, issued to subscribers;
two copies on vellum.
Frontispiece in three states.
Knickerbocker sketches from "A history of New York." By Wash-
ington Irving. Illustrated by F. O. C. Darley. Philadelphia,
J. B. Lippincott co., 1886.
Knickerbocker's History of New York . . . London, Cassell [1886?]
2 v. (Cassell's national library, v. 77, 70)
Knickerbocker's History of New York . . . New York, 1887. 2 v.
Edited by H. Morley.
. . . A history of New-York . . . The author's revised edition . . .
New York, G. P. Putnam's sons [1889] (*Publisher's lettering:*
Irving's works)
At head of title: Hudson edition.
Knickerbocker's History of New York, by Washington Irving; with
illustrations by Edward W. Kemble . . . New York [etc.] G. P.
Putnam's sons, 1890. 2 v.
At head of title: Van Twiller edition.
Half-title: A history of New York . . . By Diedrich Knicker-
bocker.
Ornamental borders.
* A history of New York . . . The author's revised edition. Complete
in one volume. Philadelphia, David McKay, 1891.
Knickerbocker's History of New York . . . Illustrated by Ed-
ward W. Kemble . . . New York, G. P. Putnam's sons, 1894. 2 v.
Peter Stuyvesant edition.
Edition of 281 numbered copies on handmade paper.
* . . . Knickerbocker's History of New York, by Washington Irving;
with illustrations by Edward W. Kemble . . . New York [etc.]
G. P. Putnam's sons, 1894. 2 v.
At head of title: Van Twiller edition.
Half-title: A history of New York . . . By Diedrich Knicker-
bocker.
Ornamental borders.
. . . Knickerbocker's History of New York, by Washington Irving
. . . New York and London, G. P. Putnam's sons [1897] 2 v.
At head of title: Knickerbocker edition.
Half-title: A history of New York, from the beginning of the world
to the end of the Dutch dynasty . . . by Diedrich Knicker-
bocker.
. . . Knickerbocker stories from the old Dutch days of New York,
by Washington Irving. Edited with introduction and notes, by
Edward Everett Hale, jr. . . . New York, Boston and New

Orleans, University publishing co. [c 1897] (Standard literature series [no. 23])

A history of New York . . . Embellished by eight pictures from the hand of Maxfield Parrish, esq^re. New York, R. H. Russell, 1900. 8vo.

—— New York, R. H. Russell, 1900. 4to.
Typography by D. B. Updike.

A history of New York . . . Embellished by eight pictures from the hand of Maxfield Parrish, esq^re. London, John Lane, 1900.

. . . A history of New York . . . The author's revised edition . . . New York, G. P. Putnam's sons [1902] (*Publisher's lettering:* Irving's works)
At head of title: Hudson edition.
Added engr. t.-p.; vignette.

A history of New York . . . Embellished by eight pictures from the hand of Maxfield Parrish, esq^re. New York, R. H. Russell, 1903.

A history of New York . . . Embellish'd by eight pictures from the hand of Maxfield Parrish, esq^re. New York, Dodd, Mead & co., 1915.

Knickerbocker's History of New York (books iii–vii), by Washington Irving; edited with notes and an introduction by Edwin A. Green-law . . . New York, The Macmillan co., 1916. (Macmillan's pocket classics)

* —— New York, The Macmillan co., 1919.

* Diedrich Knickerbocker's A history of New York, by Washington Irving; edited with a critical introduction by Stanley Williams and Tremaine McDowell. New York, Harcourt, Brace and co. [c 1927] (*Half-title:* American authors series. General editor: Stanley T. Williams)
> A reprint of the 1809 edition, with reproduction of the original title-page and with a "reduced facsimile of the folding map."

* Knickerbocker's History of New York, by Washington Irving, edited by Anne Carroll Moore, with pictorial pleasantries by James Daugherty. Garden city, New York, Doubleday, Doran & co., 1928.
First edition.

Knickerbocker's History of New York. Edited by H. Morley. Chicago, Education publishing co. [19–?]

A history of New York . . . [New York, Belford co., 188–?]

Knickerbocker's History of New York . . . New York, Burt [19–?] (Home library)

Knickerbocker's History of New York . . . New York, H. M. Cald-well co. [189–?]

Knickerbocker's History of New York . . . New York, G. P. Put-nam [19–?] (Ariel booklets)

Knickerbocker's History of New York . . . New York, G. P. Putnam
[19–?]
Gift edition.
Knickerbocker's History of New York . . . New York, G. P. Putnam
[19–?]
Large paper edition.
Knickerbocker's History of New York . . . New York, G. P. Putnam
[19–?]
New handy volume edition.
Knickerbocker's History of New York . . . New York, G. P. Putnam
[19–?]
New Knickerbocker edition.
Knickerbocker's History of New York . . . Philadelphia, Altemus
[19–?] (Altemus' new vademecum series)
Knickerbocker's History of New York. The sketch book . . . Phila-
delphia, David McKay [19–?] (American classics series)

A play based on A history of New York was announced in The New-York
mirror, February 1, 1834.

Extracts

Knickerbocker life in New York . . . Taylorville, Ill., Parker pub-
lishing co. [19–?] (Eight page classics)
Peter Stuyvesant's voyage up the Hudson . . . *see* A book of the
Hudson.
The renowned Wouter Van Twiller . . . Taylorville, Ill., Parker
publishing co. [19–?] (Eight page classics)
* The sage decision of the renowned Governor Van Twiller. (*In* The
Intelligent reader . . . Springfield, G. and C. Merriam, 1835.
p. 159–161)
* The wrath of Peter Stuyvesant. (*In* The Magnolia for 1837. Edited
by Henry William Herbert. New York, Bancroft & Holley [etc.,
etc., c 1836] p. [254])
* —— (*In* The Magnolia for 1843 [*i.e.*, 1837] Edited by Henry William
Herbert. New-York, Robert P. Bixby & co. [1837] p. [254])

French

* Histoire de New-York, depuis le commencement du monde jusqu'à
la fin de la domination hollandaise . . . seule histoire authentique
de ces temps qui ait jamais été ou puisse être jamais publiée. Par
Diedrick Knickerbocker . . . Ouvrage traduit de l'anglais . . .
Paris, A. Sautelet et cie, 1827. 2 v.
First French edition.

German

* Humoristische Geschichte von New-York, von Anbeginn der Welt
bis zur Endschaft der holländischen Dynastie . . . In sieben

Büchern. Von Dietrich Knickerbocker . . . Aus dem Englischen übersetzt . . . Frankfurt am Main, J. D. Sauerländer, 1829. (Washington Irving's Såmmtliche Werke, Bd. 38–40)

Dietrich Knickerbocker's Humoristische Geschichte von New-York von Anbeginn der Gründung der Colonie durch Hendrik Hudson, bis zur Endschaft der holländischen Dynastie. New-York & Philadelphia, Schäfer & Koradi, 1851.

Dietrich Knickerbocker's Humoristische Geschichte von New-York, von Anbeginn der Gründung der Colonie durch Hendrick Hudson, bis zur Endschaft der holländischen Dynastie . . . New-York, Koch & Co. [18–?]

Contents. — Knickerbocker's Humoristische Geschichte von New-York. — Das Abentheuer meines Grossvaters. — Das Abentheuer des Studenten. — Rip Van Winkle. — Capitain Kitt, der Seeräuber. — Der Teufel und Tom Walker. — Das Abentheuer des Maurers. — Die aristokratischen Einwanderer.

Swedish

New-York's Historia från verldens begynnelse intill Holländska väldets slut. Af Washington Irving . . . Stockholm, B. M. Bredberg, 1827.

A HISTORY OF THE LIFE AND VOYAGES OF CHRISTOPHER COLUMBUS

* A history of the life and voyages of Christopher Columbus. By Washington Irving . . . New-York, G. & C. Carvill, 1828. 3 v. First edition.

* A history of the life and voyages of Christopher Columbus. By Washington Irving . . . London, John Murray, 1828. 4 v. Four issues of this first edition were printed, one by T. Davison and three by W. Clowes.

* A history of the life and voyages of Christopher Columbus. By Washington Irving . . . In four volumes . . . Paris, A. Galignani, 1828. 4 v.

* A history of the life and voyages of Christopher Columbus. By Washington Irving . . . Paris, Baudry, 1828. 4 v.

A history of the life and voyages of Christopher Columbus. By Washington Irving . . . New-York, G. & C. Carvill, 1829. 3 v. Second edition.

* The life and voyages of Christopher Columbus, by Washington Irving. (Abridged by the same.) . . . New York, G. & C. & H. Carvill, 1829. First edition of the issue abridged by Irving complete in one volume.

The life of Christopher Columbus, abridged by the author. London, J. Murray, 1829.

* A history of the life and voyages of Christopher Columbus, by Washington Irving . . . Paris, A. and W. Galignani, 1829. 4 v.
* The history of the life and voyages of Christopher Columbus, by Washington Irving. Paris, Baudry, 1829. 4 v.
* The life and voyages of Christopher Columbus. By Washington Irving. (Abridged by the same.) London, John Murray, 1830. (The Family library, no. 11)
* The life and voyages of Christopher Columbus, by Washington Irving, abridged by the same . . . Paris, Baudry, 1830.

The life and voyages of Christopher Columbus. By Washington Irving. (Abridged by the same.) London, John Murray, 1831. (Murray's family library, v. 34)

The voyages of Christopher Columbus. Abridged. London, John Murray, 1831. (Family library, v. 16)

* History of the life and voyages of Christopher Columbus. By Washington Irving . . . A new edition revised and corrected by the author . . . New-York, G. & C. & H. Carvill, 1831. 2 v.
* The life and voyages of Christopher Columbus. By Washington Irving. (Abridged by the same.) . . . A new edition, with additions and improvements, by the author. New-York, G. & C. & H. Carvill, 1831.

The life of Christopher Columbus. (Abridged by the author.) Leipzig, B. Tauchnitz, 1832.

The life and voyages of Christopher Columbus. By Washington Irving. Abridged by the same for the use of schools. Mit grammatikalischen Erläuterungen und einem Wörterbuche. Zum Schul- und Privatgebrauch. Leipzig, Baumgärtner, 1832.

The life and voyages of Christopher Columbus, by Washington Irving. (Abridged by the same.) . . . A new edition, with additions and improvements, by the author. New-York, J. & J. Harper, 1833.

The life and voyages of Christopher Columbus. By Washington Irving. Abridged by the same for the use of schools. Med en engelsk grammatik och pronunciations-lära samt ordbok. Läsebok i engelska språket . . . Norrköping, A. Bohlin, 1834.

* The life and voyages of Christopher Columbus, illustrated, abridged, by the author expressly for the use of schools. New York, N. & J. White, 1834.
First edition.

* History of the life and voyages of Christopher Columbus, by Washington Irving . . . A new edition, revised and corrected by the author. In two volumes . . . Philadelphia, Carey, Lea, & Blanchard, 1835. 2 v.
Same as the Carvill edition, New York, 1831.

* The life and voyages of Christopher Columbus, by Washington Irving. Abridged and arranged by the author, expressly for the use of schools. New York, N. and J. White, 1835.

— — New York, N. & J. White, 1836.

Life of Christopher Columbus. Abridged by the author. New edition with improvements. Amsterdam, Schalekamp and van de Grampel, 1836.

The life and voyages of Christopher Columbus. Abridged by the same for the use of schools. Mit grammatikalischen Erläuterungen und einem Wörterbuche. Zum Schul- und Privatgebrauche. 2., verbesserte Auflage. Leipzig, Baumgärtner, 1837.

* Life and voyages of Christopher Columbus including the author's Visit to Palos. Boston, Crosby, 1839.

* . . . Irving's Life and voyages of Columbus, with the author's Visit to Palos . . . Boston, Marsh, Capen, Lyon, and Webb, 1839. (The School library, v. 1)

Added series t.-p., engr.

Contains also special t.-p.: The life and voyages of Christopher Columbus . . . Including the author's Visit to Palos . . . Boston, Marsh, Capen, Lyon, and Webb, 1839.

* The life and voyages of Christopher Columbus. By Washington Irving. (Abridged by the same.) Including the author's Visit to Palos . . . Boston, Marsh, Capen, Lyon, and Webb, 1839. 1 p. l., [iii]–xi, [1], [9]–324 p.

* — — Boston, Marsh, Capen, Lyon, and Webb, 1839. xi, [1], [9]–325 p.

* . . . Life and voyages of Christopher Columbus with the author's Visit to Palos . . . Boston, Marsh, Capen, Lyon, and Webb, 1839. (The School library, published under the sanction of the Board of education of the State of Massachusetts, v. 1)

The American library of literature and science, v. 1.

The life and voyages of Christopher Columbus. Abridged and arranged for the use of schools. New York, Collins, Keese and co., 1839.

* History of the life and voyages of Christopher Columbus. By Washington Irving. Paris, A. and W. Galignani, 1839. 4 v.

History of the life and voyages of Christopher Columbus. By Washington Irving. Philadelphia, Carey & Lea, 1839.

* The life and voyages of Christopher Columbus. By Washington Irving. (Abridged by the same.) Including the author's Visit to Palos. With a portrait, map, and other illustrations. New York, Harper & brothers [c 1839]

History of the life and voyages of Christopher Columbus. Philadelphia, Carey & Lea, 1840.

The life and voyages of Christopher Columbus. By Washington Irving. Abridged by the same for the use of schools. Mit grammatikalischen Erläuterungen und einem Wörterbuche. Zum Schul- und Privatgebrauche. 3., verbesserte Auflage. Leipzig, Baumgärtner, 1840.

History of the life and voyages of Christopher Columbus. By Washington Irving . . . A new edition, revised and corrected by the author . . . Philadelphia, Lea & Blanchard, for G. W. Gorton, 1841. 2 v.

* The life and voyages of Christopher Columbus. By Washington Irving, (abridged by the same.) Second edition. London, T. Tegg, 1841. (Murray's family library)

* The life and voyages of Christopher Columbus, by Washington Irving. Abridged and arranged by the author expressly for the use of schools. New edition with improvements. Bath, New York, R. L. Underhill & co., 1844.

* The life and voyages of Christopher Columbus, by Washington Irving, abridged by the same . . . Paris, Baudry, 1846.

* The life and voyages of Christopher Columbus. By Washington Irving. Abridged by the same for the use of schools. Mit grammatischen Erläuterungen und einem Wörterbuche. Zum Schul- und Privatgebrauche. Vierte, verbesserte, mit Stereotypen gedruckte Auflage. Leipzig, Baumgärtner, 1846.
Vocabulary by E. Amthor.

The life and voyages of Christopher Columbus. With a copious vocabulary compiled by E. Amthor. Revised edition. Leipzig, Renger, 1846.

* The life and voyages of Christopher Columbus. By Washington Irving. (Abridged by the same.) Including the author's Visit to Palos . . . New York, Harper & brothers, 1847.
Title vignette.
Appended: Obsequies of Columbus. A glossary of the Latin, French, Spanish, and other . . . words and phrases.

The life and voyages of Christopher Columbus, by Washington Irving, abridged by the same . . . London, T. Tegg, 1847.

* The life and voyages of Christopher Columbus; to which are added those of his companions. By Washington Irving . . . Author's revised edition . . . New York, G. P. Putnam, 1849. 3 v. (*Added t.-p.:* The works of Washington Irving, v. 3–5)

* The life and voyages of Christopher Columbus, together with the voyages of his companions. London, J. Murray, 1849. 3 v.

— — London, J. Murray, 1849. 3 v.
Library edition.

The life and voyages of Christopher Columbus, together with the voyages of his companions. Author's revised edition. London, 1850. 2 v.

The life and voyages of Christopher Columbus . . . London, H. G. Bohn, 1850. 3 v. (Bohn's shilling series, v. 12–14)
Paged continuously.
Vol. 3: Voyages and discoveries of the companions of Columbus.

* The life and voyages of Christopher Columbus; to which are added those of his companions. By Washington Irving . . . Author's revised edition . . . New York, G. P. Putnam, 1850–51. 3 v. (*Added t.-p.:* The works of Washington Irving, v. 3–5)

The life and voyages of Christopher Columbus, to which are added those of his companions. By Washington Irving. New York, G. P. Putnam, 1851.

The life and voyages of Christopher Columbus. By Washington Irving. Abridged by the same for the use of schools. Mit grammatikalischen Erläuterungen und einem Wörterbuche. Zum Schul- und Privatgebrauche. 5., mit Stereotypen gedruckte Auflage. Leipzig, Baumgärtner, 1853.

* The life and voyages of Christopher Columbus. By Washington Irving. (Abridged by the same.) Including the author's Visit to Palos . . . New York, Harper & brothers, 1856.

The life and voyages of Christopher Columbus. By Washington Irving. Abridged by the same for the use of schools. Mit grammatikalischen Erläuterungen und einem Wörterbuche. Zum Schul- und Privatgebrauche. 6. Auflage. Leipzig, Baumgärtner, 1857.

The life and voyages of Christopher Columbus. By Washington Irving. (Abridged by the same.) Including the author's Visit to Palos . . . New York, Harper & brothers, 1858.

The life and voyages of Christopher Columbus . . . Author's revised edition. New York, G. P. Putnam, 1859. 3 v. (Works, v. 3–5)

* The life and voyages of Christopher Columbus. By Washington Irving . . . Author's revised edition. London, H. G. Bohn, 1859. 2 v. in 1. (Bohn's series)
Paged continuously.

The life and voyages of Christopher Columbus; to which are added those of his companions. By Washington Irving . . . Author's revised edition . . . New York, G. P. Putnam, 1860. 2 v.

— — London, Routledge, 1860.

The life and voyages of Christopher Columbus. By Washington Irving. Abridged by the same for the use of schools. Mit grammatikalischen Erläuterungen und einem Wörterbuche. Zum Schul- und Privatgebrauche. 7., mit Stereotypen gedruckte Auflage. Leipzig, Baumgärtner, 1861.

The life and voyages of Christopher Columbus hrsg. und mit einem ausführlichen Wörterbuche versehen von H. J. Lohmann. Quedlinburg, Basse, 1863.

* The life and voyages of Christopher Columbus . . . Author's revised edition . . . London, Bell & Daldy, 1866. 2 v. in 1.
Paged continuously.

The life and voyages of Christopher Columbus. By Washington Irving. Abridged by the same for the use of schools. Mit gram-

matikalischen Erläuterungen und einem Wörterbuche. Zum Schul-
und Privatgebrauche. 8., mit Stereotypen gedruckte Auflage.
Leipzig, Baumgärtner, 1866.

The life and voyages of Christopher Columbus . . . with . . . notes
[in Italian] . . . By R. J. Isnard. Genoa & Turin, 1868.

* The life and voyages of Christopher Columbus . . . Author's revised
edition . . . [New York, G. P. Putnam, 1868] 3 v. in 2. (*Added
t.-p.:* The works of Washington Irving. The Kinderhook edition,
v. 5, [11])
Includes Voyages and discoveries of the companions of Columbus.

The life and voyages of Christopher Columbus, to which are added
those of his companions. New York, G. P. Putnam's sons [c 1868]
2 v.
Hudson edition.

The life and voyages of Christopher Columbus . . . Author's revised
edition . . . New York, G. P. Putnam and son, 1868-69. 3 v.
Riverside edition.

The life and voyages of Christopher Columbus. By Washington
Irving. Abridged by the same for the use of schools. Mit grammatikalischen Erläuterungen und einem Wörterbuche. Zum Schul-
und Privatgebrauche. 9. Auflage. Leipzig, Baumgärtner, 1869.

* The life and voyages of Christopher Columbus; to which are added
those of his companions. By Washington Irving . . . Author's
revised edition . . . New York, G. P. Putnam and son, 1869. 3 v.
Knickerbocker edition.

— — New York, G. P. Putnam and son, 1869. 3 v.
Vol. 2: Philadelphia, J. B. Lippincott & co., 1871.

The life and voyages of Christopher Columbus, including the author's
Visit to Palos. Paris, 1869.

* Life and voyages of Christopher Columbus. By Washington Irving;
abridged by the same . . . Paris, Baudry, 1869. (Juvenile
library)

* The life and voyages of Christopher Columbus, by Washington Irving
. . . Author's revised edition . . . London, Bell & Daldy, 1870.
2 v.
Paged continuously.

The life and voyages of Christopher Columbus. (Condensed by the
author from his larger work) for students and young persons.
New York, G. P. Putnam's sons [c 1870] (Putnam's popular
histories)

The life and voyages of Christopher Columbus. By Washington
Irving. Abridged by the same for the use of schools. Mit grammatikalischen Erläuterungen und einem Wörterbuche. Zum Schul-
und Privatgebrauche. 10., verbesserte Auflage. Leipzig, Baumgärtner, 1873.

The life and voyages of Christopher Columbus. By Washington

Irving. Abridged by the same for the use of schools. Mit grammatikalischen Erläuterungen und einem Wörterbuche. Zum Schul- und Privatgebrauche bearbeitet und ausgestattet mit einem Wörterbuche, sowie mit erläut. Anmerkungen von J. B. Peters. Leipzig, Brauns, 1873.

The life and voyages of Christopher Columbus . . . Philadelphia, J. B. Lippincott & co., 1873. 3 v.

The life and voyages of Christopher Columbus, to which are added those of his companions . . . New York [1873?] Knickerbocker edition.

The life and voyages of Christopher Columbus with copious notes, published by Rob. J. Isnard. Nuova edizione. Genova, Beuf, 1874.

The life and voyages of Christopher Columbus . . . London, 1875.

* The life and voyages of Christopher Columbus by Washington Irving, abridged by the same . . . Paris, Mme Dramard-Baudry, 1876.

The life and voyages of Christopher Columbus, to which are added those of his companions. Bickers, 1877. 3 v.

* The life and voyages of Christopher Columbus, by Washington Irving. Vorgeschichte und erste Entdeckungsreise. Erklärt von E. Schridde. Berlin, Weidmann, 1878.

The life and voyages of Christopher Columbus. By Washington Irving. Abridged by the same for the use of schools. Mit grammatikalischen Erläuterungen und einem Wörterbuche. Zum Schul- und Privatgebrauche. 11. Auflage. Revidierte von M. von Metzsch. Leipzig, Baumgärtner, 1878.

—— 12. völlig neurevidierte Auflage. Leipzig, Baumgärtner, 1882.

* The life and voyages of Christopher Columbus by Washington Irving, abridged by the same . . . Paris, Mme Dramard-Baudry, 1882.

The life and voyages of Christopher Columbus, by Washington Irving . . . New York, J. W. Lovell co., 1883. 2 v. in 1. (Lovell's library, no. 199)

The life and voyages of Christopher Columbus, to which are added those of his companions . . . London, Cassell & co., 1885. 3 v. Author's revised edition.

The life and voyages of Christopher Columbus. Vorgeschichte und erste Entdeckungsreise. Erklärt von E. Schridde. 2. Auflage. Berlin, Weidmann, 1886.

The life and voyages of Christopher Columbus. Ausgewählt und mit Anmerkungen, sowie teilweiser Accentuierung hrsg. von D. Bendan. Berlin, Friedberg und Mode, 1886. (English authors for the use of schools, Nr. 10)

. . . Christopher Columbus. New York, J. B. Alden, 1887. (The works of Washington Irving [v. 1])

* Vie et voyages de Christoph Colomb. (Texte anglais.) Édition classique, abrégée par l'auteur et précédée d'une notice littéraire par A. Elwall. Paris, Delalain frères, 1888.

* . . . The life and voyages of Christopher Columbus, avec une introduction et des notes, par Jules Guiraud . . . Paris, Belin frères,
1891.

Washington Irving. The discovery and conquest of the New World;
containing the life and voyages of Christopher Columbus, by
Washington Irving . . . A separate account of the conquest of
Mexico and Peru, by W. W. Robertson . . . A perfect history of
the United States; from the works of Bancroft, Fiske, Blaine
[et al.] . . . Introduction, by the Hon. Murat Halstead . . .
New York, John Williams, 1892.

* . . . The life and voyages of Christopher Columbus, and The voyages
and discoveries of the companions of Columbus . . . Author's revised edition . . . New York, London, G. P. Putnam's sons, 1892.
3 v.
Quadri-centennial edition.
402 copies, numbered 1492–1893.

The life and voyages of Christopher Columbus. By Washington
Irving . . . Philadelphia, David McKay, 1892. 2 v. (American
classics)
Author's revised edition.

The life and voyages of Christopher Columbus. Zum Schul- und
Privatgebrauch hrsg. von J. Bauer und Th. Link. Mit Ques-
tionnaire, Wörterverzeichnis und Karte. München, Lindauer,
1892.

. . . Life and voyages of Christopher Columbus, by Washington
Irving . . . New York and London, G. P. Putnam's sons [c 1892]
5 v.
At head of title: Knickerbocker edition.
Title-page in red and black.
Half-title: Life and voyages of Christopher Columbus and The
voyages and discoveries of the companions of Columbus.

The life and voyages of Christopher Columbus . . . Author's revised edition. New York [etc.] G. P. Putnam's sons [c 1892] 3 v.
Isabella edition, limited to 1100 copies.

The life and voyages of Christopher Columbus, by Washington Irving.
(Condensed by the author from his larger work.) . . . New York
[etc.] G. P. Putnam's sons [c 1893] (Half-title: Heroes of the
nations)

The life and voyages of Christopher Columbus, by Washington Irving.
(Condensed by the author from his larger work.) . . . New York,
London, G. P. Putnam's sons [c 1893] (Library of American
biography, v. 4)
Appended are: A visit to Palos; Obsequies of Columbus; Glossary.

* Columbus, his life and voyages, by Washington Irving. (Condensed
by the author from his larger work.) New York, G. P. Putnam,
1896. (Heroes of the nations, 18)

Life and voyages of Christopher Columbus, by Washington Irving
. . . New York and London, G. P. Putnam's sons [1897] 5 v.
At head of title: Knickerbocker edition.

. . . The life and voyages of Christopher Columbus, to which are
added those of his companions, by Washington Irving . . . The
author's revised edition. New York, G. P. Putnam's sons [1902]
3 v. (*Publisher's lettering:* Irving's works)
At head of title: Hudson edition.

The life and voyages of Christopher Columbus, by Washington Irving
. . . with an introduction by G. Mercer Adam . . . New York,
The Perkins book co. [c 1902] ([Heroes of history])

The life and voyages of Christopher Columbus . . . London, Dean,
1905.

The life and voyages of Christopher Columbus. Vorgeschichte und
erste Entdeckungsreise, erklärt von E. Schridde. Berlin, Weidmann, 1907.

The life and voyages of Christopher Columbus . . . London, Harrap,
1909.

* Columbus, his life and voyages . . . (Condensed by the author from
his larger work). New York and London, G. P. Putnam's sons,
1914. (Heroes of the nations [18])

The life and voyages of Christopher Columbus. Con introduzione e
note di Scevola Mariotti. Roma, Albrighi, Segati e c., 1929. (Col-
lezione di classici stranieri)

The voyages of Columbus, by Washington Irving, edited by Winifred
Hulbert, illustrated by Henry Pitz. New York, The Macmillan co.,
1931. ([The Green and blue library])
Illustrated t.-p. and lining-papers.

The life and voyages of Christopher Columbus . . . New York,
American publishers [*sic*] corporation [189-?] 2 v.
Paged continuously.

Life and voyages of Christopher Columbus . . . New York, Belford
co. [188-?]

The life and voyages of Christopher Columbus, by Washington Irving.
New York, Burt [19-?] 2 v. (Columbia series)

The life and voyages of Christopher Columbus, by Washington Irving.
New York, Burt [19-?] (Home library)

The life and voyages of Christopher Columbus . . . New York,
Hurst & co. [189-?]
Sleepy Hollow edition.

The life and voyages of Christopher Columbus, by Washington Irving.
New York, G. P. Putnam's sons [19-?] 5 v.
New Knickerbocker edition.

The life and voyages of Christopher Columbus, by Washington Irving.
Abridged edition. New York, G. P. Putnam's sons [19-?] (Heroes
of the nations [18])

The life and voyages of Christopher Columbus, by Washington Irving.
Philadelphia, David McKay [19-?]   2 v.   (American classics
series)

Extracts

Christopher Columbus. Discovery of America. The first voyage.
Im Auszuge hrsg. von Ed. Paetsch. Ausgabe B. Bielefeld, Vel-
hagen & Klasing, 1892. (English authors, 58)
— — Bielefeld, Velhagen & Klasing, 1897.
Christopher Columbus. Discovery of America. The first voyage.
Im Auszug mit Anmerkungen und einer Karte zum Schulgebrauche
neu hrsg. von Max Fuhrmann. Bielefeld, Velhagen & Klasing,
1921. (English authors, Bd. 58)
. . . The discovery of America. From Irving's Life of Columbus.
With geographical and explanatory notes. New York, E. May-
nard & co. [c 1890] (Historical classic readings, no. 1)
Discovery of America . . . Taylorville, Ill., Parker publishing co.
[19-?] (Eight page classics)
The first landing of Columbus in the New World. Bearbeitet von
Josef Bausenwein. Leipzig, G. Freytag, 1926. (Freytags Sammlung fremdsprachlicher Schriftwerke. Kurztexte. Englisch.
10/11)
* Touron, Antoine. Opening chapter of American missionary history
. . . Compiled from the French of Touron and Charlevoix. With
an appendix from the writings of Washington Irving, etc. By one
of the Dominican fathers of New York. New York, P. O'Shea,
1871.
Extract from Irving's Life of Columbus, New York, 1866: p.
[105]-118.

Translations

Catalan

Colomb. Colomb á Barcelona. (*In* Prosadors nord-americans.
Barcelona, 1909)

Czech

[The life and voyages of Christopher Columbus.] Praga, 1881.
Translation by Doucha.
. . . Život a plavby Krištofa Kolumba. Z anglického přełožil Fran-
tišek Doucha . . . Praga, B. Stýbla [n.d.]
Second edition.

Dutch

* Het leven en de reizen van Cristoffel Columbus, door H. Irving . . .
Uit het Engelsch . . . Haarlem, Bij de wed. A. Loosjes, 1828-29.
4 v.
Translation by P. J. Steenbergen van Goor.
— — Haarlem, 1828-34. 5 v.

French

* Histoire de la vie et des voyages de Christophe Colomb, par M. Washington Irving, traduite de l'anglais par C.–A. Defauconpret, fils. Paris, C. Gosselin, 1828. 4 v.
First Continental edition.

* Histoire abrégée de la vie et des voyages de Christophe Colomb, traduite de l'anglais par J.–A. Dufour. Genève, 1835.

* Histoire de la vie et des voyages de Christophe Colomb, par Washington Irving . . . traduite de l'anglais par C.–A. Defauconpret, fils . . . 2. édition, revue et corrigée . . . Paris, C. Gosselin, 1836. 4 v.

* Voyages et aventures de Christophe Colomb. Traduit de l'anglais de Washington Irving par Paul Merruau . . . Paris, Lavigne, 1837. (Bibliothèque des familles)

* — — Paris, Lavigne, 1837. (Bibliothèque des familles) 2. édition.

* — — Paris, Lavigne, 1838. (Bibliothèque des familles)

* Voyages et aventures de Christophe Colomb. Traduit de l'anglais de Washington Irving par Paul Merruau . . . Tours, A. Mame et fils, 1843. (Bibliothèque des écoles chrétiennes)

* Histoire de Christophe Colomb d'après D. Fernand Colomb, Robertson et Washington Irving. 2e édition. Lille, L. Lefort, 1850.

* Voyages et aventures de Christophe Colomb. Traduit de l'anglais de Washington Irving par Paul Merruau . . . 4. édition. Tours, A. Mame et fils, 1851. (Bibliothèque des écoles chrétiennes)

* — — 5. édition. Tours, A. Mame et fils, 1853. (Bibliothèque des écoles chrétiennes)

* — — 6. édition. Tours, A. Mame et fils, 1857. (Bibliothèque des écoles chrétiennes)

* — — 7. édition. Tours, A. Mame et fils, 1860. (Bibliothèque des écoles chrétiennes)

* — — Tours, A. Mame et fils, 1861. (Bibliothèque des écoles chrétiennes)

* — — 8. édition. Tours, A. Mame et fils, 1863. (Bibliothèque des écoles chrétiennes)

* . . . Vie et voyages de Christophe Colomb. Traduction de l'anglais par G. Renson . . . Paris, Librairie internationale; Bruxelles, A. Lacroix, Verboeckhoven et cie, 1864. 3 v. (Collection d'historiens contemporains)

* Voyages et aventures de Christophe Colomb. Traduit de l'anglais de Washington Irving par Paul Merruau . . . 9. édition. Tours, A. Mame et fils, 1866. (Bibliothèque des écoles chrétiennes)

* — — 10. édition. Tours, A. Mame et fils, 1869. (Bibliothèque de la jeunesse chrétienne)

* — — 11. édition. Tours, A. Mame et fils, 1873.

* W. Irving. Vie et voyages de Christophe Colomb. Édition classique abrégée par l'auteur et précédée d'une notice littéraire, par E. Sedley. Paris, J. Delalain et fils, 1876.
* Washington Irving. La vie et les voyages de Christophe Colomb. Édition abrégée . . . par Émile Chasles . . . Paris, Hachette, 1879.
* Vie et voyages de Christophe Colomb, d'après Washington Irving, par J. Girardin. Paris, Hachette, 1880. (Bibliothèque des écoles et des familles)
* Voyages et aventures de Christophe Colomb. Traduit de l'anglais de Washington Irving par Paul Merruau . . . Tours, A. Mame et fils, 1881. (Bibliothèque des familles et des maisons d'éducation)
* Washington Irving. La vie et les voyages de Christophe Colomb. Édition abrégée . . . par Émile Chasles . . . Paris, Hachette, 1881.
Vie et voyages de Christophe Colomb . . . Paris, 1882.
* Voyages et aventures de Christophe Colomb. Traduit de l'anglais de Washington Irving par Paul Merruau . . . Nouvelle édition, revue et corrigée. Tours, Alfred Mame et fils, 1883.
* W. Irving. Vie et voyages de Christophe Colomb. Édition classique abrégée par l'auteur et précédée d'une notice littéraire, par A. Elwall . . . Paris, Delalain frères, 1883.
* Vie et voyages de Christophe Colomb, d'après Washington Irving, par J. Girardin. Paris, Hachette, 1883. (Bibliothèque des écoles et des familles)
2. édition.
* Washington Irving. La vie et les voyages de Christophe Colomb. Édition abrégée . . . par Émile Chasles . . . Paris, Hachette, 1884.
* Voyages et aventures de Christophe Colomb. Traduit de l'anglais de Washington Irving, par Paul Merruau . . . Tours, A. Mame et fils, 1885.
* Washington Irving. La vie et les voyages de Christophe Colomb, abrégée par l'auteur lui-même pour l'usage des classes. Édition annotée, accentuée et précédée d'une notice sur l'auteur, par R. Milne . . . Paris, Garnier frères, 1886.
* Vie et voyages de Christophe Colomb, d'après Washington Irving, par J. Girardin. Paris, Hachette, 1886. (Bibliothèque des écoles et des familles)
3. édition.
* Washington Irving. La vie et les voyages de Christophe Colomb, avec notes . . . par E. Haussaire . . . Classe de quatrième et 3ᵉ année de l'enseignement secondaire spécial. Paris, Delagrave, 1887. (Cours de langue anglaise . . . Les auteurs du programme, extraits reliés par des analyses)
* Washington Irving. La vie et les voyages de Christophe Colomb.

Édition abrégée . . . par Émile Chasles . . . Paris, Hachette,
   1887.
* Voyages et aventures de Christophe Colomb. Traduit de l'anglais
   de Washington Irving par Paul Merruau . . . Tours, A. Mame et
   fils, 1887.
* W. Irving. Vie et voyages de Christophe Colomb. Édition classique
   abrégée par l'auteur et précédée d'une notice littéraire, par E. Sedley. Paris, J. Delalain, 1888.
* — — Another issue.
* Washington Irving. La vie et les voyages de Christophe Colomb
   abrégée par l'auteur lui-même pour l'usage des classes. Édition
   annotée, accentuée et précédée d'une notice sur l'auteur, par
   R. Milne . . . Paris, Garnier frères, 1888.
* Vie et voyages de Christophe Colomb, d'après Washington Irving,
   par J. Girardin. Paris, Hachette, 1891. (Bibliothèque des écoles
   et des familles)
   4. édition.
* — — Paris, Hachette, 1894. (Bibliothèque des écoles et des familles)
   5. édition.
* Washington Irving. La vie et les voyages de Christophe Colomb.
   Édition abrégée . . . par Émile Chasles . . . Paris, Hachette,
   1896.
* — — Paris, Hachette, 1898.
* Vie et voyages de Christophe Colomb, d'après Washington Irving, par
   J. Girardin. Paris, Hachette, 1898. (Bibliothèque des écoles et
   des familles)
   6. édition.
* Washington Irving. La vie et les voyages de Christophe Colomb.
   Édition abrégée . . . par Émile Chasles . . . Paris, Hachette,
   1901.
* — — Paris, Hachette, 1916.
   Histoire de la vie et des voyages de Christophe Colomb, par Wash-
   ington Irving, traduite de l'anglais par C. A. Defauconpret fils
   . . . Paris, Cherboulliez [n.d.]

German

Die Geschichte des Lebens und der Reisen Christoph's Columbus, von
   Washington Irving. Aus dem Englischen übersetzt von Ph. A. G.
   von Meyer. Frankfurt a. M., Sauerländer, 1828–29. 4 v.
   1. Auflage.
Des Christoph Columbus Leben und Reisen. Aus dem Englischen
   von F. H. Ungewitter. Frankfurt a. M. [Wesché'sche Vrlsh.]
   1828–29. 4 v.
Die Geschichte des Lebens und der Reisen Christoph's Columbus.
   Im Auszuge für die Jugend bearbeitet von Rudolf Friedner. Neu-
   stadt a. d. Haardt, Christmann, 1829.

Die Geschichte des Lebens und der Reisen Christoph's Columbus.
Aus dem Englischen übersetzt von Ph. A. G. von Meyer. Neue
Ausgabe. Frankfurt a. M., Sauerländer, 1832. 12 v. (Sämmtliche
Werke, 20.–31. Bdchn.)
Christoph Columbus Leben und Reisen. Auszug von dem Verfasser.
Aus dem Englischen übersetzt. Stuttgart, Cotta, 1833.

Greek

Ὁ Χριστοφορος Κολομβος, ἤτοι ἱστορία της ζωης και των θαλασ-
σοποριων αύτου κατα τον Ὁ. Ἰρβιγγ. Ἐκ του Γαλλικου ὑπο
Γ. Ἀ. Ἀριστειδου. Ἐν Ἀθηναις, 1858.

Italian

* Storia della vita e dei viaggi di Cristoforo Colombo, scritta da Wash-
ington Irving . . . prima versione italiana, corredata di note . . .
Genova, Dalla tipografia dei Fratelli Pagano, 1828. 4 v. in 2.
Storia e viaggi di Cristoforo Colombo. Genova, 1829. 4 v.
* Storia della vita e viaggi di Cristoforo Colombo scritta da Wash-
ington Irving, americano. Trad. dall' inglese . . . Firenze, Coen
e comp., 1829–30. 4 v.
Storia della vita di Cristoforo Colombo. Genova, 1830. 4 v.
Storia e viaggi di Cristoforo Colombo. Milano, Bestetti, 1876.

Polish

[History of the life and voyages of Christopher Columbus.] [Warsaw?
18–?]

Russian

Исторія жизни и путешествій Христофора Колумба.   St.-
Petersburg, 1836–37. 4v.
Vol. 1 contains maps.
Translated from the French by Nikolaï Bredikhin.

Spanish

* Historia de la vida y viajes de Cristóbal Colón, escrita en inglés por el
caballero Washington Irving, y traducida al castellano por Don
José García de Villalta. Madrid, José Palacios, 1833–34. 4 v. 24°.
* — — Madrid, José Palacios, 1833–34. 4 v. 16mo.
* Historia de la vida y viajes de Cristóbal Colón . . . Madrid, Gaspar
y Roig, 1851. (Biblioteca ilustrada de Gaspar y Roig)
Historia de la vida y viajes de Cristóbal Colón . . . Santiago de
Chile, Belín y cia., 1851.
* . . . Vida y viajes de Cristóbal Colón . . . Madrid, Gaspar y Roig,
1851. (At head of title: Biblioteca de Gaspar y Roig)
Illustrations.
Printed in parallel columns.

—— Madrid, Gaspar y Roig, 1852.
* Historia de la vida y viajes de Cristóbal Colón . . . Madrid, Gaspar y Roig [1852?] (Biblioteca ilustrada de Gaspar y Roig)
* Historia de la vida y viajes de Cristóbal Colón . . . Traducida por E. M. Ortega. México, Boix, Besserer y cia., 1853. 2 v.
* Vida y viajes de Cristóbal Colón, por Washington Irving. 3. edición . . . Madrid, Gaspar y Roig, 1854. (*At head of title:* Biblioteca ilustrada de Gaspar y Roig)
  Title vignette.
  Translated by José García de Villalta.
  Printed in parallel columns.
* Historia de la vida i viajes de Cristóbal Colón. Santiago [Chile] Impr. del Ferrocarril, 1859. 4 v. (Bibliotecas populares)
* —— Madrid, 1884.
  Vida y viajes de Cristóbal Colón . . . Madrid, Guijarro, 1892. 4 v.
* Vida y viajes de Cristóbal Colón escrita en inglés por Washington Irving; edición abreviada por el mismo autor para uso de la juventud, i mandada traducir i publicar por el Ministerio de instrucción pública de Chile. Valparaíso, Imp. de "La patria," 1893.
  Translated by Alberto Berguecio.
* García de Villalta, José. Prospecto de la Historia y viajes de Cristóbal Colón, escrita en inglés por Waakington [*sic*] Irving y traducida al castellano con appéndices é ilustraciones. Madrid, Imp. de José Palacios [n.d.]

Extracts

Historia del descubrimiento del Nuevo-Mundo, estractada de la Vida y viajes de Cristóbal Colón, por Washington Irving. (*In* Campoamor, Ramón de. Colón. Poema. Valencia, 1853)

Swedish

Christopher Columbus, dess lefnad och resor. Öfversättning från engelskan. Stockholm, Hierta, 1839. (I Nytt läse-bibliothek)
  Translation by Gustav Holmström.
Kristoffer Columbus, hans lefnad och resor . . . Öfversättning. Stockolm [*sic*] Hellsten, 1862. (Böcker för folket, 4)
Kristofer Columbus, hans lefnad och resor, af Washington Irving . . . Chicago, Engberg-Holmberg publishing co. [c 1893]
  Illustrated half-title and cover-title.
—— [Washington, Engberg-Holmberg publishing co., 1893]
Kristoffer Columbus, hans lefnad och resor. Stockholm, A. Bonnier, 1894.

LETTERS OF JONATHAN OLDSTYLE, GENT.

See also, Spanish Papers

* Letters of Jonathan Oldstyle, gent. By the author of The sketch
  book. With a biographical notice [of Irving, by Samuel Wood-
  worth.] New-York, Published by William H. Clayton; Clayton &
  Van Norden, printers, 1824.
  First edition.
  Originally published in parts, numbered I–IX, in The Morning
    chronicle, November 15, 1802; November 20, 1802; December 1,
    1802; December 4, 1802; December 11, 1802; January 17, 1803;
    January 22, 1803; February 8, 1803; April 23, 1803.
  — — (*In* The Chronicle express. New York, 1802–03. November
    25, 1802; December 2, 1802; December 6, 1802; December 13,
    1802; January 20, 1803; January 24, 1803; February 10, 1803;
    April 25, 1803)
  Letters II–IX reprinted, without dates, and numbered I–VIII.
  — — (*In* The Kaleidoscope . . . 1824)
  Two letters.
* Letters of Jonathan Oldstyle, gent. By the author of The sketch
  book. With a biographical notice [of Irving, by Samuel Wood-
  worth.] Second edition. London, Effingham Wilson, 1824.
* Letters of Jonathan Oldstyle, gent. By the author of The sketch
  book. With a biographical notice [of Irving, by Samuel Wood-
  worth.] London, Effingham Wilson, 1824.
  Third edition.
  Letters of Jonathan Oldstyle, gent. By the author of The sketch
  book. With a biographical notice [of Irving, by Samuel Wood-
  worth.] London, Effingham Wilson, 1824.
  Fifth edition.
  Letters of Jonathan Oldstyle, gent. Heretofore included in volume
  entitled "Biographies and miscellanies." (*In* Irving, Washington;
  Paulding, J. K.; and Irving, William. Salmagundi. New York,
  London, 1897. v. 2, p. 201–234)

TRANSLATIONS

German

* Jonathan Oldstyle's Briefe. Aus dem Englischen des Washington
  Irving übersetzt von S. H. Spiker. Berlin, Duncker und Humblot,
  1824.
  Jonathan Oldstyle's Briefe . . . (*In* Gesellschafter; oder, Blätter
  für Geist und Herz. Berlin, Maurer, 1824. No. 140)
  Extracts.

LIFE OF GEORGE WASHINGTON

* Life of George Washington. By Washington Irving . . . New York, G. P. Putnam & co., 1855–59. 5 v.
First edition.
Vol. I and II, 1855; v. III, 1856; v. IV, 1857; v. V, 1859.
Vol. I and II have on t.-p.: In III volumes. The extension to five volumes was announced in v. III.

* Life of George Washington. By Washington Irving . . . New York, G. P. Putnam & co., 1855–59. 5 v.
Vol. I, 1855; v. II, 1856; v. III, 1856; v. IV, 1857; v. V, 1859.
Edition of 110 copies.

* Life of George Washington. By Washington Irving . . . London, H. G. Bohn, 1855–59. 5 v.

The early and military life of Washington; including a comprehensive history of the American revolution, by Washington Irving. New-York, 1855–57. 4 v.

Life of George Washington. By Washington Irving. Author's edition. Leipzig, B. Tauchnitz, 1856–59. 5 v. (*Half-title:* Collection of British authors, v. 342, 349, 368, 406, 484)
Titles vary slightly: Vol. I–II: In three volumes; v. III–V: In five volumes.

* Life of George Washington. By Washington Irving . . . New York, G. P. Putnam & co., 1856–59. 5 v.

Life of George Washington. By Washington Irving. Illustrated edition. New York, G. P. Putnam & co., 1856–59. 5 v.

* Washington's earlier years. Being the first volume of the Life of Washington. By Washington Irving. Illustrated with portraits and original drawings. New York, G. P. Putnam & co.; London, Sampson Low & co., 1857.
Added engr. t.-p.: Life of George Washington. By Washington Irving. New York, G. P. Putnam & co.; London, Sampson Low & co., 1856.
Title vignette.

Life of George Washington . . . New York, G. P. Putnam & co., 1857–59. 5 v., portfolios.
Illustrations only, of the limited edition, 1855–59; proofs, on India paper. From designs by F. O. C. Darley and others.

Life of George Washington. By Washington Irving. New York and London, G. P. Putnam's sons, 1857. 5 v. (Irving's works. Hudson edition, v. 22–26)
Vol. 4 has added engr. t.-p.

Life of George Washington. By Washington Irving . . . [New York, G. P. Putnam's sons, c 1857] (Works. Kinderhook edition, v. [8, 9, 10])

Life of George Washington. By Washington Irving . . . New York
and London, G. P. Putnam's sons [c 1857] 8 v.
At head of title: Knickerbocker edition.
Title-page in red and black.
* Illustrations to Irving's Life of Washington. To his inauguration as
President . . . New York, G. P. Putnam, 1859.
Life of George Washington. By Washington Irving. New York,
G. P. Putnam, 1860. 5 v.
Life of George Washington. By Washington Irving . . . New York,
Putnam [1860?]
Illustrated edition.
— — New York, Putnam [1860?]
Library edition.
— — New York, Putnam [1860?]
Mount Vernon edition.
— — New York, Putnam [1860?]
Popular edition.
— — New York, Putnam [1860?]
Quarto edition.
— — New York, Putnam [1860?]
Sunnyside edition.
Life of George Washington, including a comprehensive history of the
American revolution. By Washington Irving . . . With numer-
ous illustrations on steel, from original designs by Darley and
others . . . New York, E. B. Treat & co., 1867.
Life of George Washington. By Washington Irving. New York,
G. P. Putnam and son, 1869. 5 v.
Knickerbocker edition.
Added engr. t.-p.
Life of George Washington. By Washington Irving. New York,
G. P. Putnam and son, 1869. 5 v.
Riverside edition.
The life and times of Washington. By Washington Irving. Illus-
trated edition. New York, G. P. Putnam & sons [etc.] 1872.
Added engr. t.-p.
At head of title: The American republic: its origin and early history.
Life of George Washington. By Washington Irving. New York,
G. P. Putnam, 1873. 5 v.
Knickerbocker edition.
Life of George Washington. By Washington Irving . . . New York
and London, G. P. Putnam's sons [1882] 5 v.
Vol. [22–26] of a uniform edition in cloth, having at head of title
"Hudson edition" (first issued in 1882) and lettered: Irving's
works.
Copyright date: 1857.
Vol. 4 has added engr. t.-p.

* The life of Washington, and the history of the American revolution
. . . New York, Putnam, 1883.
Abridged.
Centennial edition.

* Life of George Washington . . .   New York, G. P. Putnam's sons,
1885–87.   5 v.
People's edition.
Each volume has also added engr. t.-p.

The life of George Washington . . .   New York, J. B. Alden,
1887.

Washington and his country; being Irving's Life of Washington
abridged for the use of schools, with introduction and continuation,
giving a brief outline of United States history from the discovery
of America to the end of the Civil War, by John Fiske. Boston,
Ginn & co., 1887.   (Classics for children)

— — Boston, Ginn & co., 1888.

— — Boston, The Howe memorial press, 1888.   3 v.
In raised letters for the use of the blind.

— — Boston, Ginn & co., 1889.

* . . . The life of George Washington. By Washington Irving. Illustrated . . .   New York and London, G. P. Putnam's sons, 1889.
5 v.
At head of title: Limited centennial edition.

— — New York and London, G. P. Putnam's sons [1889]   5 v.
At head of title: Limited centennial edition.

Life of George Washington illustrated by Thomas Addis Emmet, M.D.
[New York] 1896.   10 v.

* Life of George Washington. By Washington Irving . . .   New York
and London, G. P. Putnam's sons, 1897.   8 v.
Knickerbocker edition.

. . . Life of George Washington, by Washington Irving . . .   New
York, G. P. Putnam's sons [1902]   5 v.
At head of title: Hudson edition.
Vol. 1, 3–5 have added engr. t.-p., with vignettes.

. . . Life of Washington . . .   New York, The Collegiate society,
1905.   5 v. (*At head of title:* The complete writings of Washington
Irving, including his life)
National edition.
500 numbered copies.

The life of George Washington, by Washington Irving. Revised
edition. New York, Thomas Y. Crowell co. [1916?]   4 v. in 2.

Life of Washington . . .   Philadelphia, David McKay [19–?]   4 v.
(American classics series)

Extracts

* The battle of Bunker Hill, June 17, 1775. [Boston, Oak Hall cloth-
ing co., 1875?]
Broadside.
Illustration by John Andrew.
Chapter 41 of Irving's Life of George Washington.
Irving's Life of Washington. An unique collection of portraits, views,
plans of battles, autograph letters, etc. . . . gathered . . . by
W. G. Craddock, for illustrating . . . Irving's Life of Washington.
Philadelphia, S. V. Henkels [1900]

TRANSLATIONS

Dutch

Het leven van George Washington. Een leseboek voor de jeugd.
Naar het Engelsch. Haarlem, 1838.

German

Das Leben George Washingtons, von Washington Irving. Aus dem
Englischen von W. C. Drugulin. Leipzig, Lorck, 1855–60. 5 v.
Bd. 1–3: Moderne Geschichtschreiber, Bd. 5–7.
Bd. 4–5 edited by F. Bülau.
* Lebensgeschichte Georg Washington's, von Washington Irving. Aus
dem Englischen von dem Uebersetzer der Werke Prescott's . . .
Leipzig, F. A. Brockhaus, 1856–59. 5 v.
Bd. 1 translated by J. H. Eberty; Bd. 2–5 by F. M. Kirbach.
Schneebeli, J. Washington. Sein Lebensbild nach Washington
Irving von J. Schneebeli. Hrsg. von der zürcherischen Schulsynode.
Zürich, J. Schabelitz, 1872.

Extracts

* George Washington's Abstammung. (*In* Magazin für die Literatur
des Auslandes. Berlin, Veit & Comp., 1855. 48. Bd., p. 404)

Swedish

George Washingtons lefnad. Öfversättning . . . Stockholm, E. T.
Bergegren, 1857–59.
Published in parts.
Translation by O. V. Ålund.

THE LIFE OF OLIVER GOLDSMITH

The miscellaneous works of Oliver Goldsmith, with an account of his
life and writings . . . Paris, A. and W. Galignani, 1825. 4 v.
(Collection of English literature)
Engraved portraits of Irving and Goldsmith.
Edited by Irving.

The miscellaneous works of Oliver Goldsmith, with an account of his life and writings. Stereotyped from the Paris edition, edited by Washington Irving . . . Philadelphia, J. Crissy, 1834.

— — Philadelphia, J. Crissy, 1835.

The miscellaneous works of Oliver Goldsmith, with an account of his life and writings. Edited by Washington Irving . . . Paris, Baudry, 1837. 4 v. (Collection of ancient and modern British authors, v. 150–153)

The miscellaneous works of Oliver Goldsmith, with an account of his life and writings. A new edition . . . Edited by Washington Irving . . . Paris, A. and W. Galignani and co., 1837. 4 v.

* The life of Oliver Goldsmith, with selections from his writings. By Washington Irving . . . New-York, Harper & brothers, 1840. 2 v. (*On cover:* The Family library, no. 121–122)

First edition.

Contents. — v. 1. Biographical sketch. Poetical extracts. Miscellaneous essays. From The Bee. From The citizen of the world. — v. 2. The citizen of the world continued. Miscellaneous.

* — — Another issue without note on cover.

The miscellaneous works of Oliver Goldsmith, with an account of his life and writings. Philadelphia, J. Crissy, 1841.

The life of Oliver Goldsmith, with selections from his writings. By Washington Irving . . . New-York, Harper & brothers, 1844. 2 v. (Harper's family library, no. 121–122)

Oliver Goldsmith: a biography. By Washington Irving. London, G. Routledge, 1849. (The Popular library)

* Oliver Goldsmith: a biography. By Washington Irving. London, John Murray, 1849. (Murray's colonial and home library)

* Oliver Goldsmith: a biography. By Washington Irving. New-York, G. P. Putnam; London, John Murray, 1849. (*Added t.-p.:* The works of Washington Irving. New edition, revised. Vol. 11. Oliver Goldsmith. New-York, G. P. Putnam, 1849)

* — — Another issue without added t.-p.

* Oliver Goldsmith. A biography. By Washington Irving. With illustrations. New-York, G. P. Putnam; London, John Murray, 1849.

* Life of Oliver Goldsmith. By Washington Irving. New York, F. M. Lupton publishing co. [1849?]

Preface dated 1849.

Oliver Goldsmith: a biography. By Washington Irving. New-York, G. P. Putnam [etc., etc.] 1850. (*Added t.-p.:* The works of Washington Irving . . . New edition, revised, v. 11)

Oliver Goldsmith: a biography . . . Leipzig, B. Tauchnitz, jun., 1850. (Collection of British authors, v. 193)

Oliver Goldsmith: a biography. By Washington Irving. London, H. G. Bohn, 1850. (Bohn's shilling series)

* Oliver Goldsmith: a biography. By Washington Irving. London, H. G. Clarke & co., 1850.
* Oliver Goldsmith: a biography. By Washington Irving. London, George Routledge & co., 1850. (The Popular library)

The miscellaneous works of Oliver Goldsmith, with an account of his life and writings. Stereotyped from the Paris edition, ed. by Washington Irving . . . Philadelphia, Crissy & Markley, 1850.

Oliver Goldsmith: a biography. By Washington Irving . . . New-York, G. P. Putnam & co., 1853.

* Oliver Goldsmith. A biography. By Washington Irving. London, W. Tweedie, 1853.
Added engr. t.-p.

A history of the earth and animated nature . . . [by Oliver Goldsmith] with an introductory view of the animal kingdom, tr. from the French of Baron Cuvier. And copious notes embracing accounts of new discoveries in natural history, a life of the author, by Washington Irving . . . London, A. Fullerton & co., 1853. 2 v.

— — London, A. Fullerton & co., 1855. 2 v.

The miscellaneous works of Oliver Goldsmith . . . Paris, Baudry's European library, 1857. 4 v. (Collection of ancient and modern British authors, v. 150–153)

Oliver Goldsmith, a biography, by Washington Irving . . . New York, G. P. Putnam, 1860. (Works. New edition, revised, v. 11)

* Oliver Goldsmith: a biography. By Washington Irving. With illustrations. New-York, G. P. Putnam, 1861. (*Added t.-p.:* The works of Washington Irving. New edition, revised, v. 11)
On shelf-back: National edition.
Title vignette.

Oliver Goldsmith. A biography. By Washington Irving . . . New York, G. P. Putnam's sons [1864]
Half-title: Irving's Goldsmith. Riverside edition.

Oliver Goldsmith. A biography. The author's revised edition . . . New York, G. P. Putnam's sons [c 1864]
Hudson edition.

Oliver Goldsmith. A biography. By Washington Irving. Author's revised edition. [New York, G. P. Putnam's sons, c 1864] (The works of Washington Irving. The Kinderhook edition, v. 7)

Oliver Goldsmith: a biography. By Washington Irving . . . New York, G. P. Putnam and son, 1868.
Added engr. t.-p.

Oliver Goldsmith. A biography . . . New York, G. P. Putnam and sons, 1869.
Knickerbocker edition.
Added engr. t.-p.

Oliver Goldsmith: a biography. By Washington Irving. Philadelphia, J. B. Lippincott & co., 1872.
Added engr. t.-p.; vignette (port.)

Oliver Goldsmith. A biography. By Washington Irving. Phila-
delphia, J. B. Lippincott & co., 1873.
People's edition.
Added engr. t.-p.; vignette.

Oliver Goldsmith: a biography. By Washington Irving. New York,
G. P. Putnam [1873?]
Knickerbocker edition.

Life of Oliver Goldsmith: a biography. By Washington Irving. London & Edinburgh [1879?] (Routledge's biographical library)

Life of Oliver Goldsmith. By Washington Irving. New York, J. W.
Lovell co. [1883] (On cover: Lovell's library, v. 6, no. 310)

Oliver Goldsmith, a biography . . . (Author's autograph edition).
New York, London, G. P. Putnam's sons, 1897. 2 v.
Edition limited to 500 sets.
Contents. — v. 1. Oliver Goldsmith. — v. 2. Oliver Goldsmith . . .
and Margaret Davidson.

. . . Oliver Goldsmith, a biography, by Washington Irving . . .
New York and London, G. P. Putnam's sons [1897] 2 v.
At head of title: Knickerbocker edition.
Half-title of v. 2: Oliver Goldsmith, a biography, to which is added
the Memoir of Margaret Davidson . . .

. . . Oliver Goldsmith, a biography, by Washington Irving. The
author's revised edition . . . New York, G. P. Putnam's sons
[1902] (Publisher's lettering: Irving's works)
At head of title: Hudson edition.

Oliver Goldsmith, a biography, by Washington Irving; edited, with
notes and an introduction by Gilbert Sykes Blakely . . . New
York, London, The Macmillan co., 1903. ([Macmillan's pocket
American and English classics])

. . . Irving's Oliver Goldsmith: edited with notes and an introduction
by Lewis B. Semple . . . New York, London [etc.] Longmans,
Green, and co., 1903. (Longmans' English classics)

* Irving's Oliver Goldsmith. A biography. Edited with introduction
and notes by Charles Robert Gaston . . . Boston, Ginn & co.,
1903. (On cover: Standard English classics)

* — — Boston, Ginn & co. [c 1903]

* . . . Oliver Goldsmith. A biography. By Washington Irving. The
author's revised edition with introduction and notes by Willis
Boughton . . . Boston [etc.] Houghton, Mifflin and co.; Cambridge, The Riverside press [c 1903] (The Riverside literature
series, no. 155)

* Oliver Goldsmith. A biography. By Washington Irving. Edited
with notes and an introduction by Gilbert Sykes Blakely . . .

New York, The Macmillan co.; London, Macmillan & co., ltd., 1904.

* . . . Oliver Goldsmith. A biography. By Washington Irving. Edited for school use by George Philip Krapp . . . Chicago, Scott, Foresman and co., 1904. (*At head of title:* The Lake English classics)

Oliver Goldsmith, a biography, by Washington Irving; edited, with introduction, notes, and questions, by H. E. Coblentz . . . Boston, D. C. Heath & co., 1904. (Heath's English classics)

Life of Oliver Goldsmith, with introduction and notes by R. Adelaide Witham . . . Boston, and Chicago, Allyn and Bacon [1904] (The Academy series of English classics)

Oliver Goldsmith, a biography, by Washington Irving; with biography, critical opinions, and explanatory notes. New York, Maynard, Merrill, & co. [1904] (Maynard's English classic series — Special number)

* . . . Oliver Goldsmith. A biography. By Washington Irving. Edited for school use by George Philip Krapp . . . Chicago, Scott, Foresman and co., 1905. (*At head of title:* The Lake English classics)

Oliver Goldsmith, a biography, by Washington Irving; edited, with notes and an introduction by Gilbert Sykes Blakely . . . New York, London, The Macmillan co., 1905. ([Macmillan's pocket American and English classics])

* . . . Irving's Oliver Goldsmith; edited with notes and an introduction by Lewis B. Semple . . . New York, London [etc.] Longmans, Green, and co., 1905. (Longmans' English classics)

* . . . Oliver Goldsmith. A biography. By Washington Irving. Edited, with introduction, notes, and questions by H. E. Coblentz . . . Boston, D. C. Heath & co., 1906. (*At head of title:* Heath's English classics)

Oliver Goldsmith, a biography, by Washington Irving; edited with notes and an introduction by Gilbert Sykes Blakely . . . New York, London, The Macmillan co., 1911. ([Macmillan's pocket American and English classics])

Oliver Goldsmith. A biography. By Washington Irving. Edited for school use by George Philip Krapp . . . Chicago, Atlanta [etc.] Scott, Foresman and co. [c1923] (The Lake English classics) At head of title: Revised edition with helps to study.

Life of Oliver Goldsmith. Edited by H. E. Coblentz. Boston, Heath [192–?] (Golden key series)

Oliver Goldsmith's Works. Poems, comedies, essays, Vicar of Wakefield. With Life by Washington Irving . . . London, C. Daly [187–?] Added engr. t.-p.

Life of Oliver Goldsmith . . . New York, Belford co. [188–?]

Life of Oliver Goldsmith. By Washington Irving. New York, T. Y.
Crowell [189–?] (Astor prose series)

Oliver Goldsmith. A biography. By Washington Irving. New York
and London, G. P. Putnam's sons [192–?] (*Lettered on back:*
Irving's works)
At head of title: Handy volume edition.
Title vignette.

Oliver Goldsmith. A biography. By Washington Irving. New York
and London, G. P. Putnam's sons [192–?]
Hudson edition.

Oliver Goldsmith. A biography. By Washington Irving. New York
and London, G. P. Putnam's sons [192–?]
New Knickerbocker edition.

Oliver Goldsmith. A biography. By Washington Irving. New York
and London, G. P. Putnam's sons [192–?]
Student's edition.

Translations

French

Vie de Goldsmith . . . Paris, 1849.

German

* Oliver Goldsmith. Eine Lebensbeschreibung von Washington Irving.
Aus dem Englischen. Berlin, G. Mertens, 1858.

Welsh

Hanes y ddaear a'r creadwriaid byw, gan O. G.; gyda Golygiad
arweiniol o'r deyrnas anifeilaidd, gan y Baron Cuvier . . . a
bywgraffiad yr awdwr gan W. Irving. Wedi ei gyfieithu a'i olygu
gan R. E. Williams. 2. cyf. Edinburgh, a Llundain [1868]

Louis XVIII. (*In* Galignani's messenger. Paris, 1824. Sept. 18?)

MAHOMET AND HIS SUCCESSORS

* Mahomet and his successors. By Washington Irving . . . New-
York, G. P. Putnam, 1850. 2 v. (*Added t.-p.:* The works of
Washington Irving . . . Vol. 12–13)
First American edition.
Title-pages also read Mohamet and Mohomet.

* Lives of Mahomet and his successors. By Washington Irving . . .
London, John Murray, 1850. 2 v.
First English edition.
Each volume has also individual t.-p.
Advertisements at the end of each volume dated respectively
January and July, 1850.

* Life of Mahomet. By Washington Irving. London, H. G. Bohn, 1850.
  (Bohn's shilling series, 2)
* The life of Mahomet. By Washington Irving. London, George
  Routledge & co., 1850.
* The life of Mahomet. By Washington Irving. Leipzig, B. Tauchnitz,
  1850. (Collection of British authors, 191)
* Lives of the successors of Mahomet. By Washington Irving. Leipzig,
  B. Tauchnitz, 1850. (Collection of British authors, 192)
* Lives of the successors of Mahomet. By Washington Irving. London,
  H. G. Bohn, 1850. (Bohn's shilling series, 5)
  May have appeared before the edition by Murray.
* Lives of the successors of Mahomet. By Washington Irving. Lon-
  don, H. G. Bohn, 1850. (Bohn's library edition)
* Lives of the successors of Mahomet. By Washington Irving. London,
  George Routledge, 1850. (The Popular library)
* Lives of Mahomet and his successors. By Washington Irving. Paris,
  Baudry, 1850. (Collection of ancient and modern British authors,
  t. 449)
  The life of Mahomet. By Washington Irving. London, George
  Routledge, 1851.
  The life of Mahomet. By Washington Irving. London, H. G. Bohn,
  1852. (Bohn's shilling series)
  The life of Mahomet. By Washington Irving. London, H. G. Bohn,
  1852. (Bohn's library edition)
* Mahomet and his successors. By Washington Irving . . . New York,
  G. P. Putnam, 1860. (The works of Washington Irving, v. 12)
  Mahomet and his successors, by Washington Irving . . . [New
  York, G. P. Putnam's sons, c 1868] 2 v. (. . . Works. The Kinder-
  hook edition, v. [3, 13])
  Mahomet and his successors. By Washington Irving . . . New
  York, G. P. Putnam and son, 1868-69. 2 v.
  Knickerbocker edition.
  Mahomet and his successors. By Washington Irving. New York,
  G. P. Putnam, 1869. 2 v.
  Riverside edition.
  Mahomet and his successors. By Washington Irving. Philadelphia,
  1873. 2 v.
  Knickerbocker edition.
  Mahomet and his successors. By Washington Irving . . . Phila-
  delphia, J. B. Lippincott & co., 1873. 2 v.
  People's edition.
  Added engr. t.-p.
  Lives of the successors of Mahomet. By Washington Irving. Phila
  delphia, 1879.
  The life of Mahomet. By Washington Irving. London and Edin-
  burgh [1879]

Lives of the successors of Mahomet. By Washington Irving. London, H. G. Bohn, 1880. (Bohn's shilling library)

* The life of Mahomet. By Washington Irving. London, H. G. Bohn, 1882. (Bohn's shilling library)

* Life of Mahomet. By Washington Irving. London, George Bell & sons, 1883. (Bohn's cheap series of standard works)

Mahomet and his successors. By Washington Irving. New York, J. B. Millar & co., 1884.
Contains also Moorish chronicles, with individual t.-p.

The life of Mahomet. By Washington Irving. London, H. G. Bohn, 1888. (Bohn's shilling library)

. . . Mahomet and his successors . . . New York and London, G. P. Putnam's sons [c 1896] 3 v.
At head of title: Knickerbocker edition.
Contents. — v. 1–2. Mahomet and his successors. — v. 3. Mahomet and his successors. The legend of Don Roderick. The legend of Pelayo. Abderahman.

. . . Mahomet and his successors . . . New York & London, G. P. Putnam's sons, 1896–97. 3 v.
Author's autograph edition.

. . . Mahomet and his successors, by Washington Irving . . . New York, G. P. Putnam's sons [1902] 2 v.
At head of title: Hudson edition.
Added engr. t.-p.

Life of Mahomet. By Washington Irving. London, J. M. Dent & sons, ltd.; New York, E. P. Dutton & co. [1911] (*Half-title:* Everyman's library . . . Biography)

Mahomet and his successors . . . [New York, Belford co., 188–?]

The life of Mahomet. By Washington Irving. New York, Burt [19–?] (Home library)

* Mahomet and his successors. By Washington Irving. Illustrated. New York, Thomas Y. Crowell & co. [18–?]
Preface dated 1849.

Mahomet and his successors. By Washington Irving. New York, G. P. Putnam's sons [19–?]
New Knickerbocker edition.

TRANSLATIONS

Danish

Mahomeds levnet, overs. af L. Moltke. Kjøbenhavn, Schønberg, 1858.

French

* . . . Vie de Mahomet. Traduit de l'anglais par Henry Georges. Paris, A. Lacroix, Verboeckhoven et cie, 1865.
At head of title: Washington Irving.

German

Das Leben Mohammed's, von Washington Irving. Leipzig, C. B. Lorck, 1850. (Historische Hausbibliothek, 16. Bd.)

* Geschichte der Kalifen, vom Tode Mohamed's bis zum Einfall in Spanien, von Washington Irving. Leipzig, C. B. Lorck, 1854. (Historische Hausbibliothek, 33. Bd.)

—— Leipzig, C. B. Lorck, 1865.

Das Leben Mohammed's, von Washington Irving. Leipzig, C. B. Lorck, 1865. (Historische Hausbibliothek, 16. Bd.)

—— Leipzig, Senf, 1865.
Neue Ausgabe.

Geschichte der Kalifen. Vom Tode Mohamed's bis zum Einfall in Spanien. 3. Ausg. Leipzig, Senf, 1865.

Das Leben Mohammed's . . . 3. Ausg. Leipzig, Senf, 1869.

—— Leipzig, Senf, 1874.

Geschichte der Kalifen, vom Tode Mohamed's bis zum Einfall in Spanien, von Washington Irving. Leipzig, C. B. Lorck, 1874. (Historische Hausbibliothek, 33. Bd.)

Extracts

* Muhammed's Leben, Wahrheit und Dichtung. (Nach Washington Irving und der North-American review.) (*In* Magazin für die Literatur des Auslandes. Berlin, Veit & Comp., 1851. 40. Bd., p. [333]–335, 339–340, 343–344, 346–348, 350–351)

* Washington Irving's Leben des Muhammed's und seiner Nachfolger. (*In* Magazin für die Literatur des Auslandes. Berlin, Veit & Comp., 1850. 37. Bd., p. [213]–215)
A review, with translations of selections.

Greek

Βίος τοῦ Μωάμεθ. Μετὰ παραρτήματος. Περὶ ἰσλαμικῆς θρησκείας. Ὑπὸ Οὐασιγτῶνος Ἴρβινγγος. Μετάφρασις ἐκ τοῦ ἀγγλικοῦ Ἀνδρέου Σ. Φαραοῦ. Ἐν Σακύνθῳ, Ῥαφτάνης, 1866.

Icelandic

Extracts

[Selections.] (*In* Norðri. [place?] 1853–61)

Italian

Vita di Maometto. Versione di Giuseppe de Tivoli. Milano, Guglielmini, 1854.

* . . . Vita di Maometto. Traduzione, prefazione e note di Silvia Falconcini . . . Lanciano, R. Carabba, 1928. 2v. (Antichi e moderni in versioni scelte, no. 56–57)

Polish

Życie Mahometa . . . (*In* Koran . . . z Arabskiego przekład Polski
J. Murzy Tarak Buczackiego . . . Wzbogacony objaśnieniami
W. Kościuszki. Poprzedzony zyciorysem Mahometa z W. Irving
. . . Warszawa, 1858. v. 1)

Russian

Жизнь Магомета. Moscow, 1857.
   Life of Mahomet, translated from the English by Petr Kirieevskiĭ.
*. . . Жизнь Магомета. Переводъ А. П. Никифорова.
Moscow, 1898. (Общеполезная библіотека для самообра-
зованія. № № 23 и 24, Изданіе М. Б. Клюкина)

Spanish

* Historia de Mahoma escrita en inglés por Washington Irving, tra-
ducida al español por J. S. Facio. Edicion del "Diario de Avisos."
México, Imprenta de Vicente Segura, 1857.
   Preface by Irving, dated Sunnyside, 1849.

* Poems, by William Cullen Bryant, an American. Edited by Wash-
ington Irving. London, J. Andrews, 1832.
   With a dedication by Irving to Samuel Rogers; and alterations by
   Irving in "The song of Marion's men."

THE POETICAL WORKS OF THOMAS CAMPBELL

See also, Spanish Papers

* The poetical works of Thomas Campbell. Including several poems
from the original manuscript, never before published in this country.
To which is prefixed a biographical sketch of the author, by a
Gentleman of New-York . . . Philadelphia, E. Earle; Baltimore,
P. H. Nicklin & co. [etc., etc.] 1810. 2 v.
* — — Albany, D. W. Farrand & Green [etc., etc.] 1810.
* The poetical works of Thomas Campbell. Including several pieces
from the original manuscript . . . Baltimore, P. H. Nicklin & co.
[etc., etc.] 1810.
* The poetical works of Thomas Campbell. Including several pieces
from the original manuscript, never before published in this country.
To which is prefixed a biographical sketch of the author, by a
Gentleman of New-York. Second American edition. Baltimore,
P. H. Nicklin [etc., etc., 1811]
* The poetical works of Thomas Campbell. Comprising several pieces
not contained in any former edition. To which is prefixed a re-

vised and improved biographical sketch of the author, by a Gentleman of New-York. [Philadelphia, Edward Earle, 1815]

* — — Philadelphia, Edward Earle [1815]
* — — Philadelphia, Edward Earle, 1815.
* — — [Philadelphia, Edward Earle, c 1815]
* A biographical sketch of Thomas Campbell. (*In* The Analectic
magazine. Philadelphia, M. Thomas, 1815. v. 5, p. 234–250)
[A biographical sketch of Thomas Campbell.] (*In* Specimens of the
British poets, with biographical and critical notices, and an essay
on English poetry. London, John Murray, 1819)
* The poetical works of Thomas Campbell. To which is prefixed, a
biographical sketch of the author. First complete American
edition. Philadelphia, Edward Parker, 1821.
* The pleasures of hope and other poems. By Thomas Campbell. With
portrait. New York, 1822.
First edition.
Contains A biographical sketch, by Irving.
[A biographical sketch of Thomas Campbell.] (*In* Beattie, William.
Life and letters of Thomas Campbell. New York, Harper & bro.,
1841]
* A biographical sketch of Thomas Campbell, esq. By Geoffry [*sic*]
Crayon, gent. (*In* Bolster's quarterly magazine. Cork, John
Bolster [etc., etc.] 1828 [*i.e.*, 1826] v. 1, p. 28–39)
* The poetry and history of Wyoming: containing Campbell's Gertrude,
with a biographical sketch of the author, by Washington Irving,
and the History of Wyoming . . . by William L. Stone. New-
York & London, Wiley and Putnam, 1841.
— — New York, 1844.
Second edition, enlarged.
* The poetical works of Thomas Campbell, complete: with a memoir
of the author by Washington Irving, and remarks upon his writings
by Lord Jeffrey . . . Philadelphia, Lea and Blanchard, 1845.
* [A biographical sketch of Thomas Campbell.] (*In* Beattie, William.
Life and letters of Thomas Campbell. New York, Harper & bro.,
1850. v. 1, p. xi–xvi)
— — New York, Harper & bro. [1855]
The poetry and history of Wyoming, containing Campbell's Gertrude,
with a biographical sketch of the author, by Washington Irving,
and the History of Wyoming . . . by William L. Stone. Albany,
J. Munsell, 1864.
The second edition of 1844, with a new title-page, and an index.
The history of Wyoming has an independent title-page reading:
Wyoming, and its history . . . New-York, Mark H. Newman,
1844.
— — Wilkes-Barre, C. E. Butler, 1869.
— — Wilkes-Barre, C. E. Butler, 1873.

Polly Holman's wedding. Notes by Washington Irving. Edited by Stanley T. Williams and Ernest E. Leisy. (*In* The Southwest review. Dallas, Texas. v. 19, p. 449-454)

Richelieu: a domestic tragedy, founded on fact . . . Now first printed from the author's manuscript. New York, E. M. Murden, 1826.

SALMAGUNDI

* Salmagundi; or, The whim-whams and opinions of Launcelot Langstaff, esq., & others . . . New-York, Printed & published by D. Longworth, 1807-08. 2 v. (port. in v. 1)
Paged continuously.
   * Originally published in twenty serial numbers, January 24, 1807-January 25, 1808. Written by Washington Irving, William Irving and James K. Paulding. * A second series in three volumes, entirely by Paulding, was issued in fifteen numbers May 1819-September 1820.
* — — New-York, Printed & published by D. Longworth, 1808. 2 v.
* Salmagundi; or, The Whim-whams and opinions of Launcelot Langstaff, esq., and others . . . Reprinted from the American edition, with an introductory essay and explanatory notes, by John Lambert. London, Printed for J. M. Richardson, 1811. 2 v. in 1.
* Salmagundi; or, The whim-whams and opinions of Launcelot Langstaff, esq., and others . . . A new and improved ed., with table of contents and a copious index . . . New-York, D. Longworth, 1814. 2 v.
First revised edition with plates and woodcut by Alexander Anderson.
* Salmagundi; or, The whim-whams and opinions of Launcelot Langstaff, esq., and others . . . Third edition . . . New-York, Published by Thomas Longworth and co., 1820. 2 v. 12mo.
Paged continuously.
Engravings by Anderson.
* — — New-York, Published by Thomas Longworth and co., 1820. 2 v. in 1. 16mo.
* — — New-York, Published by Thomas Longworth and co., 1820. 2 v. in 1. 18mo.
* — — New-York, Published by Thomas Longworth and co., 1820. 2 v. in 1.
Vol. 2 pub. by J. Seymour.
* Salmagundi; or, The whim-whams and opinions of Launcelot Langstaff, esq., and others. By the author of Knickerbocker's History of New York, Sketch book, and Bracebridge Hall . . . New edition. London, Printed by T. Davison for Thomas Tegg, Rodwell and Martin; Glasgow, R. Griffin and co., 1824.

* — — New edition. Corrected and revised by the author. London, Printed by T. Davison for Thomas Tegg [etc., etc.] 1824.

* Salmagundi; or, The whim-whams and opinions of Launcelot Langstaff, esq., and others . . . Paris, A. and W. Galignani, 1824. 2 v.

* Salmagundi; or, The whim-whams and opinions of Launcelot Langstaff, esq., and others . . . In two volumes. Paris, Baudry, 1824.

Salmagundi; or, The whim-whams and opinions of Launcelot Langstaff, esq., and others . . . London, J. Limbird, 1824.

* — — London, John Bumpus, 1825.

Salmagundi . . . Third edition. London, T. Tegg, 1825.

Salmagundi . . . London, 1830.

* Salmagundi . . . Corrected by the authors. New York, Harper, 1835. 4 v.

Contains first and second series.

Salmagundi . . . First series . . . A new edition, corrected by the authors. New-York, Harper & brothers, 1835. 2 v. (*Publisher's lettering:* Paulding's works. I–II)

* Salmagundi . . . New edition, corrected and revised by the author. London, Printed for Thomas Tegg [etc., etc.] 1839.

* Salmagundi . . . London, Published by C. Daly, 1841. (Miniature classical library)

Added engr. t.-p.

* — — London, C. Daly, 1841. (Miniature classical library)

* Salmagundi. (*In* Five hundred curious and interesting narratives and anecdotes . . . Glasgow, Richard Griffin and co., 1844)

Salmagundi . . . London, H. G. Bohn, 1850. (Bohn's shilling series)

* Salmagundi . . . By Washington Irving . . . London, George Routledge & co., 1850.

Salmagundi . . . London [1850] (The Popular library)

* Salmagundi . . . New York, G. P. Putnam & co., 1857. (*On cover:* Putnam's railway classics)

Added t.-p. with vignette.

Frontispiece engraved by Alexander Anderson.

Salmagundi . . . New York, G. P. Putnam, 1859.

* Salmagundi . . . By William Irving, James Kirke Paulding, and Washington Irving . . . Printed from the original edition with a preface and notes, by Evert A. Duyckinck. New York, G. P. Putnam, 1860.

Salmagundi . . . By William Irving, James Kirke Paulding, and Washington Irving . . . Printed from the original edition with a preface and notes, by Evert A. Duyckinck. [New York, G. P. Putnam's sons, c 1860] (The works of Washington Irving. The Kinderhook edition [v. 13])

Salmagundi . . . By William Irving, James Kirke Paulding, and Washington Irving . . . Printed from the original edition with a preface and notes, by Evert A. Duyckinck. Philadelphia, J. B. Lippincott, 1870.

Riverside edition.

Salmagundi . . . By William Irving, James Kirke Paulding, and Washington Irving . . . Printed from the original edition with a preface and notes, by Evert A. Duyckinck. Philadelphia, J. B. Lippincott, 1872.

People's edition.

Salmagundi . . . Philadelphia, J. B. Lippincott, 1873.

Knickerbocker edition.

Salmagundi . . . London, George Bell and sons, 1876. (Bohn's cheap series of standard works)

Salmagundi . . . By William Irving, James Kirke Paulding, and Washington Irving . . . Printed from the original edition with a preface and notes, by Evert A. Duyckinck. New York, G. P. Putnam's sons [1882]

Copyright date: 1860.

Vol. [18] of a uniform edition in cloth, having at head of title "Hudson edition" (first issued in 1882) and lettered: Irving's works.

Added engr. t.-p.

* Salmagundi. By Washington Irving . . . New York, J. B. Alden, 1883. (*On cover:* The Irving library, December 19, 1883)

Salmagundi . . . By William Irving, James Kirke Paulding, and Washington Irving . . . New York & London, G. P. Putnam's sons, 1897. 2 v.

Author's autograph edition.

Edition limited to 500 sets, not numbered.

Vol. 2 includes Letters of Jonathan Oldstyle, gent., and Biographical sketches.

Salmagundi, by William Irving, James Kirke Paulding, and Washington Irving . . . New York and London, G. P. Putnam's sons [1897] 2 v.

At head of title: Knickerbocker edition.

Half-title of v. 2: Salmagundi; or, The whim-whams and opinions of Launcelot Langstaff, esq., and others, Letters of Jonathan Oldstyle, gent., and Biographical sketches.

Salmagundi . . . By William Irving, James Kirke Paulding, and Washington Irving . . . Printed from the original edition, with a preface and notes, by Evert A. Duyckinck. New York, G. P. Putnam's sons [1902] (*Publisher's lettering:* Irving's works)

At head of title: Hudson edition.

Salmagundi . . . [New York, Belford co., 188–?]

* Salmagundi. By Washington Irving . . . New York, The New York publishing co. [n.d.]

Contents. — Salmagundi. — The adventures of Captain Bonneville.

Salmagundi . . . New York, Putnam [19–?]
New handy volume edition.
Salmagundi . . . New York, Putnam [19–?]   2 v.
New Knickerbocker edition.

Salmagundi. Second Series

* Salmagundi. Second series. By Launcelot Langstaff, esq. Phila-
delphia, Published by M. Thomas; New York, J. Haly and C.
Thomas; J. Maxwell, printer, 1819–20. 3 v.
Imprint varies.
Issued in 15 numbers, May 30, 1819–Sept. 2, 1820. By James
Kirke Paulding.

Extracts

* Lambert, John. Travels through lower Canada and the United
States of North America, in the years 1806, 1807, and 1808. To
which are added, biographical notices and anecdotes of some of
the leading characters in the United States; and of those who have,
at various periods, borne a conspicuous part in the politics of that
country. By John Lambert. In three volumes. With engravings
. . . London, Printed for Richard Phillips, 1810. 3 v.
Contains extracts from Salmagundi.
The second edition, 1814, does not contain the extracts from Irving.

TRANSLATIONS

German

* Eingemachtes von Washington Irving. Aus dem Englischen. Frank-
furt am Main, J. D. Sauerländer, 1827. (Washington Irving's
Sämmtliche Werke. Uebersetzt von Mehreren und hrsg. von
C. A. Fischer. 19. Bdchn.)

Extracts

[My uncle John. German translation.] (*In* Morgenblatt für gebildete Stände. Stuttgart und München, J. G. Cotta, 1824. No.
132)

Swedish

Bref från den hjeltemodiga Mustapha Rub-a-Dub Keli Kahn, under
hans fångenskap i New-York t. sina vänner i Tripolis. Stockholm,
Beijer, 1872.

THE SKETCH BOOK

* The sketch book of Geoffrey Crayon, gent. . . . New-York, Printed
by C. S. Van Winkle, 1819–20.
First American edition.
Issued in seven parts; parts I–V, 1819; parts VI–VII, 1820.
Parts I–V paged continuously.

— — New-York, Printed by C. S. Van Winkle, 1819–20.
Second American edition.
Published in parts; parts I–V, 1819; parts VI–VII, 1820.
Parts I–II paged continuously.

* The sketch book of Geoffrey Crayon, gent. . . . London, John
Miller, 1820. 2 v.
Published at Irving's expense in February, 1820.

* The sketch book of Geoffrey Crayon, gent. London, John Murray,
1820. 2 v.
Third edition, published in July, 1820, after the failure of the firm
of John Miller.

The sketch book of Geoffrey Crayon, gent. London, John Murray,
1821. 2 v.
Fourth edition.

* The sketch book of Geoffrey Crayon, gent. . . . Fifth edition . . .
London, John Murray, 1821. 2 v.

* The sketch book of Geoffrey Crayon, gent. . . . New edition. In
two volumes . . . London, John Murray, 1822. 2 v.

* The sketch book of Geoffrey Crayon, gent. New York, Printed by
C. S. Van Winkle, 1822–23. 2 v.
Third American edition.

* The sketch book of Geoffrey Crayon, gent., with the last corrections
of the author . . . Eighth edition, complete in one volume and
embellished with three lithographic prints. Dresden, Printed for
the editor, A. Montucci, 1823.
Plates signed: del [sic] L. K.

The sketch book of Geoffrey Crayon, gent. London, John Murray,
1823. 2 v.

The sketch book of Geoffrey Crayon, gent. Paris, A. Baudry and
J. Didot, 1823. 2 v.

The sketchboock [sic] by Goffrey [sic] Crayon. Leipzig, Fleischer,
1823.

The sketch book of Geoffrey Crayon, gent. . . . 4th American edition
. . . New-York, Printed by C. S. Van Winkle, 1824. 2 v.

* The sketch book of Geoffrey Crayon, gent. . . . New edition . . .
London, John Murray, 1824. 2 v.

* The sketch book of Geoffrey Crayon, gent. . . . New edition. Paris,
A. and W. Galignani, 1824.

* The sketch book of Geoffrey Crayon. Paris, L. Baudry, 1825.

The sketch book of Geoffrey Crayon. London, 1826.

The sketch book of Geoffrey Crayon, gent. New York, 1828.
Revised edition.

The sketch book of Geoffrey Crayon, gent. Philadelphia, Carey,
Lea & Carey, 1828.

The sketch book of Geoffrey Crayon, gent., with life of the author.
Paris, 1830. 2 v.

The sketch-book of Geoffrey Crayon, gent. . . . Seventh American edition. Philadelphia, Carey & Lea, 1831. 2 v.

* The sketch book of Geoffrey Crayon, gent. . . . Paris, L. Baudry, 1831. Seventeenth edition.

* The sketch book of Geoffrey Crayon, gent. Paris, L. Baudry, 1831. 2 v. Eighteenth edition.

The sketch book of Geoffrey Crayon, gent. Paris, L. Baudry, 1831. Extracts from t. 2.

The sketch book of Geoffrey Crayon, gent. . . . Philadelphia, Carey & Lea, 1832. 2 v.

— — Philadelphia, Carey & Lea, 1833. 2 v.

* The sketch book of Geoffrey Crayon, gent. . . . Paris, Baudry, 1834. 2 v.

* The sketch book of Geoffrey Crayon, gent. Paris, Cormon and Blanc, 1834. 2 v.

* The sketch-book of Geoffrey Crayon, esq. A new edition . . . London, John Murray, 1834. 2 v. Illustrations by Leslie.

* The sketch-book of Geoffrey Crayon, esq. A new edition . . . London, John Murray, 1834. 2 v. (The Family library, v. 39–40)

The sketch book of Geoffrey Crayon, gent. Philadelphia, Carey & Lea, 1834. 2 v.

The sketch book of Geoffrey Crayon, gent. New edition. Philadelphia, 1835.

The sketch-book of Geoffrey Crayon, gent. . . . A new edition. Philadelphia, Carey, Lea, & Blanchard, 1836. 2 v.

* The sketch-book of Geoffrey Crayon, esq. (Washington Irving.) Paris, Baudry, 1836. (Collection of ancient and modern British authors, 99)

The sketch-book of Geoffrey Crayon. London, John Murray and Thomas Tegg and sons, 1838.

The sketch book of Geoffrey Crayon. Bremen, 1840.

The sketch book. Mit einer Einleitung über Irving's Leben und Schriften und erklärenden Anmerkungen hrsg. von E. A. Toel. Lüneburg, Herold und Wahlstab, 1840.

The sketch-book of Geoffrey Crayon, gent. . . . Philadelphia, Lea & Blanchard, 1842. 2 v. New edition.

* The sketch book of Geoffrey Crayon, esq. (Washington Irving.) With the portrait of the author. Leipzig, B. Tauchnitz, 1843. (Collection of British authors, v. 33)

— — Leipzig, B. Tauchnitz, 1845. (Collection of British authors, v. 33)

The sketch book of Geoffrey Crayon. [place?] 1845. 2 v.

* The sketch book of Geoffrey Crayon. Paris, Baudry, 1846. 2 v.

— — Paris, Galignani, 1846.

The sketch book of Geoffrey Crayon, gent. New edition. [London?] 1847. (The Parlour library, v. 41)

* The sketch book of Geoffrey Crayon, gent^n. Author's revised edition, with original designs by F. O. C. Darley, engraved by Childs, Herrick, etc. New-York, G. P. Putnam, 1848.
Added engr. t.-p.
Edition of 50 copies.

The sketch book of Geoffrey Crayon, gent^n. The author's revised edition. Complete in one volume. New-York, Putnam, 1848. (*Added t.-p.*: The works of Washington Irving. New edition, revised, v. 2)

The sketch-book, by Washington Irving. New York, G. P. Putnam's sons [1848?] 2 v.
Preface dated 1848.
Pocket edition.

* The sketch book of Geoffrey Crayon, gent^n. The author's revised edition. Complete in one volume. New-York, Putnam, 1848. (*Added t.-p.*: The works of Washington Irving. New edition, revised, v. 2)

* The sketch book of Geoffrey Crayon, gent^n . . . With a new introduction by the author. Illustrated with original designs. London, John Murray, 1849.

The sketch book of Geoffrey Crayon, gent. London, H. G. Bohn, 1850. (Bohn's shilling series)

The sketch book of Geoffrey Crayon, gent^n . . . Author's revised edition. With original designs by F. O. C. Darley, engraved by Herrick, etc. New-York, G. P. Putnam & co., 1852.

The sketch book of Geoffrey Crayon, gent^n . . . The author's revised edition. Complete in one volume. New-York, G. P. Putnam & co., 1853. (*Added t.-p.*: The works of Washington Irving. New edition, revised, v. 2)

— — New-York, G. P. Putnam & co., 1855. (*Added t.-p.*: The works of Washington Irving. New edition, revised, v. 2)

The sketch book . . . Philadelphia, Childs & Peterson [c 1855]
Illustrated by F. O. C. Darley.

* The sketch book, by Washington Irving . . . New York, G. P. Putnam & co., 1857. (Putnam's railway classics)

* The sketch book of Geoffrey Crayon, gent^n . . . The author's revised edition. Complete in one volume. New York, G. P. Putnam & co., 1857. (*Added t.-p.*: The works of Washington Irving. New edition, revised, v. 2)

— — New York, G. P. Putnam & co., 1858. (*Added t.-p.*: The works of Washington Irving. New edition, revised, v. 2)

— — New York, G. P. Putnam & co., 1859. (*Added t.-p.*: The works of Washington Irving. New edition, revised, v. 2)

Sketches of a traveller. Aus dem Sketch-book und Bracebridge Hall von Washington Irving. Leipzig, Gerhard, 1859. (Bibliothek der englischen Literatur für Schule und Haus. Hrsg. von H. Robolsky. Hft. 4)

* The sketch-book of Geoffrey Crayon, gent. New York, G. P. Putnam, 1860. (*Added engr. t.-p.:* Irving's works)
A prospectus of the National edition of: Irving's works.

The sketch book. Für Schulen und zum Privatunterrichte in der englischen Sprache. Mit Erläuterungen und einem ausführlichen Wörterbuche versehen von J. H. Lohmann. Quedlinburg, Basse, 1861.

* The sketch-book of Geoffrey Crayon, gent. . . . The author's revised edition. Complete in one volume. New York, G. P. Putnam; Boston, Ticknor and Fields, 1864.

The sketch book . . . London, 1864.

The sketch book of Geoffrey Crayon, gent. London, Bell & Daldy [1864] (Bell & Daldy's pocket volumes)

* The sketch-book of Geoffrey Crayon, gent. . . . The author's revised edition. Complete in one volume. New York, G. P. Putnam's sons [c 1864]

* Sketch book of Geoffrey Crayon, gent. Artist's edition . . . New York, G. P. Putnam, 1864.

— — New York, G. P. Putnam; Hurd & Houghton, 1865.

* The sketch book of Geoffrey Crayon, gent. Artist's edition . . . London, Bell and Daldy, 1865.

Sketch book of Geoffrey Crayon, gent. Artist's edition . . . New York, G. P. Putnam, 1865.
Added illustrated t.-p.

Blossoms of The sketch book. Mit erläuternden Anmerkungen zum Schul- und Privatunterricht bearbeitet von P. Weeg. Münster, Brunn, 1867. (Sammlung gediegener und interessanter Werke der englischen Literatur, 3)

The sketch-book of Geoffrey Crayon, gent. . . . The author's revised edition. Complete in one volume. New York, G. P. Putnam and son, 1867.
Added engr. t.-p.

The sketch book . . . London, Routledge, 1867.

* The sketch book . . . New York, G. P. Putnam and son, 1868.

The sketch book . . . Illustrated . . . [place?] 1869.

The sketch-book. Für Schulen und zum Privatunterrichte in der englischen Sprache. Mit Erläuterungen und einem ausführlichen Wörterbuche versehen von J. H. Lohmann. Quedlinburg, Basse, 1869.

A selection from The sketch-book of Washington Irving. With a memoir of the author and explanatory notes. Leipzig, E. Fleischer, 1872. (Collection of British and American standard authors, 7)

The sketch-book of Geoffrey Crayon, gent. . . . The author's re-
vised edition . . . Philadelphia, J. B. Lippincott & co., 1873.
On half-title: People's edition.
Added engr. t.-p.; vignette; head and tail pieces.
The sketch book of Geoffrey Crayon, gent. Author's revised edition.
New York [1873?]
Knickerbocker edition, with illustrations.
[The sketch book of Geoffrey Crayon, gent.] Paris, Hachette, 1875.
Sketch book of Geoffrey Crayon, gent. (Washington Irving). Cabi-
net edition. Illustrated with one hundred and twenty engravings
on wood, from original designs . . . Philadelphia, J. B. Lippincott
& co. [c 1875]
* The sketch-book of Geoffrey Crayon, gent. . . . The author's revised
edition. Complete in one volume. New York, G. P. Putnam, 1878.
On cover: Pocket edition.
. . . Six selections from Irving's Sketch-book. Consisting of sketches
from the list made by the supervisors for the Boston high schools.
With a notice of Irving's life and times, notes, questions, etc. For
home and school use. By Homer B. Sprague . . . assisted by
M. E. Scates . . . Boston, Ginn and Heath, 1878.
The sketchbook of Geoffrey Crayon, gent. Erklärt von Emil Pfund-
heller. Mit Skizze der Westminster-Abtei. Berlin, Weidmann,
1880.
The sketch-book of Geoffrey Crayon, gent. . . . Author's revised
edition. New York, G. P. Putnam's sons [1880] (Half-title:
Irving's works. Geoffrey Crayon edition, v. 2)
Added engr. t.-p.
The sketch book of Geoffrey Crayon, gent. . . . Author's revised
edition. [New York, G. P. Putnam's sons, c 1880] (Works. Kin-
derhook edition, v. 2)
* The sketch-book of Geoffrey Crayon, gent. . . . The author's re-
vised edition . . . New York, G. P. Putnam's sons, 1881.
The sketch book of Geoffrey Crayon, gent. London, Ward, Lock &
co. [1881]
* The sketch book. By Washington Irving. New York, S. W. Green's
son, 1882.
* Sketch book of Geoffrey Crayon, gent. (Washington Irving.) Édition
de luxe. Philadelphia, J. B. Lippincott & co., 1882.
Edition of 500 copies.
* Rip Van Winkle, and other sketches, by Washington Irving. New
York, The Useful knowledge publishing company, 1882.
Contents. — Rip Van Winkle. — The wife. — The broken heart. —
Art of book-making. — The widow and her son. — Boar's Head
tavern, Eastcheap. — Mutability of literature. — Rural funerals.
— The spectre bridegroom. — Westminster Abbey. — Stratford-
on-Avon. — John Bull. — The legend of Sleepy Hollow.

The sketch-book . . . Author's revised edition. New York and London, G. P. Putnam's sons [1882?]

Vol. [19] of a uniform edition in cloth, having at head of title "Hudson edition"(first issued in 1882) and lettered: Irving's works.

The sketch-book. (Christmas and other sketches. Being the second series of the Sketch book.) London, Paterson, 1883. 2 v. (Paterson's shilling library)

The sketch book of Geoffrey Crayon, gent. . . . London, Cassell [1883] (Cassell's Red library)

The sketch-book of Geoffrey Crayon, gent. . . . The author's revised edition. New York, G. P. Putnam's sons, 1884.

At head of title: Stratford edition.

The sketch book of Geoffrey Crayon, gent., by Washington Irving; reprinted from the original edition. New York, R. Worthington, 1884.

The sketch book. By Washington Irving . . . New York, J. B. Millar & co., 1884.

Each part has special t.-p.; no general t.-p.

Contents. — The sketch book. — A history of New York.

* Washington Irving. The sketch book. Texte anglais annoté par M. l'abbé A. Julien . . . Paris, Poussielgue frères, 1885. ([Alliance des maisons d'éducation chrétienne])

The sketch-book . . . Mit Erläuterungen versehen von J. H. Lohmann. 2., völlig umgearbeitete Auflage von G. Langreuter. Quedlinburg, Basse, 1885.

Sketch book of Geoffrey Crayon, gent. (Washington Irving.) . . . Philadelphia, J. B. Lippincott co., 1886.

Cabinet edition.

"Illustrations from original designs, engraved on wood by Richardson. Portrait of the author (from Stuart Newton) engraved by Hall."

The sketch-book. A selection. Erläutert und mit Wörterbuch versehen von A. Matthias. Berlin, Simion, 1886. (Rauch's English readings, 31)

* The sketch book. By Washington Irving. London and New York, G. Routledge and sons, 1886. (Routledge's pocket library, 6)

The sketch-book of Geoffrey Crayon, gent. Leipzig, Gressner und Schramm, 1886.

A selection from The sketchbook of Washington Irving. Mit Anmerkungen und einem Wörterverzeichniss hrsg. von Hugo Wernneke. Berlin, Friedberg und Mode, 1886. (English authors for the use of schools, 9)

English sketches, from "The sketch book" by Washington Irving . . . Philadelphia, London, J. B. Lippincott co. [1886]

The sketch-book of Geoffrey Crayon, gent. London, George Routledge, 1887. (Routledge's pocket library)

* The sketch-book, by Washington Irving. Édition complète avec notices et notes par L. G. Rosensweig. Paris, A. Fouraut, 1887.
* Six selections from Irving's Sketch-book. With notes, questions, etc. For home and school use. By Homer B. Sprague . . . assisted by M. E. Scates. Boston, Ginn & co., 1888.
* Washington Irving. The sketch book. Avec notes et notices biographique et littéraire, par E. Haussaire. Classe de rhétorique et 5e année de l'enseignement secondaire spécial. Paris, C. Delagrave, 1888. (Cours de langue anglaise conforme aux derniers programmes)
* Washington Irving. The sketch book. Texte anglais annoté par M. l'abbé A. Julien . . . Paris, Poussielgue frères, 1888. ([Alliance des maisons d'éducation chrétienne])
    2. édition.
The sketch book of Geoffrey Crayon, gent. Erklärt von Emil Pfundheller. Mit . . . Skizze der Westminster-Abtei. Berlin, Weidmann, 1889.
    2. Auflage.
The sketch-book. Mit Erläuterungen von G. H. Lohmann. 2., umgearbeitete Auflage von G. Langreuter. Quedlinburg, Braunschweig, Wissmann, 1889.
Zehn charakteristische Skizzen aus dem Sketch book, mit Anmerkungen versehen von Karl Deutschbein. 2. Auflage. Cöthen, Schulze, 1889.
The sketch book. Hrsg. von K. Boethke. Bielefeld, Velhagen & Klasing, 1889. 2 v. (English authors, 47)
American tales . . . Erklärt von Gustav Wolpert. Leipzig, Renger [1889?] (Französische und englische Schulbibliothek, 48)
English sketches [aus: The sketch-book] Erklärt von Geo. Wolpert. Mit einem Plan der Westminster-Abtei. Leipzig, Renger [1889?] (Französische und englische Schulbibliothek, 60)
* The sketch book. By Washington Irving. London, George Bell and sons, 1890. (Chiswick series)
The sketch-book of Geoffrey Crayon, gent. . . . The author's revised edition. New York, G. P. Putnam's sons [1890] (*Publisher's lettering:* Irving's works)
    At head of title: Hudson edition.
    General half-title and added engr. t.-p.; vignette.
English sketches . . . Erklärt von Geo. Wolpert. Mit einem Plan der Westminsterabtei. Leipzig, Renger, 1891. (Französische und englische Schulbibliothek, 60)
The voyage and other English essays from The sketch book, by Washington Irving, with explanatory notes and questions and topics for study . . . Boston, New York [etc.] Houghton Mifflin & co., 1891. (The Riverside literature series, no. 52)

The sketch book, by Washington Irving. New York, T. Y. Crowell &
co. [c 1891]
Illustrated t.-p.

. . . Essays from The sketch book, by Washington Irving with a
biographical sketch, introduction and notes. Boston, New York
[etc.] Houghton Mifflin co. [c 1891] (The Riverside literature
series)

The voyage, and other English essays from The sketch book, by
Washington Irving. With notes. Boston and New York, Houghton
Mifflin co. [c 1891] (Riverside literature series [no. 52])

Westminster Abbey and Christmas sketches. Westminster Abbey.
Christmas Eve. Christmas Day. The Christmas dinner. By
Washington Irving. With introductory and explanatory notes.
New York, E. Maynard & co. [c 1891] (English classic series,
no. 93)

Ten selections from The sketch book . . . New York and Cincinnati,
The American book co., 1892. (English classics for schools)

Zehn charakteristische Skizzen aus dem Sketch book. (*In* Deutschbein, Karl. Methodisches Irving-Macaulay-Lesebuch mit Vor-
stufen, Anmerkungen, Karten und Anh. 2., verb. und verm.
Auflage. Cöthen, Schulze, 1892.

Ten selections from The sketch-book, by Washington Irving . . .
New York, The American book co. [c 1892] (Eclectic English
classics)

. . . The sketch book . . . edited by Elmer E. Wentworth. Boston,
Allyn & Bacon, 1894. (Academy classics)

* Sketch book . . . London, J. M. Dent & co., 1894. 2 v.

Selections from The sketch book. Arranged by Isaac Thomas.
Boston and New York, Leach, Shewell & Sanborn, 1894.

The sketch book. Bdchn. 1. Mit Anmerkungen zum Schulgebrauch
hrsg. von E. Boethke. Bielefeld, Velhagen & Klasing, 1894.
(Velhagen & Klasings Sammlung französischer und englischer
Schulausgaben. English authors, Lfg. 47b)
Wörterbuch by B. Klatt.

* The sketch-book of Geoffrey Crayon, gent. . . . by Washington
Irving . . . New York [etc.] G. P. Putnam's sons, 1895. 2 v.
Van Tassel edition.
Title and text within colored ornamental border.

The sketch book. With illustrations by Arthur Rackham and others.
New York, 1895.

The sketch book, by Washington Irving; the author's revised edition;
edited by William Lyon Phelps . . . Students' edition. New York
[etc.] G. P. Putnam's sons, 1895.

The sketch book. 2. Bdchn. . . . Hrsg. von G. Knauff. Bielefeld,
Velhagen & Klasing, 1896. (English authors, 67. Lfg.)

The sketch book, by Washington Irving. Edited by James Chalmers.

New York [etc.] Silver, Burdett & co., 1896. (Silver series of English classics)

Selections from Irving's Sketch book . . . as published in the Eclectic English classics. (*In* Select American classics . . . New York, American book co. [c 1896])

. . . The sketch-book of Geoffrey Crayon, gent. . . . by Washington Irving . . . New York [etc.] G. P. Putnam's sons, 1897.
Title and text within ornamental border.
At head of title: Van Tassel edition.

The sketch-book, by Washington Irving . . . New York and London, G. P. Putnam's sons [1897] 2 v.
At head of title: Knickerbocker edition.
Half-title: The sketch-book of Geoffrey Crayon, gent.

The sketch book. Selections. Zum Schul- und Privatgebrauch hrsg. von A. Englert. Mit Wörterverzeichnis und einem Plan. München, J. Lindauer, 1898.

. . . Eight selections from The sketch book, by Washington Irving; with an introduction for the use of schools and academies. Chicago, Ainsworth & co., 1900. (The Lakeside series of English readings [no. 30])
On cover: Nine selections.

* Washington Irving. The sketch book. Texte anglais annoté par M. l'abbé A. Julien . . . Paris, Poussielgue frères, 1900. ([Alliance des maisons d'éducation chrétienne])
3. édition.

* . . . The sketch-book, by Washington Irving. (A selection.) Transcribed into Gabelsberger-Richter Phonography, by Richard Preuss. Dresden, W. Reuter, 1900. (Reuter's Bibliothek für Gabelsberger-Stenographen, Bd. 105)

The sketch book by Washington Irving; with notes and introduction. . . . New York, The Macmillan co.; London, Macmillan & co., ltd., 1900. (Macmillan's Pocket English classics)

The sketch book of Geoffrey Crayon, gent. Reprinted from the original edition. By Washington Irving. Chicago, W. B. Conkey co. [c 1900]

. . . Essays from The sketch-book, by Washington Irving. With introductory and explanatory notes, and with grammatical notes upon two selections specially prepared to meet the requirements of regents of New York, by Florence J. Parker . . . New York, Maynard, Merrill & co. [c 1900] (Maynard's English classic series, no. 223-224)

* Irving's Sketch book. Complete edition, edited with introduction and notes by Mary E. Litchfield. Boston [etc.] Ginn and co., 1901. (Standard English classics)

* The sketch book, by Washington Irving, with illustrations by Edmund J. Sullivan. London, George Newnes, 1902. 2 v.

Life and customs in Old England. From The sketch book. By Washington Irving. Für den Schulgebrauch bearbeitet von J. Klapperich. Glogau, C. Flemming, 1902. (Englische und französische Schriftsteller der neueren Zeit, 16)

Selections from The sketch book. By Washington Irving. With introduction and notes by E. E. Kellett, M.A., and F. H. Marseille. Leipzig, Rossberg, 1902. (Neusprachliche Reformbibliothek, 11)

The sketch-book of Geoffrey Crayon, gent. . . . The author's revised edition. New York, G. P. Putnam's sons [1902] (*Added t.-p.:* Irving's works)
Hudson edition.

Selections from Irving's Sketch-book, prepared and edited by Claude Towne Benjamin, A.B. New York, Cincinnati [etc.] American book co. [c 1902]
Regents' edition.

Life and customs in Old England. From The sketch book. Bearbeitet von O. Voigt. Berlin und Glogau, C. Flemming, 1903. (Englische und französische Schriftsteller der neueren Zeit. Für Schule und Haus hrsg. von J. Klapperich, 16)

The sketch book. 1. Bdchn. Hrsg. von K. Boethke. Bielefeld, Velhagen & Klasing, 1904. (English authors, 47. Lfg.)

The sketch book. 2. Bdchn. Hrsg. von G. Knauff. Bielefeld, Velhagen & Klasing, 1905. (English authors, 67. Lfg.)

The sketch-book . . . by Washington Irving; with an introduction, suggestions for critical reading, and notes. New edition, under the editorial supervision of Edward E. Hale, jr. . . . New York, Boston [etc.] University publishing co. [c 1905] 2 v. (Standard literature series [v. 17, 61])
"The text of these selections is that of 'The author's revised edition' of 1848."
Contents. — pt. 1. Stories. — pt. 2. Essays.

Washington Irving's Sketch book. With an introduction by Brander Matthews . . . and with notes by Armour Caldwell . . . New York [etc.] Longmans, Green and co., 1905. (Longmans' English classics)

The sketch book. Abridged for schools. With preface and annotations by K. Boethke and Arthur Lindenstead. Bielefeld, Velhagen & Klasing, 1905. (Velhagen & Klasings Sammlung französischer und englischer Schulausgaben. Reform-Ausgabe mit fremdsprachlichen Anmerkungen, Nr. 12)

A selection from The sketch book of Geoffrey Crayon, gent. With an introduction, some notes, and a list of words which are not to be found in the dictionaries. Ed. by R. Nuck. Karlsruhe, F. Gutsch, 1905. (Collection of famous authors. For the use of schools, 3)

. . . The sketch book, by Washington Irving; edited with introduction and notes by George Philip Krapp . . . Chicago, Scott, Foresman & co., 1906. (The Lake English classics)

— — Chicago, Scott, Foresman & co. [c 1906] (The Lake English classics)

Tales from The sketch book. Für den Schulgebrauch erklärt von Geo. Wolpert. Leipzig, Renger, 1906. (Französische und englische Schulbibliothek, 60. Bd.)

Rural life in England, by Washington Irving; illustrated by Alan Wright and Vernon Stokes. London, G. Routledge & sons; New York, E. P. Dutton & co. [1906] (*Half-title:* The Photogravure and colour series)

The sketch-book of Geoffrey Crayon, gent., by Washington Irving; with introductory and explanatory notes. New York, Maynard, Merrill, & co. [c 1906] (Maynard's English classic series — Special number)

The sketch-book of Geoffrey Crayon, gent., together with Abbotsford and other selections from the writings of Washington Irving . . . edited with comments, notes, bibliography, and topics for study, by H. A. Davidson, M.A. Boston, D. C. Heath & co., 1907.

The sketch book. 1. Bdchn. Neu hrsg. von Alfr. Roedel. Bielefeld, Velhagen & Klasing, 1907. (English authors, 47. Lfg.)

* . . . Selections from Irving's Sketch-book; edited by Martin W. Sampson . . . New York, Cincinnati [etc.] American book co. [c 1907] (*Half-title:* The Gateway series of English texts. General editor: Henry Van Dyke)

The sketch book of Geoffrey Crayon, gent., by Washington Irving. London, J. M. Dent & co.; New York, E. P. Dutton & co. [1908] (*Half-title:* Everyman's library . . . Essays) "First edition, August, 1906; reprinted, June, 1908."

Selections from The sketch book by Washington Irving; edited with teaching material by Lewis Worthington Smith . . . Chicago, A. Flanagan co. [c 1909]

The sketch-book of Geoffrey Crayon, gent., together with Abbotsford and other selections from the writings of Washington Irving . . . Edited with comments, notes, bibliography, and topics for study, by H. A. Davidson . . . Boston, D. C. Heath & co., 1910.

The sketch book . . . With notes and introduction. New York & London, Macmillan, 1910. (Macmillan's pocket American and English classics)

Selections from Irving's Sketch-book, edited by Robert P. St. John . . . New York, Cincinnati [etc.] American book co. [c 1910] (Eclectic English classics)

Irving's The sketch-book; text of supplementary essays to accompany the edition edited by H. A. Davidson . . . Boston, D. C. Heath & co., 1911.

Irving's Sketch book, edited by Arthur Willis Leonard . . . New York, H. Holt and co., 1911. (*Half-title:* English readings for schools. General editor: W. L. Cross)

The sketch book. Texte anglais annoté par M. l'abbé Julien. 4ᵉ édition. Paris, J. de Gigord, 1911.

The sketch-book of Geoffrey Crayon, gent., by Washington Irving . . . edited with introduction and notes by Charles Addison Dawson . . . New York, Charles E. Merrill co. [c 1911] (Merrill's English texts)

The sketch book . . . Edited with an introduction and notes by T. Balston. New York, Oxford university press, 1912. (The World's classics)

The sketch book. 1. Bdchn. Neu hrsg. von Alfr. Roedel. Bielefeld, Velhagen & Klasing, 1912. (English authors, 47)

The sketch book. Für den Schulgebrauch hrsg. von Franz Eigl. Leipzig, G. Freytag, 1912. (Freytag's Sammlung französischer und englischer Schriftsteller)

The sketch book. Abridged for schools. With preface and annotations by K. Boethke and Arthur Lindenstead. Bielefeld, Velhagen & Klasing, 1912. (Velhagen & Klasings Sammlung französischer und englischer Schulausgaben. Reform-Ausgabe mit fremdsprachlichen Anmerkungen, Nr. 12)

Sketch-book, with an introduction by Brander Matthews . . . and with notes by Armour Caldwell . . . New York, Longmans, Green co. [1912] (Longmans' English classics)

Selections from The sketch-book, by Washington Irving; with biographical sketch, explanatory notes, critical opinions and directions to teachers, by A. J. Demarest . . . Philadelphia, Christopher Sower co. [c 1912] (Classics in the grades)
On cover: Demarest's classics in the grades.

The sketch book. 2. Bdchn. Hrsg. von G. Knauff. Bielefeld, Velhagen & Klasing, 1913. (English authors, 67. Lfg.)

The sketch book. Edited with an introduction and notes by T. Balston. New York, Oxford university press, 1913.

* Tales from The sketch book and The Alhambra, with an introduction and notes by Henri Hovelaque. Paris, Didier, 1913.

The sketch-book. Selections edited by Emil Markert. Introduction and notes revised by Herbert Wright. Bamberg, C. C. Buchner, 1914. (Neusprachliche Klassiker mit fortlaufenden Präparationen. Hrsg. von Christoph Beck und Heinrich Middendorf, 14. Bd.)

The sketch book . . . Kattowitz, Phönix-Verlag, 1914. (Präparationen nebst Übersetzung für neusprachlichen Unterricht, Nr. 22–24)

The sketch book . . . London, New York, Oxford university press, 1917. (The World's classics)

* Tales from The sketch book and The Alhambra. With an introduction and notes by Henri Hovelaque. Paris, H. Didier, 1917.

The sketch book. 2. Bdchn. Hrsg. von G. Knauff. Bielefeld, Velhagen & Klasing, 1919. (English authors, 67. Lfg.)

The sketch book. Abridged for schools. With preface and annotations by K. Boethke and Arthur Lindenstead. Bielefeld, Velhagen
& Klasing, 1920. (Velhagen & Klasings Sammlung französischer
und englischer Schulausgaben. Reform-Ausgabe mit fremdsprachlichen Anmerkungen, Nr. 12)

The sketch book, by Washington Irving, edited for school use by
George Philip Krapp . . . Chicago, New York, Scott, Foresman
and co. [c 1920] (Lake English classics)
At head of title: Revised edition with helps to study.

* The sketch book of Geoffrey Crayon, gent. By Washington Irving.
With an introduction by T. Balston. London, New York, Oxford
university press, H. Milford [1921] (The World's classics, 173)

The voyage and other English essays from The sketch book, by
Washington Irving, with explanatory notes and questions and
topics for study. New edition. Boston, New York [etc.] Houghton
Mifflin & co., 1923. (The Riverside literature series, no. 52)

* The sketch book. By Washington Irving. With notes and introduction. New York, The Macmillan co.; London, Macmillan & co.,
ltd., 1924. (The Macmillan pocket classics)

The sketch book. 1. Bdchn. Mit Anmerkungen zum Schulgebrauch
neu hrsg. von Alfred Roedel. Bielefeld, Velhagen & Klasing, 1925.
(English authors, 47)
Neue Ausgabe.

The sketch book. By Washington Irving. New York and London,
G. P. Putnam's sons, 1925. 2 v.

The sketch-book, by Washington Irving. New York and London,
G. P. Putnam's sons [1925?] 2 v. in 1. (On back of cover: Irving's
works)
At head of title: Handy volume edition.
Title vignette.

* The sketch book. By Washington Irving. With notes and introduction. New York, The Macmillan co.; London, Macmillan & co.,
ltd., 1928. (The Macmillan pocket classics)

Tales from The sketch book. Selected and edited by Carl Van Doren.
New York, Oxford university press, 1928. (The World's classics)

The sketch-book, edited by Elmer E. Wentworth. Boston, New York
[etc.] Allyn and Bacon [c 1928] (The Academy classics)

* The sketch book by Washington Irving. With an introduction by
Talcott Williamson. New York, The Macmillan co., 1929. (The
Modern readers' series)

The sketch book. Washington Irving; revised by H. Y. Moffett,
illustrated by Curtiss Sprague. [New York] The Macmillan co.
[c 1929] (Half-title: New pocket classics)

The sketch-book. Selections edited by Emil Markert. Introduction
and notes revised by Herbert Wright. Bamberg, C. C. Buchner,
1930. (Neusprachliche Klassiker mit fortlaufenden Präparationen.

Hrsg. von Christoph Beck und Heinrich Middendorf, 14. Bd.)
2. Auflage.

The sketch book. Edited with introduction, notes, and lesson helps by H. A. Davidson. Boston, Heath [1930?] (Golden key series)

* The sketch book of Geoffrey Crayon, gent., by Washington Irving. With an introduction by T. Balston. London, Oxford university press [1931]

The sketch book . . . [Paris?] Masson, 1932.

American and English essays from The sketch book . . . Boston, Houghton, Mifflin [19–?] 2 v. (Riverside literature series)

The sketch book. Edited by William T. Vlymen. Brooklyn, Schwartz, Kirwin & Fauss [19–?]

The sketch book of Geoffrey Crayon, gent. Reprinted from the original edition. Chicago [etc.] Belford, Clarke & co. [188–?]

The sketch book . . . Chicago, Donohue & co. [19–?]

The sketch book . . . Chicago, Educational publishing co. [19–?] School edition.

Seven selections from The sketch book . . . Chicago, Farquhar & Albright co. [19–?] (Lakeside classics)

The sketch book . . . Chicago, Flanagan [19–?] (Standard author series)

The sketch book. Handy edition. Chicago, Sanborn [19–?] (Student's series of English classics)

The sketch book. Introduction and notes by Edward A. Parker. Dansville, N. Y., Owen publishing co. [19–?] (Excelsior library series)

The sketch book . . . Dansville, N. Y., Owen publishing co. [19–?] (Instructor literature series)

More selections from The sketch book. Dansville, N. Y., Owen publishing co. [19–?] (Instructor literature series)

The sketchbook of Geoffrey Crayon . . . Leipzig, F. Fleischer [n.d.]

* The sketch book. By Washington Irving . . . A new edition. London, George Routledge and sons [n.d.]

Rural life in England . . . Illustrated by Alan Wright and Vernon Stokes. London, G. Routledge & sons; New York, E. P. Dutton & co. [n.d.] (The Photogravure and colour series)

Sketch book . . . New York, Belford co. [188–?]

The sketch book . . . New York, Burt [19–?] (Cornell series)

The sketch book . . . New York, Burt [19–?] (Home library)

The sketch book . . . New York, Burt [19–?] (New pocket edition of standard classics)

The sketch book . . . New York, Burt [19–?] (Oxford series)

The sketch book . . . New York, Collins [19–?] (Arcadian books)

The sketch book . . . New York, Collins [19–?] (Collins's illustrated pocket classics)

* The sketch book of Geoffrey Crayon, gentᵃ . . . Revised edition. New York, T. Y. Crowell & co. [n.d.]

The sketch book . . . New York, T. Y. Crowell [19–?] (Luxembourg illustrated library)

The sketch book . . . New York, Funk [19–?] (People's library)

Synopsis of The sketch book . . . New York, Globe book co. [19–?] (Guides to English classics series)

The sketch book . . . New York, Grosset & Dunlap [19–?]

The sketch book of Geoffrey Crayon, gent., by Washington Irving. Reprinted from the original edition. New York, J. W. Lovell co. [18–?]

The sketch book . . . New York, Nelson [19–?] (Nelson new century library)

The sketch book . . . New York, G. P. Putnam [19–?] Gift edition.

The sketch book . . . New York, G. P. Putnam [19–?] Large paper edition.

The sketch book . . . Philadelphia, Altemus [19–?] (Altemus' new vademecum series)

The sketch book . . . Philadelphia, David McKay [19–?]

The sketch book . . . Racine, Wisconsin, Whitman [19–?]

Selection from The sketch-book. Zürich, Rudolphi und Klemm [188–?] (English library, 13)

Extracts

[Selections from The sketch book.] (*In* Literary gazette. London, W. Pople, 1819. v. 3, p. 617–620, 634–635, 648–650)

* The angler, by Washington Irving. With etched illustrations by Louis K. Harlow. Boston, S. E. Cassino, 1892.

* The angler . . . [Portland, Maine] Privately printed for A. S. W. Rosenbach, December, 1931.
"Printed by Fred Anthoensen, The Southworth press, Portland, Maine, in the month of December, 1931, in an edition limited to one hundred and fifty copies."

* The Boar's Head tavern . . . [London? 1820?] (Shakespeareana. Miscellaneous essays . . . v. 3 [no. 4])

Christmas . . . Für den Schulgebrauch erklärt von Gustav Tanger. Leipzig, Renger, 1883. (Französische und englische Schulbibliothek, 4)

* Christmas, by Washington Irving; from The sketch book. [New York, W. E. Rudge] Privately printed, 1931.
Title-page printed in brown and black.
"Printed by William Edwin Rudge III and Frederick G. Rudge to carry on a tradition. To all of Father's and our friends a very happy and prosperous New Year."

Christmas at Bracebridge Hall . . .   New York, Barse & Hopkins
[19–?] (Pocket classics)

Christmas at Bracebridge Hall . . . Illustrated by Arthur A. Dixon.
London, Ernest Nister; New York, E. P. Dutton & co. [n.d.]

Christmas Day, from The sketch book of Geoffrey Crayon, gent., by
Washington Irving. New York, Privately printed, 1931.
Printed for George A. Nelson by Frederic Warde.
245 copies.

Christmas Day . . . New York, Graham [19–?] (Acalia series)

The Christmas dinner, from "The sketch book," by Washington
Irving. New York, William Edwin Rudge, 1925.
Illustrations by R. Caldecott.
T.-p. in red and black; running title in red.

The Christmas dinner, from The sketch book by Washington Irving.
Illustrations by Gordon Ross. New York, W. E. Rudge, 1929.
Title vignette; head and tail pieces.

* The Christmas dinner, from The sketch book, by Washington Irving.
Haarlem, Joh. Enschedé en zonen, 1931.
"Two-hundred copies printed by Joh. Enschedé en zonen to accompany their best wishes for Christmas and the New Year to
their good friends at home and abroad."

Christmas Eve . . . Boston, Seaves-Howland press, 1914. (The
Waverly chap-books, no. 14)

Christmas Eve, from "The sketch-book," by Washington Irving.
New York, Harmon & Irwin, 1928.
Title within red ornamental border.
"This little volume is sent to you by Harmon & Irwin, Inc. with their
very best wishes for a merry Christmas & a happy New Year."
Colophon: Four hundred copies printed at the Harbor press and
bound by Harmon & Irwin, New York city.

Christmas Eve . . . New York, Graham [19–?] (Acalia series)

Christmas Eve . . . London, Hodder & Stoughton [19–?]

Christmas Eve and Christmas Day. By Washington Irving. Boston,
Houghton Mifflin, 1923. (Evergreen series)

* Christmas in England. Papers from the "Sketch-book" of Washington Irving. With illustrations by eminent artists. New York,
G. P. Putnam [etc.] 1867.

Christmas sketches. Washington Irving. New York, T. Y. Crowell
& co. [19–?]
Title within colored ornamental border.

Christmas stories. By Dickens, Irving, Scott, Goddard, Andersen.
Ausgewählt und erklärt von F. J. Wershoven. Paderborn, F.
Schöningh, 1912. (Ferd. Schöningh's französische und englische
Schulbibliothek, II. Serie, 9. Bd.)

The country church . . . Illus. by Roberta F. C. Waudby. New
York, Dutton, 1930. (Aldine chapbooks)

* English writers on America. (*In* The Chautauquan, New York, Chautauqua press, 1907. v. 48, p. 409–415)

The headless horseman. A play . . . Belmar, N. J., Edgar S. Werner & co. [19–?]

See also, II. Selected works. Three stories . . . 1930.

* The Hudson legends. Rip Van Winkle. Sleepy Hollow. From The sketch-book. Illustrated with original designs by eminent artists. New York, G. P. Putnam, 1864.

* — — New York, G. P. Putnam, 1867.

John Bull. Kempton . . . München, Verlag für zeitgen. Sprach-methodik, 1923. (English library, Nr. 2)

* The Kaaterskill region. Rip Van Winkle and Sleepy Hollow, by Washington Irving. [New York] The Kaaterskill publishing co., 1884.

On cover: Haunts of Rip Van Winkle.

Advertising medium of the Hotel Kaaterskill.

* — — [n.p., n.d.]

* The keeping of Christmas at Bracebridge Hall, by Washington Irving. With 24 coloured illustrations by C. E. Brock. London, J. M. Dent & co.; New York, E. P. Dutton & co., 1906.

The keeping of Christmas at Bracebridge Hall . . . London, William Glaisher, 1924.

Illustrations by C. E. Brock.

The keeping of Christmas at Bracebridge Hall. With coloured illustrations by C. E. Brock. New York, Dutton, 1927. (Series of English idylls)

* Knickerbocker papers, being Rip Van Winkle & The legend of Sleepy Hollow. London, P. L. Warner, 1914. 8vo.

Edition limited to 1000 numbered copies printed on handmade Riccardi paper.

Printed for the Medici society at the Riccardi press.

— — London, P. L. Warner, 1914. 4to.

— — London, P. L. Warner, 1914. (The Riccardi press booklets) 1012 copies printed.

The Legend of Sleepy Hollow

See also, II. Selected Works. Three stories; *and* A book of the Hudson. *See also, above,* The headless horseman.

* Illustrations of The legend of Sleepy Hollow, designed and etched by Felix O. C. Darley, for the members of the American art-union. [New York, The American art-union] 1849.

Contains the text of The legend of Sleepy Hollow.

Legend of Sleepy Hollow. From "The sketch book" of Washington Irving. Illustrated with original designs by Huntington, Kensett, Darley [*et al.*] New York, G. P. Putnam, 1864.

Legend of Sleepy Hollow. From "The sketchbook" of Washington

Irving. Illustrated with original designs by Huntington, Kensett, Darley [*et al.*] New York, G. P. Putnam; Hurd and Houghton, 1867.

* The legend of Sleepy Hollow, and The spectre bridegroom. From the "Sketch book" by Washington Irving. Illustrated with original designs by eminent artists. Philadelphia, London, J. B. Lippincott & co. [1875]

The legend of Sleepy Hollow . . . In the reporting style of phonography. London, F. Pitman, 1883.

The legend of Sleepy Hollow. (From the "Sketch-book.") By Washington Irving. Edited for school and home use by Albert F. Blaisdell . . . New York, E. Maynard & co. [c 1883] (English classics, no. 41)

The legend of Sleepy Hollow, and The spectre bridegroom. From the "Sketch book," by Washington Irving. Illustrated with original designs by eminent artists. Philadelphia [etc., J. B. Lippincott & co., 1885]

The land of Sleepy Hollow and the home of Washington Irving. A series of photogravure representations, with descriptive letter-press by J. L. Williams. Together with Irving's "Legend of Sleepy Hollow," with illustrations by F. O. C. Darley, and selections from "The chronicle of Wolfert's Roost." Limited letter-press edition. New York and London, G. P. Putnam's sons, 1887.
Edition of 600 copies.
Contents. — The legend of Sleepy Hollow. — Wolfert's Roost. — Washington Irving, by J. L. Williams.

The legend of Sleepy Hollow . . . In the reporting style of phonography. London [I. Pitman & sons, etc., etc.] 1889.

The legend of Sleepy Hollow. By Washington Irving . . . Philadelphia, J. B. Lippincott, 1891.
Illustrated.

The legend of Sleepy Hollow . . . In the reporting style of phonography. London, Sir I. Pitman & sons, 1895.

The legend of Sleepy Hollow, by Washington Irving. Philadelphia, H. Altemus [c 1896]

The legend of Sleepy Hollow, from The sketch book of Washington Irving. New York, R. H. Russell [c 1897]

The legend of Sleepy Hollow, by Washington Irving. New York & London, G. P. Putnam's sons, 1899.
Title-page and text within colored ornamental borders.

The legend of Sleepy Hollow, by Washington Irving. In the advanced corresponding style of Graham's standard phonography. New York, Andrew J. Graham & co. [c 1899]

The legend of Sleepy Hollow . . . Boston, D. Estes & co. [1900]

Two selections. The legend of Sleepy Hollow and Rip Van Winkle, from Sketch book by Washington Irving; with notes, questions, suggestions on teaching, etc. for school use, by J. W. Graham . . . San Francisco, The Whitaker & Ray co., 1902. (*On cover:* Practical aids to literature, no. 1)

The legend of Sleepy Hollow . . . Printed in the easy reporting style of phonography, in accordance with the "Manual of phonography," by Benn Pitman and Jerome B. Howard. Cincinnati, The Phonographic institute co., 1902.

— — Cincinnati, The Phonographic institute co., 1903.

The legend of Sleepy Hollow; designed and hand colored by Lolita Perine. New York, Dodge pub. co., 1903.

The legend of Sleepy Hollow . . . Printed in the easy reporting style of phonography, in accordance with the "Manual of phonography," by Benn Pitman and Jerome B. Howard. Cincinnati, The Phonographic institute co., 1904.

The legend of Sleepy Hollow . . . New York, G. P. Putnam's sons [1905] (Ariel booklets)

* The legend of Sleepy Hollow, by Washington Irving. Drawings by Arthur I. Keller. (*In* The Reader . . . Nov., 1906)

— — Indianapolis, Bobbs-Merrill [1906]

The legend of Sleepy Hollow . . . Printed in the easy reporting style of phonography, in accordance with the "Manual of phonography," by Benn Pitman and Jerome B. Howard. Cincinnati, The Phonographic institute co., 1908.

The legend of Sleepy Hollow and other essays by Washington Irving. Topeka, Kan., Crane & co., 1908. (The Crane classics, no. 38)

The legend of Sleepy Hollow, and other selections from The sketch book, by Washington Irving. Chicago, New York, Rand, McNally & co. [c 1909] (Golden classics)
Title within colored ornamental border.

The legend of Sleepy Hollow . . . Printed in Gregg shorthand. New York [1916]

The legend of Sleepy Hollow, by Washington Irving, in Graham shorthand. [New York, Van Rees press, c 1918]
Cover-title.

* The legend of Sleepy Hollow, found among the papers of the late Diedrich Knickerbocker, by Washington Irving; with illustrations in color by Edna Cooke. Philadelphia & London, J. B. Lippincott co. [c 1924]

The legend of Sleepy Hollow. (*In* Schweikert, H. C., *ed.* Short stories . . . New York, Harcourt, Brace and co. [c 1925])

* The legend of Sleepy Hollow. By Washington Irving, with other fanciful tales. Illustrated by Frances Brundage and Lillian Sturges.

Akron, Ohio, and New York, The Saalfield publishing co. [c 1926]
(Old trail series)

The legend of Sleepy Hollow, by Washington Irving; illustrated by
Arthur Rackham. Philadelphia, David McKay co. [1928]
Illustrated lining-papers.

The legend of Sleepy Hollow, by Washington Irving; illustrated by
Arthur Rackham. London, George G. Harrap & co., ltd. [1928]

— — London, George G. Harrap & co., ltd. [1928]
Large paper edition.
375 copies.

The legend of Sleepy Hollow, by Washington Irving, illustrated with
original etchings by Bernhardt Wall. New York, Cheshire house,
1931.
Edition of 1200 copies.

The legend of Sleepy Hollow . . . Akron, Ohio, Saalfield publishing
co. [19–?] (John Newbery series)

The legend of Sleepy Hollow . . . Chicago, Beckley-Cardy co.
[19–?] (Progressive school classics)

The legend of Sleepy Hollow and Rip Van Winkle . . . Chicago,
Farquhar & Albright [19–?] (Lakeside classics)

The legend of Sleepy Hollow . . . Chicago, A. Flanagan co. [19–?]
(Little classic series)

The legend of Sleepy Hollow . . . Dansville, N. Y., F. A. Owen
publishing co. [19–?] (Instructor literature series)

* The legend of Sleepy Hollow, by Washington Irving. In the reporting style of Pitman's shorthand. London, Sir I. Pitman & sons,
ltd. [191–?] 62 p.
Twentieth century edition.

— — Another issue. 63 p.

* The legend of Sleepy Hollow, by Washington Irving. Printed in the
advanced stage of Pitman's shorthand . . . London, Sir I. Pitman
& sons, ltd. [192–?]
New era edition.
Text in shorthand and English.

* The legend of Sleepy Hollow . . . Advanced style of Pitman's shorthand . . . London, Sir I. Pitman & sons [19–?]
Centenary edition.

* — — Another issue.

The legend of Sleepy Hollow . . . New York, Barse & Hopkins
[19–?] (Golden books)

The legend of Sleepy Hollow . . . New York, Barse & Hopkins
[19–?] (Pocket classics)

The legend of Sleepy Hollow . . . New York, Barse & Hopkins
[19–?] (Savoy series)

The legend of Sleepy Hollow . . . New York, T. Y. Crowell [19–?]
(Laurel series)

The legend of Sleepy Hollow, in Gregg shorthand, with introduction by William J. Pelo. New York, Gregg publishing co. [19-?]

The legend of Sleepy Hollow. Revised. Printed in Gregg shorthand . . . New York, Gregg publishing co. [192-?] (*On cover:* English classics in Gregg shorthand)

The legend of Sleepy Hollow . . . New York, Merrill [19-?] (Maynard's English classics)

The legend of Sleepy Hollow . . . Printed in the advanced stage of Pitman's shorthand. New era edition. New York, Sir I. Pitman & sons, ltd. [192-?]
Text in shorthand and English.

* The legend of Sleepy Hollow . . . [Pittsfield, Mass., The Caxton society, 19-?] (The Caxton brochures, Series A, No. 15)

* A legend of the Kaatskill mountains . . . New York, G. P. Putnam and sons, 1870.
Cover-title: Irving's Rip Van Winkle. The Jefferson Booth's theatre edition, illustrated. Henry L. Hinton, publisher.
Two leaves of advertising matter preceding t.-p.

* Little Britain, together with The spectre bridegroom and A legend of Sleepy Hollow . . . London, Sampson Low, 1880.
Illustrations by Charles O. Murray.

Little Britain, together with The spectre bridegroom and A legend of Sleepy Hollow . . . London, Sampson Low, Marston, Searle and Rivington [n.d.]
Illustrated by Charles O. Murray.

Old Christmas

Old Christmas, from The sketch book of Washington Irving, with illustrations by Randolph Caldecott . . . London, Macmillan [1875]

* Old Christmas, from The sketch book of Washington Irving, illustrated by R. Caldecott. London, Macmillan & co., 1876. 2 v.
Second edition.

Old Christmas, from The sketch book of Washington Irving, illustrated by R. Caldecott. London, Macmillan & co., 1878.
Third edition.

* Old Christmas, from Washington Irving's Sketch-book. With upwards of one hundred illustrations by R. Caldecott. Engraved by James D. Cooper. London, Macmillan & co., 1882.
Printed by R. & R. Clark, Edinburgh.

Old Christmas, with illustrations by R. Caldecott. London, Macmillan, 1882. 8vo.

* — — London, Macmillan, 1882. 4to.

* Old Christmas: from The sketch book of Washington Irving. Illustrated by R. Caldecott. New York, Macmillan & co., 1886.
Contents. — Christmas. — The stage coach. — Christmas Eve. — Christmas Day. — The Christmas dinner.

Old Christmas, from The sketch book of Washington Irving. With many full page illustrations by R. Caldecott. New York, Macmillan, 1892. (Cranford series)
Edition limited to 250 copies.

Old Christmas, illustrated by R. Caldecott. [London?] 1894.
Title and illustrations colored by hand.

Old Christmas, by Washington Irving. Philadelphia, H. Altemus [c 1896]
Contents. — Christmas. — Christmas Eve. — Christmas Day. — The Christmas dinner.

Old Christmas, from The sketch book of Washington Irving. London, Macmillan, 1899.
Illustrated by R. Caldecott.

Old Christmas. [By] Washington Irving. New York and Boston, H. M. Caldwell co. [c 1900]
Contents. — Christmas. — The stage-coach. — Christmas Eve. — Christmas Day. — The Christmas dinner.

* Old Christmas. By Washington Irving. Pictured by Cecil Aldin. New York, Dodd, Mead & co. [1908]
— — London, Hodder & Stoughton [1908]

Old Christmas . . . Pictured by Cecil Aldin. New York, Dodd, Mead & co. [1910]
Engr. t.-p.

Old Christmas, by Washington Irving; illustrated by Frank Dadd. New York and London, G. P. Putnam's sons [c 1916]
Title within ornamental border; illustrated lining-papers.
Contents. — Christmas. — The stage coach. — Christmas Eve. — Christmas Day. — The Christmas dinner.

* Old Christmas and Bracebridge Hall. Illustrated by Lewis Baumer. [New York, Houghton Mifflin] 1918.

Old Christmas and Bracebridge Hall . . . with illustrations by Lewis Baumer. London, Constable and co., ltd., 1918.

Old Christmas and Bracebridge Hall. From The sketch-book of Washington Irving. With illustrations by Lewis Baumer. Boston, Houghton Mifflin co., 1919.

Old Christmas, from The sketch book of Washington Irving, illustrated by R. Caldecott. London, Macmillan and co., 1925.

Old Christmas, illustrated by R. Caldecott. New York, Macmillan & co., 1928. (Dainty books)

Old Christmas . . . New York, Barse & Hopkins [19–?] (Golden books)

Old Christmas . . . New edition. New York, Dodge publishing co. [19–?]

Old Christmas and Bracebridge Hall. Illustrated by Lewis Baumer. New York, Houghton Mifflin [19–?]
Holiday edition.

Old Christmas . . . New York, Macmillan [19–?] (Illustrated pocket classics)

Old Christmas. By Washington Irving. With . . . illustrations from original designs by Randolph Caldecott. New York, Pollard & Moss [187–?]

Old Christmas . . . Philadelphia, Altemus [19–?] (Altemus' new vademecum series)

The Old Christmas dinner. With illustrations by H. M. Brock. London, Foulis [1908]

The Old Christmas dinner. By Washington Irving. With illustrations by H. M. Brock. Philadelphia, G. W. Jacobs & co. [1909]

The Old English Christmas, by Washington Irving. With illustrations by H. M. Brock. Philadelphia, G. W. Jacobs & co. [192–?] Mounted t.-p.

* Old-fashioned Christmas dinner. (*In* The Independent. New York, Independent corporation, 1918. v. 94, p. 88–91)

The pride of the village, and other tales. From "The sketch book." By Washington Irving. Illustrated with original designs by eminent artists. Philadelphia, London, J. B. Lippincott co. [c 1886] Contents. — The pride of the village. — The widow and her son. — The broken heart. — The wife. — A royal poet. — The country church.

RIP VAN WINKLE

See also, II. Selected works. Three stories . . . 1930; *and* A book of the Hudson. *See also, above*, The Hudson legends, The Kaaterskill region, and A legend of the Kaatskill mountains.

Rip Van Winkle. (*In* The Romancist, and Novelist's library . . . London, Printed by C. Reynell, Published by J. Clements, 1839–40. v. 3, p. [78]–80)

Rip Van Winkle and Sleepy Hollow. London, Holten [1849?]

* Illustrations of Rip Van Winkle, designed and etched by Felix O. C. Darley, for the members of the American art-union, 1848. [New York, The American art-union, 1849] Contains the text of Rip Van Winkle.

Rip Van Winkle. A posthumous writing of Diederich Knickerbocker . . . Illustrated, with six etchings on steel, by Charles Simms, from drawings by Felix Darley . . . London, Joseph Cundall, 1850.

The bravo of Venice [from the German romance by J. H. D. Zschokke] (The amusing story of Rip Van Winkle; by Washington Irving.) London [1857] (The British library, 2)

Rip Van Winkle. A legend of the Kaatskill mountains, illustrated, with original designs, by eminent artists. [place? 1863]

Rip Van Winkle. A legend of the Kaatskill mountains. By Washington Irving. Illustrated with original designs by eminent artists. New York, G. P. Putnam, 1864. Illustrated by Darley and others.

Rip Van Winkle. A legend of the Kaatskill mountains. By Washington Irving. Illustrated with original designs by eminent artists. New York, G. P. Putnam; Hurd and Houghton, 1867.

Rip Van Winkle and his wonderful nap. By Edmund Clarence Stedman. With illustrations by Sol Eytinge, jr., engraved and printed in colors by Bobbett, Hooper & co. Boston, Fields, Osgood, & co., 1870. (*On cover:* The Uncle Sam series for American children)
In verse.

* Rip Van Winkle. A legend of the Kaatskill mountains. By Washington Irving. Illustrated with original designs by eminent artists. And photographs in carbon of Jefferson as Rip Van Winkle, by Sarony. New York, G. P. Putnam and sons, publishers. ⟨This edition is printed for⟩ Henry L. Hinton, publisher, 1870.
Cover-title: Rip Van Winkle. Jefferson edition.
Illustrated t.-p.
Line drawings by Darley, Hart, and others.

* Rip Van Winkle. A legend of the Kaatskill mountains. By Washington Irving. Illustrated with original designs by eminent artists. New York, G. P. Putnam and sons, publishers. ⟨This edition is printed for⟩ Henry L. Hinton, publisher, 1870.
Cover-title: Irving's Rip Van Winkle. The Jefferson Booth's theatre edition.
Illustrated t.-p.
Line drawings by Darley, Hart, and others.

Rip Van Winkle. A legend of the Kaatskill mountains. By Washington Irving. Illustrated with original designs by eminent artists. New York, G. P. Putnam and sons. ⟨This edition is printed for⟩ Henry L. Hinton, publisher, 1870.
Line drawings by Darley, Hart, and others.

Rip Van Winkle, and The legend of Sleepy Hollow. New York, 1871. Illustrated from photographs.

Rip Van Winkle, and other sketches, by Washington Irving. New York, The Useful knowledge publishing co., 1882.
Contents. — Rip Van Winkle. — The wife. — The broken heart. — Art of book-making. — The widow and her son. — Boar's Head tavern, Eastcheap. — Mutability of literature. — Rural funerals. — The spectre bridegroom. — Westminster Abbey. — Stratford-on-Avon. — John Bull. — The legend of Sleepy Hollow.

Rip Van Winkle. A posthumous writing of Diedrich Knickerbocker. New York, J. B. Alden, 1883. (Elzevir library, v. 1, no. 1)

Rip Van Winkle, and The Creole village; by Washington Irving. Printed in the easy reporting style in accordance with the Manual of phonography, by Benn Pitman and Jerome B. Howard. Cincinnati, Phonographic institute, 1886.

* Rip Van Winkle: a legend of the Hudson. By Washington Irving. Illustrated by Gordon Browne. London [etc.] Blackie & son, 1887.

Rip Van Winkle, by Washington Irving. Illustrated by Frank T.
Merrill . . . Boston, S. E. Cassino, 1888.
Illustrated t.-p.

* Rip Van Winkle. A legend of the Kaatskill mountains. By Washington Irving. Illustrated with original designs by eminent artists.
Philadelphia, London, J. B. Lippincott co., 1888.

Rip Van Winkle, and The Creole village; by Washington Irving.
Printed in the easy reporting style in accordance with the Manual
of phonography by Benn Pitman and Jerome B. Howard. Cincinnati, Phonographic institute, 1889.

Rip Van Winkle. Abridged from Irving's Sketch book. New York,
McLoughlin bro's [sic] [c 1890] (On cover: Good old stories)
Illustrated cover and t.-p.

Rip Van Winkle; a posthumous writing of Diedrich Knickerbocker.
This pamphlet was dictated to the phonograph, from which it was
set up by the operator upon the Morgenthaler linotype-machine,
the time occupied being two hours and fifty-eight minutes, including the making of corrections. New York, Linotype reporting and
printing co. [1891]

Rip Van Winkle, and other American essays from The sketch-book,
by Washington Irving. With a biographical sketch, introductions,
and notes. Boston, Houghton Mifflin co. [c 1891] (The Riverside
literature series [no. 51])
Contents. — Biographical sketch of Irving. — Rip Van Winkle. —
Legend of Sleepy Hollow. — Philip of Pokanoket.

Rip Van Winkle, and The Creole village, by Washington Irving.
Printed in the easy reporting style in accordance with the Manual
of phonography by Benn Pitman and Jerome B. Howard. Cincinnati, Phonographic institute, 1889 [i.e., 1892]
Transliteration of shorthand note on title-page, signed by J. B.
Howard, reads: This is called separate issue of 1892, but date
was not changed in plate.

* Rip Van Winkle and The legend of Sleepy Hollow. By Washington
Irving. With fifty-three illustrations by George H. Boughton . . .
London and New York, Macmillan and co., 1893. (Cranford
series)
250 copies.

* — — An issue without series note.

* Rip Van Winkle. By Washington Irving. Illustrated by Frank T.
Merrill. Boston, L. C. Page and co. [1894]

Rip Van Winkle, by Washington Irving. Illustrated by Frank T.
Merrill. Boston, J. Knight co. [c 1894]

Rip Van Winkle; Legend of Sleepy Hollow; The devil and Tom
Walker. — The voyage. — Westminster Abbey. — Stratford-on-
Avon. — The stout gentleman. New York, Doubleday & McClure
co., 1897. (Little masterpieces, edited by Bliss Perry)

Rip Van Winkle, by Washington Irving. Philadelphia, H. Altemus
[c 1896]

Rip Van Winkle; from The sketch book of Washington Irving. New
York, Published for Will Bradley by R. H. Russell [c 1897]

Rip Van Winkle; from The sketch book, of Washington Irving. New
York, Published for the University press, Cambridge, by Harper &
bros. [c 1897]

* Rip Van Winkle. Illustrated by Frederick Simpson Coburn. Borders
and cover by Margaret Armstrong. London, G. Putnam, 1899.

Rip Van Winkle and The legend of Sleepy Hollow by Washington
Irving, with an introduction to Rip Van Winkle by Joseph Jeffer-
son. New York, Reprint by the Century co., 1899.
Title, frontispiece and plate within colored borders.
"Reprinted from the Knickerbocker edition of The sketch book."

* Rip Van Winkle, by Washington Irving. New York & London, G. P.
Putnam's sons, 1899.
Colored ornamental borders.
"The photogravures in this volume are from designs by Frederick
Simpson Coburn. The borders and cover are by Miss Margaret
Armstrong."

A tale of Rip Van Winkle . . . Cleveland, Charles M. Hill, Waldo
press, 1900.
150 copies on handmade paper.
Initials illuminated by hand.

Rip Van Winkle, a legend of the Hudson, by Washington Irving,
with forty-six illustrations. Philadelphia, Henry Altemus co.,
1900. (Altemus' young people's library)
Includes The legend of Sleepy Hollow.

Rip Van Winkle. A posthumous writing of Diedrick Knickerbocker.
In Graham standard phonography, written by Edwin M. Williams,
with key in common type. New York, E. N. Miner, 1900.

Rip Van Winkle and Sleepy Hollow. [By] Washington Irving. New
York and Boston, H. M. Caldwell co. [c 1900]

Rip Van Winkle; a posthumous writing of Diedrich Knickerbocker.
Printed in the easy reporting style of phonography, in accordance
with the "Manual of phonography," by Benn Pitman and Jerome B.
Howard. Cincinnati, Phonographic institute co., 1902.

Rip Van Winkle . . . With drawings by Arthur Rackham . . .
London, William Heinemann; New York, Doubleday, Page & co.,
1905.
With figure, "Rip twenty years later."
51 colored plates, mounted on green mats.

* — — London, William Heinemann; New York, Doubleday, Page &
co., 1905.
Edition de luxe.
250 copies printed.

Rip Van Winkle. By Washington Irving. [East Aurora, N. Y.,
  Roycroft shop, 1905]
  Initials and title-page by Dard Hunter.
  "A little about the story and the play; being a foreword by Joseph
  Jefferson."
* Rip Van Winkle and The legend of Sleepy Hollow . . . Illustrations
  by George H. Boughton. London, Macmillan and co., ltd.; New
  York, The Macmillan co., 1907.
Rip Van Winkle and Sleepy Hollow . . . Chicago, New York [etc.]
  The Old Greek press [c 1907] (The Nutshell library, ed. by
  S. Cody)
  Contents. — Irving, life. — Rip Van Winkle. — The legend of
  Sleepy Hollow. — The mutability of literature. — Westminster
  Abbey.
Rip Van Winkle. A posthumous writing of Diedrich Knickerbocker,
  by Washington Irving. Printed in the easy reporting style of
  phonography, in accordance with the "Manual of phonography,"
  by Benn Pitman and Jerome B. Howard. Cincinnati, Phono-
  graphic institute co., 1908.
The child's Rip Van Winkle, adapted from Washington Irving; with
  twelve illustrations in colours by M. L. Kirk. New York, F. A.
  Stokes co. [1908]
Rip Van Winkle, by Washington Irving. Philadelphia, H. Altemus
  co. [c 1908]
Rip Van Winkle, by Washington Irving. Philadelphia, H. Altemus
  co. [c 1908] (Altemus' illustrated boys' and girls' classics)
— — Philadelphia, H. Altemus co. [c 1908] (Altemus' young people's
  library)
Rip Van Winkle and The legend of Sleepy Hollow, by Washington
  Irving. With fifty-three illustrations by George H. Bough-
  ton, A.R.A. London, Macmillan and co., limited, 1908.
Rip Van Winkle, by Washington Irving; decorations by R. W.
  Sawyer. Boston [etc.] J. W. Luce & co. [c 1909]
* Rip Van Winkle, by Washington Irving. With drawings by Arthur
  Rackham. London, W. Heinemann; New York, Doubleday, Page
  & co., 1910.
  Each plate accompanied by guard sheet with descriptive letterpress.
  Title vignettes.
  Printed in England.
Rip Van Winkle and other sketches by Geoffrey Crayon, gent. Phila-
  delphia, McKay, 1911. (McKay's young people's classics)
* Rip Van Winkle. (In De Vries, Tiemen. Dutch history, art, and
  literature for Americans . . . Grand Rapids, Eerdmans-Sevensma
  co. [1912] p. [193]–207)
Washington Irving, Rip Van Winkle. Bret Harte, Baby Sylvester.
  Mark Twain, How I edited an agricultural paper. Leipzig, O. R.

Reisland, 1912.   (Sammlung englischer und französischer Autoren, 12. Hft.)

Rip Van Winkle and The legend of Sleepy Hollow.   (*In* Almost true tales . . .   New York and London, G. P. Putnam's sons [1912?])

Rip Van Winkle, by Washington Irving.   Printed in Gregg shorthand. New York, Gregg publishing co. [1914]

Rip Van Winkle, by Washington Irving; illustrated by Charles Robinson.   London, T. C. & E. C. Jack; New York, Frederick A. Stokes co. [1915?]   (*Half-title:* Stories we love)

Rip Van Winkle, by Washington Irving.   Printed in Gregg shorthand. New York, Gregg publishing co. [1916]

. . . Rip Van Winkle and The legend of Sleepy Hollow.   By Washington Irving.   In the amanuensis style of phonography.   By Jerome B. Howard.   Cincinnati, The Phonographic institute co., 1919.
At head of title: The American system of shorthand.

Rip Van Winkle and other stories.   Wien, Rhombus Verlag, 1920. (Rhombus edition, Nr. 8)

Rip Van Winkle, by Washington Irving, pictures & decorations by N. C. Wyeth.   Philadelphia, David McKay co. [c 1921]
Illustrated t.-p. and lining-papers.

Rip Van Winkle, by Washington Irving.   Revised.   Printed in Gregg shorthand . . . from no. 40 of "Riverside literature series"; shorthand plates written by Harriet M. Johnson.   New York, Chicago [etc.] The Gregg publishing co. [c 1921]   (*On cover:* English classics in Gregg shorthand)
Introduction by William J. Pelo.

Rip Van Winkle, and other American essays from The sketch book, by Washington Irving, with introduction, explanatory notes and questions and topics for study.   New edition.   Boston, New York [etc.] Houghton Mifflin co. [c 1922]   (The Riverside literature series [no. 51])
Contents. — Biographical sketch of Irving. — Rip Van Winkle. — Legend of Sleepy Hollow. — Philip of Pokanoket.

Demotic shorthand reader.   Irving's Rip Van Winkle, written in demotic shorthand with fonetic print key, by Godfrey Dewey . . . Lake Placid club, N. Y., Forest press, 1923.

Rip Van Winkle, written in demotic shorthand with fonetic print key, by Godfrey Dewey.   Lake Placid club, N. Y., Forest press, 1923.

* Rip Van Winkle and other sketches by Washington Irving.   Edited with an introduction, notes and exercises by Francis Kingsley Ball. Illustrated by Sears Gallagher.   Boston [etc.] Ginn and co. [c 1923]

* Rip Van Winkle.   A legend of the Kaatskill mountains.   By Washington Irving.   With illustrations in color by Edna Cooke and in line by Felix O. C. Darley.   Philadelphia & London, J. B. Lippincott co. [c 1923]   (Children's classics)

Rip Van Winkle . . . With illustrations in color by Edna Cooke and in line by Felix O. C. Darley. Philadelphia, Lippincott, 1924. (Stories all children love series)

Rip Van Winkle and The legend of Sleepy Hollow, by Washington Irving, with illustrations in color by Edna Cooke and in line by Felix O. C. Darley. Philadelphia, J. B. Lippincott co. [c 1924]

Rip Van Winkle . . . illustrated by George Boughton. New York, Macmillan, 1925. (Cranford series)

* Rip Van Winkle, and The legend of Sleepy Hollow, by Washington Irving; illustrated by Eric Pape. New York, The Macmillan co., 1925. ([The Macmillan children's classics])

Rip Van Winkle. A posthumous writing of Diedrich Knickerbocker. Hrsg. von W. Prönnecke. Bielefeld, Velhagen & Klasing, 1926. (Französische und englische Lesebogen, Nr. 12)

Rip Van Winkle; a tale of the Hudson, by Washington Irving, illustrated by Frances Brundage. Akron, Ohio, New York, The Saalfield publishing co. [c 1927] ([John Newbery series])

— — Akron, Ohio, New York, The Saalfield publishing co. [c 1927] (Old trail series)

Rip Van Winkle. Introduction by Blanche Weekes. Philadelphia, John C. Winston co., 1928. (Child's garden of charming books)

Rip Van Winkle and The legend of Sleepy Hollow. With a preface and illustrations by George H. Boughton. New York, Macmillan, 1928. (Dainty books)

* Rip Van Winkle and The legend of Sleepy Hollow, by Washington Irving; with introduction and notes by Blanche E. Weekes, illustrated by John Fitz, jr. Philadelphia, Chicago [etc.] The John C. Winston co. [c 1928] ([The Winston large-type classics for little folks])

. . . Rip Van Winkle, a posthumous writing of Diedrich Knickerbocker, with an introduction by Mark Van Doren. New York, The Limited editions club, 1930.

"This edition . . . consists of fifteen hundred copies made for the members of the Limited editions club, with illustrations reproduced from engravings by Felix Darley; printed in Kaatskill type designed & cut for the book by Frederic W. Goudy . . . and printed at the Walpole printing office, New Rochelle, New York."

"The text of the first edition . . . as it was originally printed in the Sketch book."

* Rip Van Winkle, The legend of Sleepy Hollow, The great Mississippi bubble. New Rochelle, N. Y., Walpole printing office, Random house, 1930. 3 v.

Edition limited to 750 sets.

— — London, Rodker, 1930. 3 v.

* Rip Van Winkle, by Washington Irving. New York, The Gregg
   publishing co. [1930?]
   "Printed in Gregg shorthand . . . from No. 51 of the Riverside
   literature series."
   "Shorthand plates written by Winifred Kenna Richmond."
Rip Van Winkle. Printed in Gregg shorthand. New York, Gregg, 1931.
Rip Van Winkle, by Washington Irving; with drawings by Victor
   Perard. New York, Frederick A. Stokes co., 1933.
   Illustrated t.-p.
Rip Van Winkle, a posthumous writing of Diedrich Knickerbocker,
   by Washington Irving; with pictures by Anne Heyneman and
   printing by Helen Gentry. San Francisco, 1934.
Rip Van Winkle . . . Edited by C. M. Stebbins. Brooklyn, Stebbins
   & co. [19–?] (Studies in English classics)
Rip Van Winkle . . . Chicago, Beckley-Cardy co. [19–?]
Rip Van Winkle . . . Chicago, A. Flanagan co. [19–?] (Little
   classic series)
Rip Van Winkle . . . Chicago, Farquhar & Albright co. [19–?]
   (Lakeside classics)
Rip Van Winkle . . . Dansville, N. Y., Owen publishing co. [19–?]
Rip Van Winkle and The legend of Sleepy Hollow. London, Holten
   [18–?]
* . . . Rip Van Winkle. By Washington Irving. Illustrated by Harry
   Rountree. London, E. Nister; New York, E. P. Dutton & co.
   [19–?] (The Laurel wreath series)
Rip Van Winkle, by Washington Irving, printed in the advanced
   stage of Pitman's shorthand . . . London, Sir I. Pitman & sons,
   ltd. [19–?]
   New era edition.
Rip Van Winkle . . . New York, Barse & Hopkins [19–?] (Golden
   books)
Rip Van Winkle and The legend of Sleepy Hollow. New York, Dodge
   publishing co. [19–?] (Remarque edition of literary masterpieces)
Rip Van Winkle . . . New York, Doran [19–?] (Little leather
   classics)
Rip Van Winkle and other stories. New York, Dutton [19–?] (King's
   treasuries of literature)
Rip Van Winkle. Revised. Printed in Gregg shorthand . . . New
   York, Gregg publishing co. [192–?] (*On cover:* English classics in
   Gregg shorthand)
Rip Van Winkle . . . In the reporting style of Pitman's shorthand
   . . . New York, I. Pitman & sons [190–?]
   Twentieth century edition.
Rip Van Winkle . . . New York, Putnam [19–?] (Ariel booklets)
* Rip Van Winkle. Illustrated by F. O. C. Darley. [place? date?]
   Printed in parallel columns.

Rip Van Winkle — Dramatizations

Akerman, William. Rip Van Winkle. A romantic opera, in three acts. (Founded on Washington Irving's romance.) Written by William Akerman. Music by Franco Leoni . . . London, G. Ricordi & co. [c 1897]
Libretto; English words.

Burke, Charles. . . . Rip Van Winkle, a legend of the Catskills. A romantic drama, in two acts. Adapted from Washington Irving's Sketch book, by Charles Burke . . . New York, S. French [186–?] (French's standard drama. Acting edition, no. 174)

Jefferson, Joseph. Rip Van Winkle. The play, as performed by Joseph Jefferson. Now for the first time published. New York, Dodd, Mead and co., 1895.

— Rip Van Winkle. New York, Dodd, Mead and co., 1899.

* — Rip Van Winkle as played by Joseph Jefferson, now for the first time published. With illustrations. New York, Dodd, Mead and co., 1899.

* — Rip Van Winkle, as played by Joseph Jefferson, now for the first time published. With illustrations. New York, Dodd, Mead and co., 1903.
Title within ornamental border.
Introduction by Joseph Jefferson.

Ould, Herman. . . . Rip Van Winkle. [London] Oxford university press [c 1924] (*At head of title:* New plays from old stories)
Cover-title.
In five scenes.

Wainright, J. H. Rip Van Winkle: an original American opera in three acts [founded on the story by Washington Irving] Music by G. F. Bristow . . . London, T. H. Lacy [18–?] (Lacy's acting edition of plays, v. 39)

See also, The life of Washington Irving, I, 433.

* Sketch of William Roscoe, by Washington Irving. Liverpool, Printed by Harris and co. [1853]

The spectre bridegroom; or, A ghost in spite of himself. A farce founded on a story of the same name, in The sketch-book. By W. T. Moncrief, esq., author of Giovanni in London, etc. New-York [1822?]
Cf. Literary and scientific repository and critical review, January, 1822, p. 251.

* The spectre bridegroom; story. (*In* The Golden book. New York, Review of reviews corporation, 1929. v. 10, no. 60, p. 78–84)

The stage coach . . . Taylorville, Ill., Parker pub. co. [19–?] (Eight page classics)

* Stratford-upon-Avon, from "The sketch book" of Washington Irving.

With notes and original illustrations. Edited by Richard Savage
and William Salt Brassington . . . Stratford-upon-Avon, Edward
Fox, 1900.
75 copies.

Stratford-on-Avon. Hrsg. von Franz Heinrich Schild. Frankfurt a.
M., M. Diesterweg, 1926. (Diesterwegs neusprachliche Lesehefte.
Englische Reihe, Nr. 125)

Stratford-on-Avon. Ausgewählt und bearbeitet von Heimo Manfred
Schultze. Kiel, Lipsius und Tischer, 1930. (Französische und
englische Schullektüre, Erg.-Hft. 51)

Two selections. The legend of Sleepy Hollow and Rip Van Winkle,
from The sketch book by Washington Irving; with notes, questions,
suggestions on teaching, etc., for school use, by J. W. Graham.
San Francisco, The Whitaker & Ray co., inc., 1902. (Practical
aids to literature, No. 1)

Two tales from The sketch book. [Rip Van Winkle; The widow and
her son] Hrsg. von Walther Preusler. 1.-3. unveränderte Auflage. Frankfurt a. M., M. Diesterweg, 1926-30. (Diesterwegs
neusprachliche Lesehefte [Englische Reihe] Nr. 101)

The voyage and other English essays from The sketch book, *see
above*, Complete text, including volumes of selections.

Westminster Abbey. Hrsg. von G. Knauff. Bielefeld, Velhagen &
Klasing, 1925. (Französische und englische Lesebogen, Nr. 10)

Westminster Abbey. Ausgew. vom Hrsg. A[dalbert] Hämel. Leipzig, G. Freytag, 1926. (Freytags Sammlung fremdsprachlicher
Schriftwerke. Kurze Texte. Englisch, 9)

Westminster Abbey and Christmas sketches, *see above*, The sketch
book [c 1891]

* Westminster Abbey. Washington Irving . . . New York, G. M.
Allen co., 1893.

The wife. (*In* The Kaleidoscope, 1819, August 24)
A note contains the phrase "That elegant scholar George Washington Irving."
Probably the first version of a part of The sketch book published
in Great Britain.

* The wife. (*In* Roberts' semi-monthly magazine. Boston, G. Roberts,
1841. v. 1, p. 55-57)

* The wife. (*In* Sands of gold . . . New York, Morris & Willis, 1844.
p. 31-32)

Shorthand (*English*)

See, above, The legend of Sleepy Hollow, 1883, 1889, 1895, [c 1899],
1902, 1903, 1904, 1908, [1916], [c 1918]; London [19-?], London [191-?], London [192-?]; New York [19-?], New York
[192-?]; Rip Van Winkle, 1886, 1889, 1892, 1900, 1902, 1908,
[1914], [1916], 1919, [c 1921], 1923, [1930?], 1931.

TRANSLATIONS

Catalan

La vida rural á Anglaterra. (*In* Prosadors nord-americans. Barcelona, 1909)

Czech

Washington Irving: Náčrty. (The sketch-book.) Výbor povídek a črt. Z Angličiny přeložil Karel Mušek. Prague, J. Otty, 1904.

Extracts

* Rip Van Winkle az álmōs-völgy legendája két rajz irta Washington Irwing. Angol eredetibōl forditotta Bartha László. Budapest, 1916.
On slip pasted over imprint: Budapest, A népszava-könyvkereskedés kiadása, 1919.

* . . . Rip Van Winkle. By Washington Irving. Budapest, Lampel, 1920. (*At head of title:* Angol könyvtár, szerkeszti Dr. Rózsa Dezsö, 1)

Danish

Skizzer, overs. af W. Mariboe. Kjøbenhavn, Schønberg, 1858.

Dutch

* . . . Schetsen en portretten, in Engeland en Amerika, naar het leven geteekend door Geoffrey Crayon, (Washington Irving.) . . . Uit het Engelsch. Leeuwarden, Steenbergen van Goor, 1823.

Extracts

Rip Van Winkle, met 50 chromo's naar teekeningen van Arthur Rackham. Amsterdam, Van Holkema & Warendorf, 1906.

Rip Van Winkle . . . Teekeningen van Arthur Rackham. Antwerpen, 1906.

Rip Van Winkle . . . Antwerpen, G. Janssens [n.d.] (Keurboeking voor reizigers, no. 3)

Esperanto

* Washington Irving. El La skizlibro. El la angla originalo tradukis H. L. Elvin. Leipzig, F. Hirt & Sohn, 1924. (Internacia mondliteraturo, v. 6)

* . . . La abatejo de Westminster . . . Eldonita esperante de J. C. O'Connor . . . London, Central esperanto institute [n.d.] (La "Verd-stelo" serio, No. 1)

French

* Esquisses morales et littéraires, ou, Observations sur les mœurs, les usages et la littérature des Anglois et des Américains . . . traduites de l'anglois sur la 4ᵉ édition, par MM. Delpeux et Villetard . . . Paris, C. LeTellier fils, 1822. 2 v.

* Voyage d'un Américain à Londres, ou, Esquisses sur les mœurs anglaises et américaines; traduit de l'anglais de M. Irwin Washington . . . Paris, Ponthieu, 1822. 2 v.
First edition.
A complete Sketch book, omitting only "A Sunday in London," "London Antiques," and "L'envoy."

* Esquisses morales et littéraires, ou, Observations sur les mœurs, les usages et la littérature des Anglois et des Américains par M. Washington Irving, traduites de l'anglois sur la quatrième édition, par MM. Delpeux et Villetard . . . Paris, C. Le Tellier fils, 1827. 2 v.
Second edition.

* Voyage d'un Américain à Londres, ou, Esquisses sur les mœurs anglaises et américaines; traduit de l'anglais de M. Washington Irving. Paris, Ponthieu, 1829. 2 v.
Second edition.

* Washington Irving. Le livre d'esquisses, traduit de l'anglais par Théodore Lefebvre. Paris, Poulet-Malassis, 1862.

* Washington Irving. Le livre d'esquisses. Traduction française littérale. Paris, Poussielgue frères, 1885. (Alliance des maisons d'éducation chrétienne)

Le livre d'esquisses (Sketch book). Extraits publiés avec une introduction, une notice et des notes par P. Fiévet. Paris, Hachette et cie, 1890.

* — — Paris, Hachette et cie, 1891.
* — — Paris, Hachette et cie, 1894.
* — — Paris, Hachette et cie, 1898.
"Édition portant le nom de l'auteur."
* — — Paris, Hachette et cie, 1901.
* — — Paris, Hachette et cie, 1904.
* — — Paris, Hachette et cie, 1906.

* Washington Irving. Choix d'esquisses (The sketch book). Avec des notes par Jules Guiraud. Paris, Garnier frères, 1908.

Le livre d'esquisses (Sketch book). Extraits publiés avec une introduction, une notice et des notes par P. Fiévet. Paris, Hachette et cie, 1909.
"Édition portant le nom de l'auteur."

* — — Paris, Hachette et cie, 1912.
* — — Paris, Hachette et cie, 1920.

Extracts

Le fiancé-fantôme. Traduit de l'anglais par L. Bocquet. Paris et Bruxelles, Éditions de la renaissance de l'occident, 1921.

* Le flacon de Rip. (Conte traduit d'Irving.) Par Henry Vesseron. Sedan, J. Laroche, 1867.

* [Rip Van Winkle and The spectre bridegroom] (*In* Contes, mor-

ceaux et anecdotes tirés de W. Irving, Gally Knight, W. Scott, etc., suivis de quelques poésies . . . Paris, Derache, 1840)

Rip Van Winkle. Par Washington Irving. Traduction exacte, par le major L. DuBos . . . Philadelphia, Claxton, Remsen & Haffelfinger, 1877.

* Rip, la légende du dormeur . . . Paris, H. Gautier [1891] (Nouvelle bibliothèque populaire à 10 centimes. No. 257)
   "Notice" by Charles Simond, p. 1–4, states that Irving's ignorance of German acquits him of plagiarism.

Rip. Le fiancé fantôme. La légende du Vallon-endormi. Le legs du maure. Traduction de George Elwall. Paris, Delagrave, 1897.

* — — Paris, Delagrave, 1898.

* Rip, suivi du Vallon Enchanté et Le fiancé d'outre-tombe. Traduits par Léonora C. Herbert. Paris, J. Rouff et cie, 1905.

Rip Van Winkle. Album illustré de 50 pl. en couleurs par A. Rackham. Paris, Hachette et cie, 1905.

* . . . Rip . . . traduit par Léonora C. Herbert. Paris, J. Rouff [1905]

* Rip Van Winkle, par Washington Irving. Illustré par Arthur Rackham. Nouvelle édition. Paris, Hachette et cie, 1906.
   "Illustrations photographiques en couleurs, montées sur bristol brun."
   Edition of 200 numbered copies.

* Washington Irving. Rip Van Winkle. Extrait du "Livre d'esquisses" (The sketch book.) Publié, avec une introduction, une notice et des notes par P. Fiévet. Paris, Hachette et cie, 1907. (Auteurs français et étrangers désignés pour l'examen du brevet supérieur)

* Rip Van Winkle, par Washington Irving. Adaptation française par M. Fernand Gillard . . . Paris, Larousse [n.d.] (Les Livres roses pour la jeunesse. No. 142)

* Le Val Dormant, récit arrangé par B.–H. Révoil . . . (In Reid, Mayne. La Baie d'Hudson . . . Paris, 1878)

* — — Paris [n.d.]

German

* Gottfried Crayon's Skizzenbuch . . . Aus dem Englischen des Washington Irving übersetzt von S. H. Spiker . . . Berlin, Duncker und Humblot, 1825. 2 v.

* Gottfried Crayon's Skizzenbuch. Von Washington Irving. Aus dem Englischen übersetzt von S. H. Spiker. Wien, Chr. Fr. Schade, 1826. 2 v.

* Gottfried Crayon's Skizzenbuch . . . Frankfurt, Sauerländer, 1826. 6 v. in 1. (Washington Irving's Sämmtliche Werke, 1. Bd.)
   Also issued in 3 v. and 2 v.

Gottfried Crayon's Skizzenbuch. 2., sorgfältig verbesserte Auflage. Frankfurt-am-Main, Sauerländer, 1846. (Ausgewählte Schriften. Hrsg. von J. V. Adrian. Th. 1)

* Gottfried Crayon's Skizzenbuch, von Washington Irving. Aus dem Englischen. 3., sorgfältig verbesserte Auflage. Frankfurt a. M., Sauerländer, 1870.

Skizzenbuch von Washington Irving. Deutsch von Jenny Piorkowska. Leipzig, Violet, 1876. 4 v. (Haus-Bibliothek ausländischer Classiker, 8–12)

Washington Irving's Skizzenbuch. Übersetzt, mit Biographie und Anmerkungen hrsg. von Karl Theodor Gaedertz. Leipzig, Reclam, 1877. (Universal-Bibliothek, 1031–1034)

— — Leipzig, Reclam [1882] (Universal-Bibliothek, 1031–1034)

Das Skizzenbuch von Geoffrey Crayon, Esquire. Wortgetreu nach H. R. Mecklenburg's Grundsätzen aus dem Englischen übersetzt von R. T. Berlin, H. R. Mecklenburg, 1884–85. 3 v.

* Gottfried Crayons Skizzenbuch von Washington Irving. Gesamt-Ausgabe. Halle a. d. S., Otto Hendel [1888] (Bibliothek der Gesamt-Litteratur des In- u. Auslandes, Nr. 241–244)

Gottfried Crayons Skizzenbuch. Gesamtausgabe. Berlin, Hendel [1924] (Hendel-Bücher, 241/44) Neudruck.

Skizzenbuch. Übersetzung und mit einer biographischen Einleitung und Anmerkungen hrsg. von Karl Theodor Gaedertz. Leipzig, Ph. Reclam, Jun. [1926] (Reclams Universal-Bibliothek, Nr. 1031–1034) Neudruck.

Extracts

Landleben in England. Bruchstück aus Godfried Crayon Esquire's Skizzenbuch. Neu York, 1819. (*In* Morgenblatt für gebildete Stände. Stuttgart und München, J. G. Cotta, 1819. Nr. 283)

Die Legende von der Schlafhöhle. Dolph Heyliger . . . Aus dem Englischen von Adolf Strodtmann. Leipzig, Bibliographisches Institut [1889?] (Meyer's Volksbücher, Nr. 651–652)

Rip Van Winkle. Illustriert durch 50 Aquarelle von Arthur Rackham. Leipzig, E. A. Seemann, 1905.

Rip Van Winkle. Übersetzt von R. Diehl. 1.–20. Tausend. Wiesbaden, H. Staadt, 1909. (Wiesbadener Volksbücher, Nr. 124)

Rip Van Winkle und anderes. Englische Bearbeitung und Übertragung ins Deutsche von E. Springer und Hans Lebede. Berlin, A. Scherl, 1912. (Sprachenpflege, System August Scherl, Englisch, 11. Bd.)

Rip Van Winkle. Hrsg. und mit Anmerkungen versehen von Karl Richter. München, M. Kellerers Verlag, 1926. (Kellerers englische Ausgaben, Bd. 21)

Rip Van Winkle. Wolfenbüttel, Heckners Verlag, 1930. (Stenogr. Jugendbibliothek, Bd. 64) In short-hand.

Die Seereise. Bruchstück aus Godfried Crayon Esquire's Skizzenbuch. Neu York, 1819. (*In* Morgenblatt für gebildete Stände. Stuttgart und München, J. G. Cotta, 1819. Nr. 269–270)

* Stratford am Avon. Nach Washington Irving, deutsch von K. v. W. [Karoline von Woltmann.] (*In* Der Kranz; oder, Erholungen für Geist und Herz. Eine Unterhaltungsschrift für gebildete Leser hrsg. von Karoline von Woltmann. Prag, 1824. Jahrg. 1824, 1. Hft.)

[Translation of some of Irving's remarks on criticism, from The sketch book.] (*In* Literarisches Conversationsblatt. Leipzig, Brockhaus, 1825. No. 174, p. 696)

Shorthand (German)

See, above, Rip Van Winkle, 1930.

Hebrew

ריפ וואן ווינקל. מעשה. תרגם א. טבק. [Rip Van Winkle, tr. by A. Tabak. Tel-Aviv, [5] 688 (A.D. 1928)]

Italian

Racconti di Natale. Traduzione di Pompeo Bettini. Milano, Pietro Faverio, 1893.
    Contents. — 1. Il Natale. — 2. La diligenza. — 3. La vigilia. — 4. La giornata di Natale. — 5. Il pranzo.

* . . . Il libro degli schizzi. A cura di G. L. Brezzo. Torino, Unione tip. edit. torinese, 1931. (I Grandi scrittori stranieri: collana di traduzioni, no. 7)

Extracts

L'abazio di Wetsminster [*sic*] e Stratfore su l'Avone. Traduzione di Mariano Bertolami dal Libro degli schizzi. Messina, Tip. Alicò e Zuccaro, 1920.

L'abazio di Westmister [*sic*] (*In* Mondo nuovo e cose vecchie, di G. B. Carta. Milano, Presso Omobono Manini [183–?])

Filippo di Pokanoket. (*In* Mondo nuovo e cose vecchie, di G. B. Carta. Milano, Presso Omobono Manini [183–?])

La moglie. Novella di Washinton [*sic*] Irving, tradotta in italiano da F. Frank. Rovigo, Minelli, 1841.

La moglie . . . Mantova, Mondovi, 1874.

La montagna prodigiosa (Rip Van Winkle.) Prima versione italiana di Federigo Verdinois. Napoli, Soc. ed. Partenopea, F. Ricciardi, 1911. (Libro economico: serie racconti di fate)

Rip Van Winkle: racconto di Washington Irving, con disegni di Arturo Rackham . . . Bergamo, Istituto italiano d'arti grafiche [1908]

Rip Van Winkle. Con brevissimi cenni sulla vita dell' autore e sulle sue opere più importante del prof. F. N. Piagnucco. Novara, Tip. E. Cattaneo, 1930.

Lo spettro del fidanzato.   Prima versione italiana di O. Roux-Rocca.
S. Cascianao, Cappeler, 1880.

. . . Lo spettro del fidanzato.   Torino, Meyer, 1884.   (Biblioteca
antica e moderna, 27)
At head of title: Alla caccia di un taccuino [not identified]

La sposa.   (*In* Passatempi morali . . . Londra, 1826)

La vedova e suo figlio . . .   (*In* Passatempi morali . . . Londra,
1826)

Il viaggio.   (*In* Mondo nuovo e cose vecchie, di G. B. Carta.   Milano,
Presso Omobono Manini [183–?])

La vigilia di Natale.   (*In* Mondo nuovo e cose vecchie, di G. B. Carta.
Milano, Presso Omobono Manini [183–?])

La vittima del crepacuore . . .   (*In* Passatempi morali . . . Londra,
1826)

Norwegian

Skissebogen af Washington Irwing . . .   Oversat af Hans Brekke.
Fagerstrand, Høvik, 1887.   3 v.   (Bibliothek for de tusen hjem, 52,
63, 96)

— — 2. tildels ændrede opl. Fagerstrand, Høvik, 1888.   v. 1–2.
(Bibliothek for de tusen hjem, 52, 63)

Polish

Rysy moralności i literatury, albo postrzeżenia we względzie obycza-
jów i literatury Anglików i Amerykanów.   Wilno, 1830.   2 v.
Translated from the fourth edition.

Russian

Extracts

Безголовый мертвецъ.   (*In* Московскій Телеграфъ.   Moscow,
1826.   v. 9, p. 116–142, 161–187)
The legend of Sleepy Hollow.

Spanish

* . . . Washington Irving.   Apuntes literarios.   Traducción y prólogo
de Miguel Álvarez Aguilar.   Madrid, Compañía ibero-americana
de publicaciones [1930?]   (*At head of title:* Las Cien mejores obras
de la literatura universal, v. 6)

Extracts

El caballero sin cabeza.   (*In* Leyendas extraordinarias.   Traducción
del inglés por M. Juderías Bénder.   Madrid, Manuel Tello, 1882.
v. 3, p. 39–79)

* Costumbres inglesas.   La Noche buena.   (*In* El Museo mexicano;
6, Miscelanea pintoresca de amenidades curiosas é instructivas.

México, Lo imprime y publica Ignacio Cumplido, 1844. v. 4, p. 522–523)

El espectro desposado. Tr. by E. de O. (*In* Horas de invierno. Madrid, 1836. No. 16, p. 137–168)

* La leyenda del Valle Encantado. (*In* Cuentos clásicos del norte. Nueva York, Doubleday, Page & co., 1920. 2. série, p. [43]–96)

* Rip Van Winkle. (*In* Cuentos clásicos del norte. Nueva York, Doubleday, Page & co., 1920. 2. série, p. [9]–42)

Rip Van Winkle. Tr. por Gutiérrez Nájera. [place? date?]

* El serrano de las Alpujarras. (*In* Tareas de un solitario; 6, Nueva colección de novelas. [Por D. Jorge W. Montgomery.] Madrid, Imprenta de Espinosa, 1829. p. 63–94)

Rip Van Winkle.

— (*In* Novelas españolas. Brunswick [Maine] 1830)

— (*In* Novelas españolas. New York, 1842)

— (*In* Novelas españolas. Brunswick [Maine] 1845)

* El sueño. (*In* Tareas de un solitario; 6, Nueva colección de novelas. [Por D. Jorge W. Montgomery.] Madrid, Imprenta de Espinosa, 1829. p. [1]–15)

Swedish

Ur skizzboken. Öfv. af Erik G. Folcker. Stockholm, Fahlcrantz & k., 1888.

Extracts

Rip Van Winkle. Öfversättning af Elisabeth Carlson. Med illustrationer af Arthur Rackham. Stockholm, Norstedt & söners [1905]

* Sagan om Sofdalen af Didrick Knickerbocker. Efter hans död utgifven af Washington Irving. Öfversättning af Vitalis. Stockholm, Bredberg, 1827.

Yiddish

... ריפ וואן ווינקל. די לעגענדע פון פערשלאָפענעם טאל. איבערזעצט פון ענגליש פון פ. נאָוויק. ניו יאָרק: פארלאג ה. טויבענשלאג.

New York, H. Taubenschlag [c 1923]

Rip Van Winkle.

SPANISH PAPERS

See also, II. Selected Works

* Spanish papers and other miscellanies, hitherto unpublished or uncollected. By Washington Irving. Arranged and edited by Pierre M. Irving ... New York, G. P. Putnam, Hurd and Houghton, 1866. 2 v.

First edition.

Contents. — v. 1. The legend of Don Roderick [from Legends of the conquest of Spain]. Legend of the subjugation of Spain [from Legends of the conquest of Spain]. Legend of Count Julian and his family [from Legends of the conquest of Spain]. The legend of Pelayo [from The Knickerbocker; pirated by The Evergreen: a monthly magazine. 1840; also published in The Spirit of the Fair]. Abderahman [from The Knickerbocker]. Chronicle of Fernan Gonzalez, Count of Castile [published for the first time]. Chronicle of Fernando the Saint [published for the first time]. Spanish romance [from The Knickerbocker]. — v. 2. Letters of Jonathan Oldstyle. Captain James Lawrence [from The Analectic magazine, August–September, 1813]. Lieutenant Burrows [from The Analectic magazine, November, 1813]. Commodore Perry [from The Analectic magazine, December, 1813]. Captain David Porter [from The Analectic magazine, September, 1814]. Thomas Campbell [from The Analectic magazine, March, 1815]. Washington Allston [from Duyckinck's Encyclopedia of American literature]. Conversations with Talma [from The Knickerbocker gallery, 1855]. Margaret Miller Davidson. Review of the works of Robert Treat Paine [from The Analectic magazine, March, 1813]. Review of the poems of Edwin C. Holland [from The Analectic magazine, March, 1814]. Review of Wheaton's History of the Northmen [from North American review, October, 1832]. The conquest of Granada [from The Quarterly review, October, 1830]. Letter to the editor of The Knickerbocker magazine [from The Knickerbocker, March, 1839]. Sleepy Hollow [from The Knickerbocker, May, 1839]. National nomenclature [from The Knickerbocker, August, 1839]. Desultory thoughts on criticism [from The Knickerbocker, August, 1839]. Communipaw [from The Knickerbocker, September, 1839]. Conspiracy of the cocked hats [from The Knickerbocker, October, 1839; pirated by The Evergreen: a monthly magazine. 1840]. Letter from Granada [from The Knickerbocker, July, 1840]. The Catskill mountains [from The Home book of the picturesque].

— — Another issue.

Stamped on binding: J. B. Lippincott, Philadelphia.

* Biographies and miscellaneous papers by Washington Irving . . . Collected and arranged by Pierre Irving. London, Bell and Daldy, 1867.

— — London, S. Low, 1867.

Spanish papers, by Washington Irving, edited by Pierre Munro Irving. New York, G. P. Putnam's sons, 1868. (Works . . . Hudson edition, v. 20)

Spanish papers by Washington Irving . . . edited by Pierre M. Irving. [New York, G. P. Putnam's sons, c 1868] (The works of Washington Irving. The Kinderhook edition, v. 10)

Biographies and miscellanies . . . Edited by Pierre M. Irving. New York, Putnam, 1869.

Spanish papers and other miscellanies . . . edited by Pierre M. Irving . . . Philadelphia, J. B. Lippincott, 1870.
Riverside edition.

Biographies and miscellanies by Washington Irving. Edited by his literary executor, Pierre M. Irving. Philadelphia, J. B. Lippincott & co., 1871.
Knickerbocker edition.

—— Philadelphia, J. B. Lippincott & co., 1873.

Spanish papers by Washington Irving, edited by Pierre M. Irving. New York, G. P. Putnam's sons [1882]
Vol. 20 of a uniform edition in cloth, having at head of title "Hudson edition" (first issued in 1882) and lettered: Irving's works.

* . . . Biographies and miscellanies, by Washington Irving, edited by his literary executor, Pierre M. Irving. New York, G. P. Putnam's sons [1882]
Copyright date: 1866.
Vol. [17] of a uniform edition in cloth, having at head of title "Hudson edition" (first issued in 1882) and lettered: Irving's works.

. . . Spanish papers by Washington Irving. New York and London, G. P. Putnam's sons [c 1895]
At head of title: Knickerbocker edition.

—— New York and London, G. P. Putnam's sons, 1897.

Biographical sketches. Heretofore included in volume entitled "Biographies and miscellanies." (*In* Salmagundi. [Author's autograph edition.] New York and London, G. P. Putnam's sons, 1897. v. 8, p. 235–411)
Contents. — Captain James Lawrence. — Lieutenant Burrows. — Commodore Perry. — Captain David Porter. — Thomas Campbell. — Washington Allston. — Conversations with Talma.

. . . Spanish papers by Washington Irving. Edited by Pierre M. Irving. New York, G. P. Putnam's sons, 1902. (*Publisher's lettering:* Irving's works)
At head of title: Hudson edition.

. . . Biographies and miscellanies by Washington Irving; edited by his literary executor, Pierre M. Irving. New York, G. P. Putnam's sons [1902] (*Publisher's lettering:* Irving's works)
At head of title: Hudson edition.

Spanish papers . . . New York, Putnam [19–?]
New handy volume edition.

Spanish papers . . . New York, Putnam [19–?]
New Knickerbocker edition.

Extracts

* The Catskill mountains. (*In* A Landscape book, by American artists and American authors . . . New York, G. P. Putnam & son; London, Sampson Low & co., 1868. p. 22–29)

Moorish chronicles. By Washington Irving. New York, J. W. Lovell & co. [1883] ([Lovell's library, v. 6, no. 314])
    Contents. — Chronicle of Fernan Gonzalez. — Chronicle of Fernando the Saint.

Moorish chronicles. By Washington Irving. New York, J. B. Millar & co., 1884.

Moorish chronicles. By Washington Irving. [New York, Belford co., 188–?]

Moorish chronicles. By Washington Irving. New York, F. M. Lupton publishing co. [188–?]

TALES OF A TRAVELLER

* Tales of a traveller . . . by Geoffrey Crayon, gent. . . . Philadelphia, H. C. Carey & I. Lea, 1824.
    First edition.
    Published in four parts.

* Tales of a traveller, by Geoffrey Crayon, gent. . . . New York, C. S. Van Winkle, 1824. 2 v.
    Second American edition.

* Tales of a traveller. By Geoffrey Crayon, gent. . . . London, John Murray, 1824. 2 v.
    Published before the appearance of the first American edition.

* Tales of a traveller, by Geoffrey Crayon, gent. . . . Paris, L. Baudry, 1824. 2 v.

* Tales of a traveller. By Geoffrey Crayon, gent. . . . Second American edition. New-York, C. S. Van Winkle, 1825. 2 v.

* Tales of a traveller. By Geoffrey Crayon, gent. . . . New edition. In two volumes. London, John Murray, 1825. 2 v.

* Tales of a traveller. By Geoffrey Crayon, gent. . . . Paris, Baudry, 1829. 2 v.

* Tales of a traveller, by Geoffrey Crayon, gent. . . . London, John Murray, 1829. 2 v.

* — — Another issue with a notice, 1 leaf, at end.

* Tales of a traveller. By Geoffrey Crayon, gent. Paris, Baudry, 1834. 2 v.

* Tales of a traveller, by Geoffrey Crayon, gent. . . . A new edition. Philadelphia, Carey, Lea, & Blanchard, 1835. 2 v.
    Third American edition.

Tales of a traveller, by Geoffrey Crayon, gent. . . . New edition. Philadelphia, Carey, Lea, & Blanchard, 1837. 2 v.

Tales of a traveller, by Geoffrey Crayon, gent. . . . New edition. Philadelphia, Carey, Lea, & Blanchard, 1838. 2 v.

* Tales of a traveller, by Washington Irving. Mit erklärenden Anmerkungen hrsg. von Dr. E. A. Toel. Lüneburg, Herold und Wahlstab, 1841.

Tales of a traveller, with a life of the author. New York, 1844.

Tales of a traveller . . . Paris, 1844.

* Tales of a traveller . . . Paris, Baudry, 1846. (Collection of ancient and modern British authors, t. 398A)
"Édition portant le nom véritable de l'auteur."

Tales of a traveller, by Washington Irving. New York, G. P. Putnam's sons [1848?] 2 v.
Pocket edition.

* Tales of a traveller. By Geoffrey Crayon, gent. . . . Author's revised edition. Complete in one volume. New-York, G. P. Putnam, 1849.
— — Another issue. (The works of Washington Irving, v. 7)

Tales of a traveller. By Geoffrey Crayon, gent. . . . London, H. G. Bohn, 1850. (Bohn's shilling series)

Tales of a traveller . . . [London?] 1850. (The Parlour library, v. 42)

* Tales of a traveller, by Geoffrey Crayon, gent^n . . . New York, G. P. Putnam [etc.] 1850.
Added engr. t.-p.
Illustrations by Felix O. C. Darley.
Plates and illustrated added title-page are mounted proofs.

* Tales of a traveller, by Geoffrey Crayon, gent. . . . With illustrations by Felix O. C. Darley, engraved by eminent artists. New-York, G. P. Putnam, 1850.
50 copies printed.
— — New-York, G. P. Putnam, 1851.

* Tales of a traveller. By Washington Irving . . . New York, G. P. Putnam & co., 1857.

Tales of a traveller. By Geoffrey Crayon, gent. . . . Author's revised edition . . . New York, G. P. Putnam, 1860. (The works of Washington Irving, v. 7)

Tales of a traveller . . . Illustrated with steel engravings. [place? publisher?] 1860.

* Tales of a traveller. By Washington Irving. London, Bell and Daldy, 1864. (Bell and Daldy's Elzevir series of standard authors)

* Tales of a traveller, by Geoffrey Crayon, gent. Author's revised edition. New York, G. P. Putnam [etc.] 1865.
On half-title: Riverside edition.
Added engr. t.-p.

* Tales of a traveller. By Geoffrey Crayon, gent. . . . Author's revised edition . . . New York, G. P. Putnam's sons [c 1865]
Added engr. t.-p.
Riverside edition.

* Tales of a traveller, by Geoffrey Crayon, gent. . . . Author's revised edition . . . [New York, G. P. Putnam's sons, c 1865] (The works of Washington Irving. The Kinderhook edition, v. 1)

Tales of a traveller, by Geoffrey Crayon, gent. . . . The author's revised edition. Complete in one volume. New York, G. P. Putnam & son, 1868.
Knickerbocker edition.
Added engr. t.-p.: Tales of a traveller, by Washington Irving. New York, G. P. Putnam, Hurd & Houghton.

Tales of a traveller . . . New York, 1868.
Riverside edition.

Tales of a traveller. By Washington Irving. London, Bell and Daldy [1868?]

Tales of a traveller. By Geoffrey Crayon, gent. . . . Author's revised edition. Philadelphia, J. B. Lippincott & co., 1873. (On cover: Irving's works)
Half-title: . . . Riverside edition.
Added engr. t.-p.; vignette.

Tales of a traveller . . . Author's revised edition. New York [1873?]
Knickerbocker edition.

Tales of a traveller . . . London [1876]   (The Golden library)

* Tales of a traveller. By Washington Irving . . . London, George Bell and sons, 1877.

Tales of a traveller, by Geoffrey Crayon, gent. New York, G. P. Putnam, 1882.
Hudson edition.

Tales of a traveller . . . New York, J. B. Alden, 1883.
Caxton edition.

Tales of a traveller . . . New York, J. W. Lovell co. [1883] (Lovell's library, v. 4, no. 198)

* . . . Tales of a traveller . . . The author's revised edition . . . New York, G. P. Putnam's sons, 1889. (Publisher's lettering: Irving's works)
At head of title: Hudson edition.

. . . Tales of a traveller, edited by James R. Rutland . . . New York, Cincinnati [etc.] American book co., 1894. (Eclectic English classics)

* — — New York, Cincinnati [etc.] American book co. [c 1894]

* . . . Tales of a traveller . . . The author's revised edition, edited by William Lyon Phelps . . . New York, London, G. P. Putnam's sons, 1894.
Student's edition.

Tales of a traveller, by Geoffrey Crayon, gent. . . . The author's revised edition. New York and London, G. P. Putnam's sons [1894?] (Publisher's lettering: Irving's works)
At head of title: Hudson edition.
Preface dated 1894, signed W. L. P.

—— Another issue.

Without caption: Hudson edition.

Tales of a traveller . . . The author's revised edition, edited by William Lyon Phelps . . . New York, London, G. P. Putnam's sons, 1895.

Student's edition.

Washington Irving's Tales of a traveller. With an introduction by Brander Matthews, with . . . notes by G. R. Carpenter. New York, London, Longmans Green and co., 1895. (Longmans' English classics)

* Tales of a traveller . . . Buckthorne edition. New York & London, G. P. Putnam's sons, 1895. 2 v.

Title and text within ornamental border.

Tales of a traveller . . . Knickerbocker edition. New York & London, G. P. Putnam's sons, 1895.

* Tales of a traveller (selected) . . . With a biographical sketch and explanatory notes. New York, Maynard, Merrill & co. [1895] (Maynard's English classics, no. 174–175)

Tales of a traveller . . . New York and London, G. P. Putnam's sons, 1897. 2 v.

Knickerbocker edition.

Tales of a traveller . . . The author's revised edition, edited by William Lyon Phelps . . . New York, London, G. P. Putnam's sons, 1897.

Student's edition.

Washington Irving's Tales of a traveller; with an introduction by Brander Matthews, together with notes and other illustrative matter by G. R. Carpenter. New York, Longmans Green and co., 1897. (Longmans' English classics)

Tales of a traveller. With selections from The sketch book. Edited for school use by G. P. Krapp . . . Chicago, Scott, Foresman & co., 1901.

Tales of a traveller, by Geoffrey Crayon, gent. Author's revised edition. New York, G. P. Putnam's sons, 1902.

Hudson edition.

Tales of a traveller . . . With introduction and notes by Margaret A. Eaton, B.A. Boston, New York, Educational publishing co., 1907. (Classic library)

—— Boston, New York, Educational publishing co., 1907. 2 v. (Red shield English classics)

* . . . Irving's Tales of a traveller, edited by James R. Rutland. New York, Cincinnati [etc.] American book co. [c 1911] (Eclectic English classics)

Tales from Washington Irving's Traveller with illustrations by George Hood. Philadelphia & London, J. B. Lippincott co., 1913.

* Selected tales from Tales of a traveller by Washington Irving. Edited

by Jennie F. Chase . . . New York, The Macmillan co., 1913.
(Macmillan's pocket classics)

Tales of a traveller, with selections from The sketch book by Washington Irving, edited for school use by G. P. Krapp. Chicago,
New York, Scott, Foresman and co. [c 1920] (Lake English
classics)

Tales of a traveller . . . New York, Belford co. [18–?]

Tales of a traveller . . . New York, Burt [19–?] (Cornell series)

Tales of a traveller . . . New York, Burt [19–?] (Home library)

Tales of a traveller . . . New York, T. Y. Crowell & co. [n.d.]
Illustrated by Frank E. Merrill.

* Tales of a traveller. By Geoffrey Crayon, gent^n . . . Revised edition. New York, T. Y. Crowell & co. [n.d.]

Tales of a traveller . . . New York, The New York publishing co.
[188–?]
Contents. — Tales of a traveller. — Wolfert's Roost, and Miscellanies.

Tales of a traveller . . . New York, G. P. Putnam's sons [19–?]
(Ariel booklets)

Tales of a traveller . . . New York, G. P. Putnam's sons [19–?]
Gift edition.

. . . Tales of a traveller . . . New York, G. P. Putnam's sons
[190–?] 2 v.
At head of title: Knickerbocker edition.
Title in red and black.

Tales of a traveller . . . New York, G. P. Putnam's sons [19–?]
Large paper edition.

Tales of a traveller . . . New York, G. P. Putnam's sons [19–?]
New handy volume edition.

Extracts

The devil and Tom Walker: together with Deacon Grubb and the
Old Nick. Woodstock, Vt., R. & A. Colton, 1830.

Wolfert Webber, *see* A book of the Hudson.

The young robber. (*In* The Romancist, and Novelist's library . . .
London, Printed by C. Reynell, Published by J. Clements, 1839–40.
v. 2, p. [142])

— (*In* Ascanius, or The young adventurer . . . Glasgow and London
[1876])

TRANSLATIONS

Danish

En reisendes fortællinger, oversat af Wallich. København, Schubothe,
1828. 2 v.

Dutch

Verhalen van eener reiziger; uit het Engelsch vertaald, door Steenbergen van Goor. Amsterdam, C. L. Schleyer, 1827. 2 v.

French

* Œuvres complètes de M. Washington Irving, traduites de l'anglais
    . . . par M. Lebègue d'Auteuil . . . Contes d'un voyageur . . .
    Paris, Boulland, 1825. 4 v.
* Historiettes d'un voyageur, par Geoffrey Crayon . . .   Paris,
    Carpentier-Méricourt, 1825. 4 v.
    Translation by Lebègue.
* Contes d'un voyageur, par Geoffrey-Crayon, traduits de l'anglais de
    M. Washington Irving par Mme Adèle Beaurgard [*sic*].   Paris,
    Lecointe et Durey, 1825. 4 v.

Extracts

* Washington Irving.   Les chercheurs de trésors.   Paris, Librairie
    illustrée, 1892. (Chefs-d'œuvre du siècle illustrés, 22)
    Notice par H. Duclos.
    Tales of a traveller, Part IV.
* — — Paris, Librairie illustrée [1897] (Chefs-d'œuvre du siècle illus-
    trés, 22)

German

* Erzählungen eines Reisenden.   Von Washington Irving . . .   Aus
    dem Englischen übersetzt von S. H. Spiker . . .   Berlin, Duncker
    und Humblot, 1825. 2 v.
Erzählungen eines Reisenden. Übersetzt von S. H. Spiker. Wien,
    1825. 3 v.
Erzählungen eines Reisenden, von C. A. Fischer. Frankfurt, 1827.
Erzählungen eines Reisenden. Frankfurt-am-Main, Sauerländer, 1847.
    (Ausgewählte Schriften, Theil 3)
    2., verbesserte Auflage.
Erzählungen eines Reisenden . . .   Dresden, Arnold [n.d.]

Extracts

Aus den Erzählungen eines Reisenden von Washington Irving, dem
    Verfasser des Skizzenbuches. Übertragen von Th. Hell. (*In*
    Abendzeitung.   Dresden, Arnold, 1824.   No. 236–243)
    No. 236. — Geistergeschichten.   Der Jagdschmaus.
    No. 237. — Meines Onkels Abenteuer.
    No. 238. — Meines Onkels Abenteuer.
    No. 239. — Meines Onkels Abenteuer.
    No. 240. — Meiner Tante Abenteuer.

No. 241. — Meiner Tante Abenteuer.   Meines Grossvaters Abenteuer; oder, Der tapfere Dragoner.

No. 242. — Meines Grossvaters Abenteuer; oder, Der tapfere Dragoner.

No. 243. — Des deutschen Studenten Abenteuer.

Reiseabenteuer. (*In* Morgenblatt für gebildete Stände.   Stuttgart
und München, J. G. Cotta, 1822.   p. 152 ff)

Wolfert Webber. (*In* Novellenschatz des Auslandes . . .   München,
Oldenbourg [1872–75] Bd. 3, p. 1–92)

Italian

Extracts

Il fantasma, racconto di un viaggiatore (Washinton [*sic*] Irving);
traduzione di G. B. Carta. (*In* Il Presagio, ricordo di letteratura.
Strenna pel capo d'anno.   Milano, Carlo Canadelli [1841])

Lo straniero misterioso, novella del signor *Irving;* versione dall'
originale inglese di Gaetano Barbieri. (*In* Un atto di virtù, di
Carlo de Bernard.   Versione di F.–M.   Milano, per Borroni e Scotti,
1846)

Lo straniero misterioso, novella del signor Irving.   Traduzione dall'
originale inglese di G. B.   Milano, 1826.
Extract from "Il Nuovo raccoglitore" [a periodical]

Lo straniero misterioso: leggende dell' Alhambra.   Milano, Sonzogno,
1884. (Biblioteca universale, n. 94)

Russian

Extracts

Вольферъ Вебберъ, или золотые сны. (Соч. Ирв. Вашингтона)
(*In* Московскій Телеграфъ.   Moscow, 1826.   v. 7, p. 62–102,
130–150, 167–196)
Wolfert Webber.

Spanish

Extracts

Aventura de un estudiante alemán. (*In* El Artista.   Madrid [1835]
v. 1, no. 16)
The Spanish editor explains Irving's allusion to the mystic Sweden-
borg as a reference to a character in a tale of Hoffman's.

. . . Los buscadores de tesoros.   Barcelona, J. Roura; A. del Castillo,
1893. (Biblioteca ilustrada.   Primera sección, número 3)
A translation and adaptation of Tales of a traveller, Part IV.

* El cuadro misterioso. (*In* Tareas de un solitario; ó, Nueva colección
de novelas. [Por D. Jorge W. Montgomery.]   Madrid, Imprenta de
Espinosa, 1829.   p. 95–157)

— (*In* Novelas españolas. Brunswick [Maine] Imprenta de Griffin, 1830)
Edited by H. W. Longfellow.

— (*In* Novelas españolas. New York, 1842)
Edited, with a translation by Julio Soler.

— (*In* Novelas españolas. Brunswick [Maine] 1845)
Edited by H. W. Longfellow.

* Historia del joven italiano. (*In* Aventuras de un misántropo. Por X. B. Saintine. [Madrid, Barcelona, 18–?] p. 298–335)
Irving's name is not mentioned.

* El misterioso extranjero. (*In* Aventuras de un misántropo. Por X. B. Saintine. [Madrid, Barcelona, 18–?] p. 295–298)
Irving's name is not mentioned.

* El retrato misterioso, novela escrita en inglés por M. Whasington [*sic*] Irving. Traductor M. Marcial Busquets. (*In* Aventuras de un misántropo. Por X. B. Saintine. Madrid, Barcelona, 1860. p. 289–335)

Swedish

En resandes berättelser. Öfversättning af Lars Arnell. Stockholm, Hæggström, 1829.
En resandes berättelser. Öfversättning . . . Stockholm, 1865.
(Familjebibliotek, 7)

AN UNWRITTEN DRAMA OF LORD BYRON

* An unwritten drama of Lord Byron. (*In* The Gift. A Christmas and New Year's present for 1836. Edited by Miss Leslie. Philadelphia, E. L. Cary & A. Hart, 1836. p. 166–171)
Irving's sketch gives the plan of a dramatic poem, never written by Byron, based on an unidentified Spanish play (possibly by Calderón), which is supposed to be the source of Poe's "William Wilson."

* — (*In* The Americana collector. Edited by C. F. Heartman . . . Metuchen, N. J., 1925. v. 1, p. 64–66)
Introduction by Thomas Ollive Mabbott.

* — Metuchen, N. J., C. F. Heartman, 1925.
51 copies printed.

* Ein dramatischer Entwurf Lord Byron's. Von Washington Irving. (*In* Magazin für die Literatur des Auslandes. Berlin, Hayn, 1835. 8. Bd., p. [585])
"Mitgeteilt in einem unter dem Titel «The Gift etc. Weihnachts- und Neujahrsgeschenk" von Miss Leslie in Philadelphia heraus- gegebenen, Almanack für 1836."
A review, with extracts.

A VOYAGE TO THE EASTERN PART
OF TERRA FIRMA

* Pons, F. de. A voyage to the eastern part of Terra Firma, or the
Spanish Main, in South-America, during the years 1801, 1802, 1803,
and 1804 . . . With a large map of the country, &c. Translated
by an American gentleman [Washington Irving.] New-York,
Printed by and for I. Riley and co., 1806. 3 v.
The first issue with the errors in the text.
Translated by Washington Irving, Peter Irving and George Caines.
* — — New-York, Printed by and for I. Riley and co., 1806. 3 v. in 1.
* — — New-York, I. Riley and co., 1806. 3 v.

VOYAGES AND DISCOVERIES OF THE COMPANIONS
OF COLUMBUS

See also, A history of the life and voyages of Christopher Columbus

* Voyages and discoveries of the companions of Columbus. By Washington Irving . . . Philadelphia, Carey and Lea, 1831.
First edition.
4 p. of the Encyclopedia Americana bound in front of volume;
some copies have a Carey and Lea advertisement dated February,
1830.
* Voyages and discoveries of the companions of Columbus. By Wash-
ington Irving. London, John Murray, 1831.
First English edition.
* — — London, John Murray, 1831. (*On cover:* The Family library,
no. 18)
* Voyages of the companions of Columbus. By Washington Irving . . .
Paris, A. and W. Galignani, 1831.
Printed by Jules Didot.
* Voyages and discoveries of the companions of Columbus, by Wash-
ington Irving. Paris, Baudry, 1831.
* The voyages and discoveries of the companions of Columbus. Phila-
delphia, Carey, Lea, & Blanchard, 1835.
Voyages and discoveries of the companions of Columbus. Mit Noten
zur Erklårung des Textes und zur Erleichterung der Aussprache,
nebst einem Wörterbuche. Leipzig, Baumgårtners Buchhandlung,
1835.
— — Leipzig, Baumgårtners Buchhandlung, 1837.
Voyages and discoveries of the companions of Columbus. Edited with
accents and 1000 notes. Stockholm, 1837.
* Voyages and discoveries of the companions of Columbus. By Washington Irving. With a complete vocabulary compiled by Dr. E.
Amthor. Leipzig, Renger, 1840.

* — — Leipzig, Renger, 1846.
　　Revised edition.

Voyages and discoveries of the companions of Columbus . . . New York, G. P. Putnam, 1849. (The works of Washington Irving. New edition, revised, v. 5)

Voyages and discoveries of the companions of Columbus . . . London, Bohn, 1850.

Spanish voyages of discovery. By Washington Irving. New York, J. W. Lovell co. [1883] (Lovell's library, v. 6, no. 301)
　　Caption title: Voyages and discoveries of the companions of Columbus.

Spanish voyages of discovery. By Washington Irving. New York, J. B. Alden, 1883.

Voyages and discoveries of the companions of Columbus. Mit einer Einleitung und erklärenden Erläuterungen hrsg. von C. Th. Lion. Leipzig, Baumgärtner; Dresden, Kühtmann, 1885.

Voyages and discoveries of the companions of Columbus . . . with an introduction by the author, a foreword by Van Wyck Brooks, and a decoration by Edward A. Wilson. New York, Rimington & Hooper, 1929.
　　The Savoy edition of 374 copies, designed and printed by W. A. Kittredge at the Lakeside press; issue no. 4 of the Savoy edition.

Voyages and discoveries of the companions of Columbus . . . London, T. Tegg [n.d.]

Spanish voyages of discovery . . . [New York, Belford co., 188–?]

Spanish voyages of discovery. By Washington Irving. New York, F. F. Lovell & co. [187–?]

Translations
Dutch

* Ontdekkingsreisen van eenige der vroegere togtgenooten van Columbus. Naar het Engelsch van Washington Irving . . . Zijnde een aanhangsel op deszelfs Leven en reizen van Chr. Columbus. Haarlem, A. Loosjes, 1834.

French

* Histoire des voyages et découvertes des compagnons de Christophe Colomb par M. Washington Irving, suivie de l'Histoire de Fernand Cortez et de la conquête du Mexique, et de l'Histoire de Pizarre et de la conquête du Pérou. Ouvrages traduits de l'anglais par A.-J.-B. et C.-A. Defauconpret. Paris, C. Gosselin, 1833. 3 v.

* Voyages et découvertes des compagnons de Colomb, traduit de l'anglais de Washington Irving, par Henri Lebrun [pseud.] Tours, A. Mame, 1839. (Bibliothèque de la jeunesse chrétienne) 1. éd.
　　This translation omits "Micer Codro," "A visit to Palos," and "Manifesto of Alonzo de Ojeda."

* Voyages et découvertes des compagnons de Colomb. Traduit de l'anglais de Washington Irving, par Henri Lebrun [*pseud.*] Tours, A. Mame, 1841. (Bibliothèque de la jeunesse chrétienne [2. sér.]) 2. édition.

* —— Tours, A. Mame, 1843. (Bibliothèque de la jeunesse chrétienne [2. sér.]) 3. édition.

* —— Tours, A. Mame, 1851. (Bibliothèque de la jeunesse chrétienne [2. sér.]) 5. édition.

* —— Tours, A. Mame, 1858. (Bibliothèque de la jeunesse chrétienne [2. sér.]) 7. édition.

* —— Tours, A. Mame, 1861. (Bibliothèque de la jeunesse chrétienne [2. sér.]) 8. édition.

* —— Tours, A. Mame, 1864. (Bibliothèque de la jeunesse chrétienne [2. sér.]) 9. édition.

* —— Tours, A. Mame, 1867. (Bibliothèque de la jeunesse chrétienne [2. sér.]) 10. édition.

* —— Tours, A. Mame, 1870. (Bibliothèque de la jeunesse chrétienne [2. sér.]) 11. édition.

* —— Tours, A. Mame, 1873. (Bibliothèque de la jeunesse chrétienne [2. sér.]) 12. édition.

* —— Tours, A. Mame, 1876. (Bibliothèque de la jeunesse chrétienne [2. sér.]) 13. édition.

* —— Tours, A. Mame, 1879. (Bibliothèque de la jeunesse chrétienne [2. sér.]) 14. édition.

* —— Tours, A. Mame, 1882. (Bibliothèque de la jeunesse chrétienne [2. sér.]) 15. édition.

* —— Tours, A. Mame, 1885. (Bibliothèque de la jeunesse chrétienne [2. sér.]) 16. édition.

Voyages et découvertes des compagnons de Colomb d'après Washington Irving. Récits d'exploration et de découvertes par J. Girardin. Paris, Hachette et cie, 1880. (Bibliothèque des écoles et des familles)

—— 3. édition. Paris, Hachette et cie, 1893. (Bibliothèque des écoles et des familles)

German

* Reisen der Gefährten des Columbus. Übersetzt von Ph. A. G. von Meyer. Frankfurt, Sauerländer, 1831. 3 v. in 1.

Italian

Viaggi e scoperte dei compagni di Colombo, di Washington Irving. Prima traduzione dall' originale inglese di L. T. Milano, Dalla tip. di Paolo Andrea Molina, 1842.

Extracts

Viaggi di Alonso di Ojeda. Viaggio di Diego di Nicuesa. Avventure di Valdivia e dei suoi compagni e Destino dell' astrologo Micer Codro, autore Washington Irving, traduttore Bartolommeo Poli. (*In* Raccolta di viaggi, dalla scoperta del nuovo continente fino ai di nostri, compilata da F. C. Marmocchi. Prato, Tipografia Giachetti, 1840–45. v. 5)

Spanish

* Los compañeros de Colón . . . Madrid, Gaspar y Roig, 1851.
* . . . Viajes y descubrimientos de los compañeros de Colón, por Washington Irving. Madrid, Gaspar y Roig, 1854. (Biblioteca ilustrada de Gaspar y Roig)

Extracts

Vasco Nuñez de Balboa, descubridor del Océano Pacifico. Trad. por Florencio Varela. Montevideo, Imprenta del Comercio del Plata, 1845.

Swedish

Columbi följeslagare, deras resor och upptäckter. Från original språket. Stockholm, 1832.

THE WILD HUNTSMAN

* The wild huntsman, by Washington Irving (hitherto unpublished) with an introduction by George S. Hellman . . . Boston, The Bibliophile society, 1924.
  "This edition is limited to 455 copies."
  "Washington Irving's manuscript of 'The wild huntsman' is the first dramatization in English of the great German opera, 'Der Freischütz.'"
* Song from The wild huntsman. (*In* The poems of Washington Irving . . . New York, The New York public library, 1931. p. 19)

WOLFERT'S ROOST

See also, II. Selected Works

* Wolfert's Roost and other papers, now first collected. By Washington Irving. New York, G. P. Putnam & co., 1855.
First edition.
Added illus. t.-p.
Illustrations by Felix O. C. Darley.
Contains advertisements dated February, 1855, 12 p.
Contents. — Wolfert's Roost [from The Knickerbocker, April, 1839]. — The birds of spring [from The Knickerbocker, May, 1839]. — The Creole village. A sketch from a steamboat. First published in 1837 [from The Magnolia for 1837; also republished in The Crayon papers]. — Mountjoy, or, Some passages out of the life of a castle-builder [from The Knickerbocker, November–December, 1839]. — The Bermudas. A Shakespearian research [from The Knickerbocker, January, 1840]. — The widow's ordeal, or, A judicial trial by combat [from The Magnolia for 1837]. — The knight of Malta [from The Knickerbocker, February, 1840; pirated by The Evergreen: a monthly magazine, 1840]. — "A time of unexampled prosperity." [from The Knickerbocker, April, 1840; also republished in The Crayon papers with title: The great Mississippi bubble]. — Sketches in Paris in 1825 . . . [from The Knickerbocker, November–December, 1840; also republished in The Crayon papers]. — A contented man [from The Literary souvenir . . . edited by A. A. Watts . . . London, 1827; republished in The Crayon papers and in New-York American, Dec. 22, 1826]. — Broek, the Dutch paradise [from The Knickerbocker, January, 1841; also republished in The Crayon papers]. — Guests from Gibbet-Island . . . [from The Knickerbocker, October, 1839]. — The early experiences of Ralph Ringwood . . . [from The Knickerbocker, August–September, 1840; also republished in The Crayon papers]. — The Seminoles [from The Knickerbocker, October, 1840; also republished in The Crayon papers]. — The Count Van Horn [from The Knickerbocker, March, 1840]. — Don Juan: a spectral research [from The Knickerbocker, March, 1841; also republished in The Crayon papers]. — Legend of the engulphed convent [from The Knickerbocker, March, 1840]. — The phantom island [from The Knickerbocker, July, 1839]. — Recollections of the Alhambra [from The Knickerbocker, July, 1839].

* Wolfert's Roost and other tales. Now first collected. By Washington Irving. London, H. G. Bohn, 1855.

Wolfert's Roost and other tales. Now first collected. By Washington Irving. London, George Routledge, 1855.

Possibly this may have preceded the authorized edition published
by Bohn.

Chronicles of Wolfert's Roost and other papers. By Washington
Irving. Author's edition. Leipzig, B. Tauchnitz, 1855. (*Half-title:*
Collection of British authors, v. 324)

* Wolfert's Roost. Transatlantic sketches by Washington Irving.
With portrait of the author. Goettingen, G. H. Wigand, 1855.
(Wigand's pocket miscellany, v. 4)

* Chronicles of Wolfert's Roost and other papers. By Washington
Irving. Author's edition. Edinburgh, Thomas Constable and co.
[etc., etc.] 1855. (Constable's miscellany of foreign literature, v. 4)
Probably this was published by Constable earlier in 1855 as v. 10
of the same series.

Wolfert's Roost and other tales. Now first collected. By Washington
Irving. New York, G. P. Putnam, 1856.

Wolfert's Roost and other papers. Now first collected. By Washington Irving. Author's revised edition. New York, G. P. Putnam's
sons, 1865. (Works . . . Hudson edition, v. 27)
Added title-page.

Wolfert's Roost and other papers; now first collected by Washington
Irving. Author's revised edition. New York, G. P. Putnam's sons
[c 1865]
Riverside edition.

Wolfert's Roost and other papers. New York, G. P. Putnam, 1866.
Riverside edition.

Wolfert's Roost and other papers. Now first collected, by Washington Irving. Author's revised edition. New York, G. P. Putnam
and son, 1868.
On half-title: Riverside edition.
Two added half-titles, one engraved and one illustrated.

Wolfert's Roost and other papers. Now first collected, by Washington Irving. Author's revised edition. Philadelphia, J. B. Lippincott & co., 1870.
Knickerbocker edition.
Two added half-titles, one engraved and one illustrated.

Wolfert's Roost and other papers. Now first collected, by Washington
Irving. Author's revised edition. Philadelphia, J. B. Lippincott &
co., 1871.
Added engr. t.-p.

Wolfert's Roost and other papers. Now first collected, by Washington
Irving. With illustrations. New York, G. P. Putnam [1873]
Knickerbocker edition.

Wolfert's Roost and other papers. Now first collected, by Washington
Irving. Author's revised edition. New York, G. P. Putnam's sons,
1882. (Works . . . Hudson edition, v. 27)

. . . Wolfert's Roost, and other papers. Now first collected, by

Washington Irving. Author's revised edition. New York, G. P. Putnam's sons [1882]
Copyright date: 1865.
Added t.-p., illustrated.
Vol. [27] of a uniform edition in cloth, having at head of title "Hudson edition" (first issued in 1882) and lettered: Irving's works.
* Wolfert's Roost, and Miscellanies . . . New York, J. B. Alden, 1883.
* Wolfert's Roost, and Miscellanies. By Washington Irving. New York, United States book co., successors to John W. Lovell co. [1891] (Lovell's literature series, no. 172)
. . . Wolfert's Roost and other papers. Now first collected, by Washington Irving. Author's revised edition. New York, G. P. Putnam's sons [1902] (*Publisher's lettering:* Irving's works)
At head of title: Hudson edition.
Added engr. t.-p.
Wolfert's Roost, and Miscellanies . . . [New York, Belford co., 188-?]

Extracts

* The Abencerrage; or, Recollections of the Alhambra. (*In* The Romancist, and Novelist's library . . . London, Printed by C. Reynell, Published by J. Clements, 1839-40. v. 3, p. [223]-224)
Bobolink . . . Taylorville, Ill., Parker publishing co. [19-?] (Eight page classics)
* The early experiences of Ralph Ringwood . . . (*In* The Knickerbocker sketch-book . . . New-York, Burgess, Stringer and co., 1845. p. [47]-83)
* The enchanted island; or, The adalantado of the seven cities. (*In* The Romancist, and Novelist's library . . . London, Printed by C. Reynell, Published by J. Clements, 1839-40. v. 2, p. [346]-348)
* Mountjoy, or, Passages out of the life of a castle-builder. By Geoffrey Crayon, gent. (*In* The Knickerbocker sketch-book . . . New-York, Burgess, Stringer and co., 1845. p. [163]-218)
* . . . "A time of unexampled prosperity." New-York, The Rebellion record, 1864. (Reading on the rail, no. 5)
See also, II. Selected Works. Three stories . . . 1930. The great Mississippi bubble.

French

Extracts

* [The Creole village and other stories.] (*In* Contes américains, traduits de l'anglais de M. Irving, Miss Sedgwick [Paulding et Flint] . . . Paris, A. Auffray, 1832)

German

* Wolfert's Rust. Transatlantische Skizzen von Washington Irving. Aus dem Englischen von W. C. Drugulin. Leipzig, C. B. Lorck, 1855. (Conversations- und Reisebibliothek, 11)
* Wolfert's Rust . . . Stuttgart, Heffner [1882?]

Russian

Extracts

Графъ фанъ Горнъ. St.-Petersburg, 1856. (Библіотека для дачъ, v. 72)

The Count van Horn.

Островъ–привидѣніе и Адалантадо семи городовъ. St.-Petersburg, 1856. (Библіотека для дачъ, v. 72)

The phantom island.

Похожденія Ралфа Рингвуда . . . Американская быль. С. Петербургъ, 1856.

The early experiences of Ralph Ringwood.

Spanish

Extracts

* Las memorias de un gobernador. Por Washington Irving. Traducción del inglés por M. Juderías Bénder. Segunda edición. Madrid, 1882.

The early experiences of Ralph Ringwood.

Nothing is known of the first edition.

VII. WORKS ASCRIBED TO IRVING

The following titles have been repeatedly ascribed to Irving, and are listed here for the guidance of the reader. With the exception of the first item, to which Irving may have contributed, almost certainly none of these was written by him.

* Fragment of a journal of a sentimental philosopher, during his residence in the city of New-York. To which is added, A discourse upon the nature and properties of eloquence as a science, delivered to his disciples previous to his departure. Found among some papers left at his lodgings . . . New York, E. Sargeant, 1809.
Ascribed to Irving; probably written by Rodman. *See* The life of Washington Irving, I, 125.

Literary picture gallery, and admonitory epistles, to the visitors of Ballston-Spa, by Simeon Senex, esquire. Ballston-Spa, 1808.
See The life of Washington Irving, I, 75.

The manuscript of Diedrich Knickerbocker, jun. New York, Bliss & White, 1824.

— Die Handschrift Diedrich Knickerbockers des Jûngern . . . Leipzig, Rein [1825]

Recollections of a student. (*In* New monthly magazine and literary journal. London, 1823. v. 7, p. 205–210)
See The life of Washington Irving, Chap. IX, note 164.

* A word in season, touching the present misunderstanding in the Episcopal church. By a layman . . . New York, Printed by D. & G. Bruce, 1811.

VIII. LIFE AND LETTERS

* The life and letters of Washington Irving. Edited by his nephew, Pierre M. Irving . . . London, Richard Bentley, 1862–64. 4 v. 8vo.
  Vol. 1–3 have on t.-p.: In three volumes; v. 4: In four volumes.
* The life and letters of Washington Irving. Edited by his nephew, Pierre M. Irving . . . New York, G. P. Putnam, 1862–64. 4 v. 12mo.

The life and letters of Washington Irving . . . London, Bohn, 1864.

The life and letters of Washington Irving, by his nephew, Pierre M. Irving . . . [New York, Putnam, c 1869] 3 v. (The works of Washington Irving. The Kinderhook edition [v. 11–12])

The life and letters of Washington Irving . . . Revised and condensed, in three volumes. New York, G. P. Putnam, 1869.
Riverside edition.

The life and letters of Washington Irving. By his nephew, Pierre M. Irving. Revised and condensed . . . New York, G. P. Putnam's sons [c 1869] 3 v.
People's edition.

The life and letters of Washington Irving . . . New York, G. P. Putnam, 1870. 3 v.
Riverside edition.

The life and letters of Washington Irving. By his nephew, Pierre M. Irving. Revised and condensed . . . Philadelphia, J. B. Lippincott & co., 1872.
Knickerbocker edition.
Added engr. t.-p.

The life and letters of Washington Irving. By his nephew, Pierre M. Irving. New York, Putnam [1873?] 3 v.
Knickerbocker edition.

The life and letters of Washington Irving, by his nephew, Pierre M. Irving . . . New York and London, G. P. Putnam's sons [1882?] 3 v.
Vol. [12–14] of a uniform edition in cloth, having at head of title "Hudson edition" (first issued in 1882) and lettered: Irving's works.

The life and letters of Washington Irving, by his nephew, Pierre M. Irving . . . New York, G. P. Putnam's sons, 1883. 3 v.
Memorial edition.
300 numbered copies.

The life and letters of Washington Irving, by his nephew, Pierre M. Irving. Revised and condensed . . . New York, G. P. Putnam's sons, 1892–95. 3 v.
People's edition.

IX. PERIODICALS AND COLLECTIONS

TO WHICH IRVING CONTRIBUTED OR WHICH CONTAIN EXTRACTS
FROM HIS WORKS

Almost true tales. Stories by Washington Irving — Nathaniel Hawthorne — Thomas Bulfinch — M. V. Farrington — Charles Kingsley — and "Ouida." Illustrated. New York and London, G. P. Putnam's sons [1912?]

Contains Rip Van Winkle and The legend of Sleepy Hollow.

* American literature. Durham, N. C., Duke university press, 1932–34.

v. 4, p. 296. New verses by Washington Irving. By J. H. Birss; v. 6, p. 185–195. Washington Irving's letters to Mary Kennedy. By Stanley T. Williams and Leonard B. Beach; v. 5, p. 364–367. An uncollected tale by Washington Irving. By Nelson F. Adkins.

* The Americana collector. Edited by C. F. Heartman . . . Metuchen, N. J., 1925. v. 1, Nov., 1925. p. 64–66.

An unwritten drama of Lord Byron with introduction by Thomas Ollive Mabbott.

Since July, 1926, v. 2, no. 4, this periodical has been called: The American collector.

* The Analectic magazine, containing selections from foreign reviews and magazines of such articles as are most valuable, curious, or entertaining. Philadelphia, Moses Thomas, 1813–15.

Edited anonymously by Irving from late in 1812 to January, 1815. After Irving resigned, the magazine was continued under the editorship of Thomas Isaac Wharton.

Contributions by Irving

March, 1813. Review of the works of Robert Treat Paine. [Republished in Spanish papers]

August, 1813. Biography of Captain James Lawrence. [Published separately in 1813; republished in Spanish papers]

See also, VI. Individual works: Biography of James Lawrence, esq.

September, 1813. Captain Lawrence. [A note on Biography of Captain James Lawrence; included in the separately published Biography . . . 1813; republished in Spanish papers]

— The lay of the Scottish fiddle: a tale of Havre de Grace.
A notice of Paulding's poem.
Sometimes ascribed to Irving.

November, 1813. Biographical notice of the late Lieutenant Burrows.
[Republished in Spanish papers]

December, 1813. Biographical memoir of Commodore Perry. [Republished in Spanish papers]

February, 1814. Traits of Indian character. [Republished in all English editions of The sketch book, and in all American editions after the third]

March, 1814. Odes, naval songs, and other occasional poems. By Edwin C. Holland. [Republished in Spanish papers]
A review.

June, 1814. Philip of Pokanoket. An Indian memoir. [Republished in all English editions of The sketch book, and in all American editions after the third]

July, 1814. Lord Byron.
A notice.
Sometimes ascribed to Irving.

September, 1814. Biographical memoir of Captain David Porter. [Republished in Spanish papers]

March, 1815. A biographical sketch of Thomas Campbell. [Republished, with revision, from The poetical works of Thomas Campbell; republished in Spanish papers]

* The Atlantic souvenir; Christmas and New Year's offering, 1827–1828. Philadelphia, H. C. Carey & I. Lea [c 1826–27]
Imprint varies.
1827, p. 146–148. On Passaic falls; 1828, p. 294. The dull lecture; contributed by Irving.

* Bolster's quarterly magazine . . . MDCCCXXVI. Cork, John Bolster [etc., etc.] 1828 [i.e., 1826] v. 1, p. 28–39.
A biographical sketch of Thomas Campbell, esq. By Geoffry [sic] Crayon, gent.; pirated.

The Book hunter. [place?] Jan., 1932.
Contains Biography of James Lawrence.

* The Bouquet of popular literature. London, 1822. v. 1, p. 11–26.
"Review [of Bracebridge Hall], with selected extracts in illustration."

* The Casket. London, J. Murray, 1836. April.
Contains extracts from Abbotsford.

* The Chautauquan. New York, Chautauqua press, 1907. v. 48, p. 409–415.
English writers on America.

* The Chronicle express. New York, 1802–03. Nov. 25, Dec. 2, 6, 13, 1802; Jan. 20, 24, Feb. 10, Apr. 25, 1803.

Contains the last eight letters of Jonathan Oldstyle, reprinted by the editor, Peter Irving.

* The Cornhill magazine . . . London, Smith, Elder & co., 1860. v. 1, p. [582]

Written in the Deepdene album.

The Evergreen: a monthly magazine. 1840–

Pirated from The Knickerbocker, within three months of their appearance: The knight of Malta; Pelayo and the merchant's daughter; The conspiracy of Neamathla.

* Five hundred curious and interesting narratives and anecdotes; comprising The wonderful book, The anecdote book, Sailors' yarns, Salmagundi, and The domestic manners of the Americans. Embellished with numerous engravings. Glasgow, Richard Griffin and co., 1844.

Contains Salmagundi, 72 p.

Each part (*i.e.*, The wonderful book, The anecdote book, etc.) has separate pagination.

The Forget-me-not. Philadelphia, Judah Dobson, 1828.

Contains Ellen. A sketch from "Scenes and thoughts"; sometimes ascribed to Irving.

* Friendship's offering: a Christmas, New Year and birthday present, for MDCCCXLIX. Boston, Phillips & Sampson, 1849. p. [326]–330.

The haunted ship. A true story — as far as it goes. By the author of "The sketch-book."

Reprinted from Heath's book of beauty. 1836 . . .

Galignani's messenger. Paris, 1824. Sept. 18[?]

Contains an article on Louis XVIII contributed by Irving; Irving also contributed an article on Byron, probably in 1824. The only complete file of the Messenger, in Galignani's shop in Paris, is not accessible.

* The Gift. A Christmas and New Year's present for 1836. Edited by Miss Leslie. Philadelphia, E. L. Cary & A. Hart, 1836. p. 166–171.

An unwritten drama of Lord Byron; contributed by Irving.

* Godey's lady's book. New York [etc.] 1830–98.

Irving is sometimes mentioned as a contributor to Godey's lady's book, but no contributions by him have been identified.

* The Golden book. New York, Review of reviews corporation, 1929. v. 10, no. 60, p. 78–84.

The spectre bridegroom.

* Heath's book of beauty. 1836. With nineteen beautifully finished engravings, from drawings by the first artists. Edited by the Countess of Blessington. London, Longman, Rees, Orme, Brown, Green, and Longman [etc., etc., 1836] p. [253]–257.

The haunted ship. A true story — as far as it goes. By the author of "The sketch-book."

Contributed by Irving.

* Historical magazine. New York, C. B. Richardson; London, Trübner & co., 1860. v. 4, p. 181.

Written in the Deepdene album.

* The Home book of the picturesque: or, American scenery, art, and literature. Comprising a series of essays by Washington Irving, W. C. Bryant, Fenimore Cooper, Miss Cooper, N. P. Willis, Bayard Taylor, H. T. Tuckerman, E. L. Magoon, Dr. Bethune, A. B. Street, Miss Field, etc. With thirteen engravings on steel, from pictures by eminent artists, engraved expressly for this work. New-York, G. P. Putnam, 1852. p. [71]–78.

Added engr. t.-p.: The Home book of the picturesque. New York, G. P. Putnam, 1852.

Title vignette.

The Catskill mountains; contributed by Irving; reprinted in Spanish papers.

* The Independent. New York, Independent corporation, 1917–18. v. 89, p. 407–408. Legend of the rose of the Alhambra; v. 94, p. 88–91. Old-fashioned Christmas dinner.

* The Intelligent reader: designed as a sequel to The Child's guide . . . Springfield, G. and C. Merriam, 1835. p. 159–161.

On cover: Stereotype edition.

The sage decision of the renowned Governor Van Twiller; reprinted from A history of New York.

The Kaleidoscope. 1819–24.

1819, Aug. 24 contains The wife; 1824 contains two letters of Jonathan Oldstyle; reprinted.

* Kettell, Samuel. Specimens of American poetry. Boston, S. G. Goodrich and co., 1829. v. 2, p. 173–174.

The falls of the Passaic.

* The Knickerbocker, or, New-York monthly magazine. New York, Peabody & co., 1839–41.

Contributions by Irving

March, 1839. To the editor of The Knickerbocker. [Republished in Spanish papers; the first paragraph republished in A book of the Hudson]

April, 1839. A chronicle of Wolfert's Roost. [Republished in Wolfert's Roost]

May, 1839. The birds of spring. [Republished in Wolfert's Roost] — Sleepy Hollow. [Republished in Spanish papers]

June, 1839. Recollections of the Alhambra. [Republished in Wolfert's Roost]

July, 1839. The enchanted island. [Republished in Wolfert's Roost, with title: The phantom island]

August, 1839. National nomenclature. [Republished in Spanish papers]

— Desultory thoughts on criticism. [Republished in Spanish papers]

September, 1839. Spanish romance. [Republished in Spanish papers]

— Communipaw. [Republished in A book of the Hudson and in Spanish papers]

October, 1839. Conspiracy of the cocked hats. [Republished in Spanish papers]

— Guests from Gibbet-island. [Republished in A book of the Hudson and in Wolfert's Roost]

November, 1839. Mountjoy. [Republished in The Crayon papers and in Wolfert's Roost]

January, 1840. The Bermudas. [Republished in Wolfert's Roost]

— Pelayo and the merchant's daughter. [Republished in Spanish papers, with title: The legend of Pelayo]

— To the editor of The Knickerbocker.
On international copyright.

February, 1840. The knight of Malta. [Republished in Wolfert's Roost]

March, 1840. Legend of the engulphed convent. [Republished in Wolfert's Roost]

— The Count Van Horn. [Republished in Wolfert's Roost]

April, 1840. A time of unexampled prosperity. [Republished in Wolfert's Roost; and in The Crayon papers, with title: The great Mississippi bubble]

May, 1840. Abderahman. [Republished in The Crayon papers and in Spanish papers]

June, 1840. The taking of the veil. [Republished in The Crayon papers]

— The charming Letorières. [Republished in The Crayon papers]

July, 1840. Letter from Granada. [Republished in The Crayon papers and in Spanish papers]

August, September, 1840. The early experiences of Ralph Ringwood. [Republished in The Crayon papers and in Wolfert's Roost]

October, 1840. The Seminoles. [Republished in The Crayon papers and in Wolfert's Roost]

November, December, 1840. Sketches in Paris in 1825. [Republished in The Crayon papers and in Wolfert's Roost]

January, 1841. Broek: or, The Dutch paradise. [Republished in The Crayon papers and in Wolfert's Roost]

March, 1841. Don Juan: a spectral research. [Republished in The Crayon papers and in Wolfert's Roost]

October, 1841. American researches in Italy. [Republished in The Crayon papers]

* The Knickerbocker gallery: a testimonial to the editor of The Knickerbocker magazine [Lewis Gaylord Clark] from its contributors. With forty-eight portraits on steel . . . New-York, S. Hueston, 1855. p. [15]-22.
   Conversations with Talma. From rough notes in a common-place book. By the author of The sketch-book.
   Irving's name is given in the table of contents.
* The Knickerbocker sketch-book: a library of select literature. Edited by Lewis Gaylord Clark . . . New-York, Burgess, Stringer and co., 1845. p. [25]-29. The first locomotive again. By Washington Irving; p. [47]-83. The early experiences of Ralph Ringwood. By Washington Irving; p. [115]-132. Guests from Gibbet-island. A legend of Communipaw. By Washington Irving; p. [163]-218. Mountjoy: or, Passages out of the life of a castle-builder. By Geoffrey Crayon, gent.
* The Lady's cabinet album . . . New-York, Published for the booksellers [1839] p. 291.
   Added engr. t.-p.: Album. New York, Published by Elisha Sands. The dull lecture; reprinted from The Atlantic souvenir.
* The Literary gazette, and journal of belles lettres, arts, sciences, etc. . . . London, W. Pople, 1819. v. 3, p. 617-620, 634-635, 648-650. Selections from The sketch book.
* The Literary souvenir; or, Cabinet of poetry and romance. Edited by Alaric A. Watts . . . London, Longman, Rees, Orme, Brown, & Green; and John Andrews, 1827. p. [1]-9.
   A contented man. By Geoffrey Crayon, gent.; contributed by Irving; republished in The Crayon papers and in Wolfert's Roost.
* The Literary world; a journal of science, literature, and art . . . New York, E. A. & G. L. Duyckinck, 1851. Nov. 22, p. 408.
   "Correction of a misstatement respecting 'Astoria,' by Washington Irving."
   A letter to the editor, correcting the statement that he [Irving] had been paid by Astor for writing Astoria.
* The Magnolia for 1837. Edited by Henry William Herbert. New York, Bancroft & Holley [etc., etc., c 1836]
   p. [254] The wrath of Peter Stuyvesant; p. [257]-274. The widow's ordeal, or, A judicial trial by combat. By the author of the "Sketch book"; p. [315]-326. The creole [sic] village. A sketch from a steamboat. By the author of the "Sketch book."
* — The Magnolia for 1843 [i.e., 1837] Edited by Henry William Herbert. New-York, Robert P. Bixby & co. [1837]
* Missouri historical review. Columbia, Mo., 1910. v. 5, p. [15]-33. . . . Travels in Missouri and the South. Notes by F. A. Sampson. Extracts from Astoria.
The Morning chronicle. New York, 1802-03.

The letters of Jonathan Oldstyle. No. 1, Nov. 15, No. 2, Nov. 20, No. 3, Dec. 1, No. 4, Dec. 4, No. 5, Dec. 11, 1802; No. 6, Jan. 17, No. 7, Jan. 22, No. 8, Feb. 8, No. 9, Apr. 23, 1803.

New-York American. New York, 1826, Dec. 22.
Contains A contented man.

* The New-York book of poetry . . . New-York, George Dearborn, 1837. p. 105–106.
Added engr. t.-p.; vignette.
Edited by Charles Fenno Hoffman.
"By natives of the state of New York."
The falls of the Passaic; contributed by Irving.

* New-York mirror, a weekly journal, devoted to literature and the fine arts . . . New-York, 1833–36.
v. 11, p. 136 [Verse in Stratford album]; v. 12, p. 318. Advance excerpts from A tour on the prairies, The honey camp, and A bee hunt; v. 13, p. 218. A haunted ship. A true story — as far as it goes; v. 14, p. 198. Advance excerpts from Astoria.

* New York public library. Bulletin. New York, The New York public library, 1930. v. 34, p. 763–779.
The poems of Washington Irving, brought together from various sources by William R. Langfeld.

The New-York review; or, Critical journal. To be continued as occasion requires. March 1809. Containing Strictures on a pamphlet entitled "Fragments [sic] of the journal of a sentimental philosopher." . . . New-York, Inskeep & Bradford [1809]
No further issues are known to have been published; may be partly by Irving. Cf. The life of Washington Irving, I, 125.

* North American review. Boston, Gray and Bowen, 1832. v. 35, p. 342–371.
A review of Wheaton's History of the Northmen; republished in Spanish papers and in Essays from the North American review, ed. A. T. Rice. London [1879?]

* Opening addresses. Edited by Laurence Hutton. New-York, The Dunlap society, 1887. p. 22–26. (Publications of the Dunlap society, v. 3)
"Written by Washington Irving for the re-opening of the Park theater, New-York. Spoken by Thomas Abthorpe Cooper. Sept. 9, 1807."

The Plaindealer. 1887.
Jan. 28. [Letter to the editor, on the charge of Anglophilism]; Feb. 18. [Letter to William Cullen Bryant, February 16, 1837]

* The Quarterly review. London, John Murray, 1830–31. v. 43, p. 55–80. The conquest of Granada. [An article by Irving]; incorporated in the introduction to A chronicle of the conquest of Granada . . . New York, G. P. Putnam, 1850; republished in Spanish

papers; v. 44, p. [321]–342. A review of A year in Spain. By a young American [Alexander Slidell Mackenzie]

* Quinn, A. H., ed. Representative American plays. New York, The Century co., 1917. p. 141–164.
Charles the Second, by John Howard Payne and Washington Irving.

The Reader . . . Nov., 1906.
Contains The legend of Sleepy Hollow.

* Roberts' semi-monthly magazine. Boston, G. Roberts, 1841. v. 1, p. 55–57.
The wife.

* The Romancist, and Novelist's library; the best works of the best authors. London, Printed by C. Reynell, Published by J. Clements, 1839–40.
v. 2, p. [142] The young robber; p. [346]–348. The enchanted island; or, The adalantado of the seven cities. v. 3, p. [78]–80. Rip Van Winkle, a tale; p. [223]–224. The Abencerrage, or, Recollections of the Alhambra.

* Sands of gold, (sifted from the floods of fugitive literature.) Number one . . . New York, Morris & Willis, 1844. p. 31–32. (Mirror library, no. 15)
The wife.

Schweikert, H. C., ed. Short stories . . . New York, Harcourt, Brace and co. [c 1925]
Contains The legend of Sleepy Hollow.

— Enlarged edition. New York, Chicago, Harcourt, Brace and co., 1934.
Contains The legend of Sleepy Hollow.

* Scribner's magazine. New York, 1910. v. 48, p. 461–482, 597–616.
Correspondence of Washington Irving and John Howard Payne ⟨1821–1828⟩

Select American classics; being selections from Irving's Sketch book, Webster's Orations and Emerson's Essays, as published in the Eclectic English classics. New York, American book co. [c 1896]

* Select reviews of literature, and spirit of foreign magazines . . . Philadelphia, John F. Watson, 1812–1813.
Irving became the editor late in 1812. In January, 1813 the name was changed to The Analectic magazine. After Irving resigned, the magazine was continued under the editorship of Thomas Isaac Wharton.

* Sewanee review. Sewanee, Tenn., University press, 1917. v. 25, p. 1–19.
The Kennedy papers. A sheaf of unpublished letters from Washington Irving. Edited by Killis Campbell.

* The Southwest review. Dallas, Texas, Southern Methodist university, 1934. v. 19, p. 449–454.

Polly Holman's wedding. Notes by Washington Irving. Edited by Stanley T. Williams and Ernest E. Leisy.

Specimens of the British poets, with biographical and critical notices, and an essay on English poetry. London, John Murray, 1819.
Contains A biographical sketch of Thomas Campbell.

* The Spirit of the Fair . . . New York, John F. Trow, 1864. p. 126, 138-9.
Published during the Metropolitan fair for the U. S. Sanitary Commission in New York, 1864.
No. 11 (Apr. 16) and 12 (Apr. 18) contain The story of Pelayo (now published for the first time); republished in Spanish papers.

The Student's pastime, being a selection of the most esteemed works of Miss Edgeworth, W. Irving, Miss Mitford, T. Moore, to which are added numerous anecdotes and other amusing pieces, by Sidney Dawson. Paris, A. Derache, 1850.
Contains Murad the unlucky [unidentified]

* The Sunnyside book. Authors: Bryant, Curtis, Stedman, [et al.]; with choice papers from Irving. Authors: Wm. Hart, Hows, Darley [et al.] New York, G. P. Putnam & sons, 1871.
p. [18]-26. The wife; p. [32]-36. The historian of Manahatta; p. [46]-52. A contented man; p. [55]-62. Adventure of the little antiquary; p. [66]-72. Early days of Manahatta, or New York; p. [73]-81. The angler; p. [87]-93. The brigands in Italy; p. [106]-112. Capt. Kidd's treasure.

* Yale review. New Haven, Conn., Yale university press, 1927.
v. 16, p. [459]-484. Unpublished letters of Washington Irving. Spanish fêtes and ceremonies. By Stanley T. Williams; v. 17, p. [99]-117. Letters of Washington Irving. Sunnyside and New York chronicles. By Stanley T. Williams.
Reprinted in Letters from Sunnyside and Spain. By Washington Irving. Edited by Stanley T. Williams. New Haven, Yale university press; London, H. Milford, Oxford university press, 1928.

Catalan

Prosadors nord-americans. Barcelona, 1909.
Contains Colomb, Colomb á Barcelona, La vida rural á Anglaterra.

Dutch

Verhalen (Holl., Fr., Duitsche en Eng.) door Ernst Frank, A. F. E. Langbein, Washington Irving, F. H. Greb, Harrisson, A. Romien, Lawrence Sterne en andere schryvers. Amsterdam, Nayler en co. (J. H. v.d. Beek), 1842.
Selections from Irving not identified.

French

Coin des enfants. 2. série. Recueil de contes de F. Beata, W. Irving,
M. Petit, etc., etc. [Paris?] 1906. (Librairie des temps nouveaux)
Selections from Irving not identified.

* Contes américains, traduits de l'anglais de M. Irving, Miss Sedgwick
[Paulding et Flint] . . . Paris, A. Auffray, 1832.
Note at beginning: "La littérature américaine n'est guère encore
qu'à son aurore: Cooper et Irving ont seuls passé l'Atlan-
tique . . ."
Contains The Creole village and other stories by Irving.

* Contes, morceaux et anecdotes tirés de W. Irving, Gally Knight,
W. Scott, etc., suivis de quelques poésies . . . Paris, Derache, 1840.
Contains Rip Van Winkle and The spectre bridegroom.

* Reid, Mayne. La Baie d'Hudson . . . Paris, 1878.
Contains Le Val Dormant.

* — — Paris [n.d.]

* Revue encyclopédique. Paris, 1829. v. 43, p. 719.
A review of A chronicle of the conquest of Granada, with extracts.

German

Abendzeitung. Dresden, Arnold, 1824. No. 236–243.
Contains Aus den Erzählungen eines Reisenden.

Eos. München, Fleischmann, 1824. No. 143 ff. Der dicke Herr;
No. 152 ff. Die alten Sitten; No. 154–155. Duelle.

Erzählungen . . . Erstes Bdchn. Leipzig, Schurmann, 1830.
Contains Der Goldmacher nach W. Irving, von Karl Friedrich
Heinrich Strass.

Europa. [place? date?] No. 1.
Contains extracts from Abbotsford.

Gesellschafter, oder, Blätter für Geist und Herz. Berlin, Maurer,
1824. No. 140.
Contains extracts from Jonathan Oldstyle's Briefe.

Herkules und andere Sagen. Von Gustav Schwab, Washington Irving,
Ferdinand Bässler, Konrad Fischer. Hrsg. von d. Lehrer Vereini-
gung für Kunstpflege. Berlin, Reutlingen, Ensslin & Leiblin, 1823.
(Bunte Jugendbücher, 11)
Selection from Irving not identified.

* Der Kranz; oder, Erholungen für Geist und Herz. Eine Unterhaltungsschrift für gebildete Leser hrsg. von Karoline von Woltmann. Prag, 1824. Jahr. 1824. 1. Hft.
Stratford am Avon.

Literarisches Conversationsblatt. Leipzig, Brockhaus, 1825. No. 174,
p. 696.
Translation of some of Irving's remarks on criticism, from The
sketch book.

* Magazin für die Literatur des Auslandes. Berlin, Hayn [etc., etc.] 1835–55.

    1835. 7. Bd., p. [141]–142. A tour on the prairies.

    1835. 8. Bd., p. [585] Ein dramatischer Entwurf Lord Byron's.

    1836. 9. Bd., p. 19–20. Legenden aus der Zeit der Eroberung Spaniens.

    1836. 10. Bd., p. [561]–562; 566–568; 570–571; 575–576. Washington Irving's "Astoria."

    1837. 11. Bd., p. 28. Eine Menschenjagd.

    1837. 11. Bd., p. [305]–306, 311–312. Washington Irving's "Capitain Bonneville."

    1850. 37. Bd., p. [213]–215. Washington Irving's Leben des Muhammed's und seiner Nachfolger.

    1851. 40. Bd., p. [333]–335, 339–340, 343–344, 346–348, 350–351. Muhammed's Leben, Wahrheit und Dichtung.

    1855. 48. Bd., p. 404. George Washington's Abstammung.

Morgenblatt für gebildete Stände. Stuttgart und München, J. G. Cotta, 1819–24.

    1819, No. 269–270. Die Seereise; No. 283. Landleben in England; 1822, p. 152 ff. Reiseabenteuer; 1824, No. 132. [Translation of My uncle John]

Neueste Schriften . . . Hamburg, 1836. v. 3.

    Contains Die Unterjochung Spaniens. Legende nach Washington Irving in der *Literary Gazette* [by Hans Georg Lotz]

Novellenschatz des Auslandes, hrsg. von Paul Heyse und Hermann Kurz. München, Oldenbourg [1872–75] 14 v.

    Bd. 3, p. 1–92: Wolfert Webber.

Originalien aus dem Gebiete der Wahrheit, Kunst, Laune und Phantasie. Redigiert und vorgelegt von Georg Lotz. Hamburg, 1836.

    No. 12–14. Der Untergang der Familie Julian. ⟨Nach Washington Irving in der *Literary Gazette*.⟩ No. 43/53. Die Unterjochung Spaniens. Legende nach Washington Irving von Hans Georg Lotz.

Von Goldsuchern und Schatzgräbern. Erzählungen für Jugend und Volk. Donauwörth, L. Auer, 1921. (Donauwörther Volksbücher, Bd. 1)

Zeitung für die elegante Welt. Leipzig, Voss, 1822. No. 206–208.
Contains extracts from Bracebridge Hall.

Icelandic

Norðri. [place?] 1853–61.

    Edited by Bjørn Jønnson and Jøn Jønnson.

    Contains selections from Mahomet and his successors.

Ný sumargjöf. Copenhagen, 1859–62, 1865.

    Published by Páll Sveinsson; edited by Steingrímur Thorsteinsson.

    Contains translations of stories by Irving.

Italian

Un atto di virtù, di Carlo de Bernard. Versione di F.–M. Milano, per Borroni e Scotti, 1846. (*On half-title:* Florilegio romantico, terza serie, v. 23)

Contains Lo straniero misterioso.

Fiori e glorie della letteratura inglese, offerti nelle due lingue inglese ed italiana da Marcello Mazzoni, autore dei cenni biografici e delle note di cui quest' opera è corredata. Milano, Tipografia e libreria Pirotta e c., 1844.

Contains fragments from Irving's works.

Mondo nuovo e cose vecchie, di G. B. Carta. Milano, Presso Omobono Manini [183–?]

Contains Filippo di Pokanoket, leggenda indiana; L'abazio di Westmister [*sic*]; Il viaggio; La vigilia di Natale.

Nuovo raccoglitore . . . [Milano? 1826?]

Contains Lo straniero misterioso.

Passatempi morali; ossia, Scelta di novelle . . . da autori celebri inglesi e francesi, tradotte ad uso delle giovani . . . Londra, 1826.

Contains La sposa, La vedova e suo figlio, and La vittima del crepacuore.

Il Presagio, ricordo di letteratura. Strenna pel capo d'anno. Milano, Carlo Canadelli [1841]

Contains Il fantasma.

Raccolta di viaggi, dalla scoperta del nuovo continente fino ai di nostri, compilata da F. C. Marmocchi. Prato, Tipografia Giachetti, 1840–45. v. 5.

Contains Viaggi di Alonso di Ojeda, Viaggio di Diego di Nicuesa, Avventure di Valdivia e dei suoi compagni e Destino dell' astrologo Micer Codro.

Translated by Bartolommeo Poli.

Polish

Koran . . . z Arabskiego przekład Polski J. Murzy Tarak Buczackiego . . . Wzbogacony objaśnieniami W. Kościuszki. Poprzedzony zyciorysem Mahometa z W. Irving . . . Warszawa, 1858. 2 v.

Vol. 1 contains Życie Mahometa.

Russian

Московскій Телеграфъ. Moscow, 1826–28.

v. 5, p. 14, 75, 125. The haunted house; v. 5, p. 28–49; v. 6, p. 159–171. Annette Delarbre; v. 7, p. 62–102, 130–150, 167–196. Wolfert Webber; v. 9, p. 116–142, 161–187. The legend of Sleepy Hollow; v. 12, p. 14–37, 66–83. The student of Salamanca.

Spanish

El Artista.   Madrid [1835] v. 1, no. 16.
Aventura de un estudiante alemán.

* Aventuras de un misántropo. Por X. B. Saintine. Madrid, Barcelona, 1860. p. 289–335.
El retrato misterioso.

* — — [Madrid, Barcelona, 18–?]
p. 295–298. El misterioso extranjero; p. 298–335. Historia del joven italiano.

* Biblioteca de la juventud. [n.p., n.d.] (Leyendas maravillosas)
p. 35–39. Leyenda del astrólogo árabe; p. 50–75. El príncipe Ahmed al Kamel; ó, El peregrino de amor.

* Colección de novelas. Traducidas por Don Rafael García Tapia. Granada, 1849.
Contains La rosa de la Alhambra.

* La Crónica. Semanario popular económico. Colección de artículos de viages, de literatura, novelas, cuentos, anécdotas, costumbres, etc. Madrid, 1845.
p. 206–207. Amores del rey Don Rodrigo con la princesa Eliata; p. 219–222. Leyendas de la conquista de España.

* . . . Cuentos clásicos del norte. Segunda serie. Por Wáshington Írving, Nathániel Háwthorne, Édward Éverett Hale . . . Traducción de Carmen Torres Calderón de Pinillos. Nueva York, Doubleday, Page & co., 1920. (Biblioteca interamericana, 3)
p. [9]–42. Rip Van Winkle; p. [43]–96. La leyenda del Valle Encantado.

Horas de invierno. Madrid, 1836. No. 16, p. 137–168.
El espectro desposado. Tr. by E. de O.

Leyendas extraordinarias, por N. Hawthorne, E. Poe y Washington Irving. Traducción del inglés por M. Juderías Bénder. Madrid, Manuel Tello, 1882. v. 3, p. 39–79.
El caballero sin cabeza.

Museo de familias. Barcelona [1840] v. 4.
Contains El album de Waterloo.

* El Museo mexicano; ó, Miscelanea pintoresca de amenidades curiosas é instructivas. México, Lo imprime y publica Ignacio Cumplido, 1844. v. 4, p. 522–523.
Costumbres inglesas. La Noche buena.

Novelas españolas . . . Brunswick [Maine] Imprenta de Griffin, 1830.
Edited by H. W. Longfellow.
Contains El serrano de las Alpujarras and El cuadro misterioso.

— New York, 1842.
Edited with a translation, by Julio Soler.

— Brunswick [Maine] 1845.
Edited by H. W. Longfellow.

Nuevo siglo ilustrado.   Madrid, 1869.   May 2, 9.
   Contains El album de Waterloo.
Semanario pintoresco español.   Madrid, 1840.   Oct. 18, 25.
   Contains Cuento de la Alhambra.   El comandante Manco y el
   soldado.
* Tareas de un solitario; 6, Nueva colección de novelas.   [Por D. Jorge
   Montgomery.]   Madrid, Imprenta de Espinosa, 1829.
   Probably this was the first version of Irving's works in Spanish.
   p. [1]–15.   El sueño; p. 63–94.   El serrano de las Alpujarras;
   p. 95–157.   El cuadro misterioso.

X. MISCELLANEA

* Album.   New York, J. C. Riker [183–?]
  Autograph album, with illustrations of Irving's works.
* Astor library, New York. Trustees. Annual report . . . 1850–[56].
  Albany, G. Van Benthuysen, 1850–56.
  Irving was named a trustee of the Astor library in 1839 and was
     President from 1849 to 1859.
Caballero, Fernán. Two unpublished anecdotes by Fernán Caballero
  preserved by Washington Irving. Edited by E. H. Hespelt and
  S. T. Williams. (In Modern language notes. Baltimore, Johns
  Hopkins press, 1934. v. 49, p. 25–31)
Campoamor, Ramón de . . . Colón. Poema. Valencia, 1853.
  Contains Historia del descubrimiento del Nuevo-Mundo.
Colton, G. H. Tecumseh; or, The West thirty years since. A poem
  New-York, Wiley and Putnam, 1842.
  Dedicated to Irving.
Davidson, L. M. Poetical remains of the late Lucretia Maria David-
  son, collected and arranged by her mother, with a biography, by
  Miss Sedgwick. Philadelphia, Lea and Blanchard, 1841.
  Dedicated to Irving.
— — Philadelphia, Lea and Blanchard, 1843.
  Dedicated to Irving.
* Ellsworth, H. L. Washington Irving on the prairie; or, A narrative
  of a tour of the southwest in the year 1832 by Henry Leavitt Ells-
  worth, edited by Stanley T. Williams and Barbara D. Simison.
  New York, Rufus Rockwell Wilson, inc., 1936.
  Ellsworth describes Irving's experience on the prairies.
Grattan, T. C. High-ways and by-ways. London, G. and W. B.
  Whittaker, 1824. 2 v.
  Dedicated to Irving.
Guilbert, Edmund. The home of Washington Irving, illustrated . . .
  New York, 1867.
Immermann, Karl. Skizzen und Grillen. Die Gelehrte Cousine.
  (In Morgenblatt für gebildete Stände. Stuttgart und München,
  1829. No. 4, p. 13)
  Poem containing allusion to Irving.

[Irving, Theodore] Souvenirs of Old England.   By an Anglo-American.   London, 1830.
By Irving's nephew.

— — The conquest of Florida, by Hernando de Soto.   Philadelphia, Carey, Lea & Blanchard, 1835.   2 v.

* The Irving library . . .   New York, John B. Alden, 1883–

* Irving literary institute of Philadelphia.   Constitution and by-laws of the Irving literary institute, organized January 17th, 1856 . . . Philadelphia, O. P. Glessner, printer, 1859.

— — Journal . . .   Philadelphia, 1856–

* The Irving offering: a token of affection, for 1851.   New-York, Leavitt and company, 1851.

The Irving offering for 1852.   New York, Leavitt and co., 1852.

The Irving sketchbook, published semi-monthly by the Irving association.   Elmira, 1854.

[James, G. P. R.]   Delaware; or, The ruined family.   A tale.   Edinburgh, 1833.   3 v.
Dedicated to Irving.

— — Thirty years since: or, The ruined family.   A tale.   By G. P. R. James . . .   London, Simpkin, Marshall & co., 1848.

* [Kennedy, J. P.] Horse Shoe Robinson; a tale of the Tory ascendancy. By the author of 'Swallow Barn.'   Philadelphia, Carey, Lea & Blanchard, 1835.
Dedicated to Irving.

Kingsley, M. E.   Outline studies in literature.   [The legend of Sleepy Hollow.]   Boston, Palmer company [19–?]

* Latrobe, C. J.   The rambler in North America, MDCCCXXXII– MDCCCXXXIII.   New York, Harper & brothers, 1835.   2 v.
Dedicated to Irving.

Lotz, Georg.   Kerkergenossen.   Roman nach Washington Irving. Berlin, Jonas, 1840.

— Der Untergang der Familie Julian.   ⟨Nach Washington Irving in der *Literary Gazette*.⟩   (*In* Originalien aus dem Gebiete der Wahrheit, Kunst, Laune und Phantasie.   Redigiert und vorgelegt von Georg Lotz.   Hamburg, 1836.   No. 12–14)

— Die Unterjochung Spaniens.   Legende nach Washington Irving von Hans Georg Lotz.   (*In* Originalien aus dem Gebiete der Wahrheit, Kunst, Laune und Phantasie.   Redigiert und vorgelegt von Georg Lotz.   Hamburg, 1836.   No. 43/53)

— Die Unterjochung Spaniens.   Legende nach Washington Irving in der *Literary Gazette*.   (*In* Neueste Schriften.   Hamburg, 1836.   v. 3)

Lynch, Virginia.   Washington Irving footprints, etched by Bernhardt Wall.   New York city, Bernhardt Wall, 1922.

* [Macnish, Robert] The man with the mouth.   (*In* Blackwood's Edinburgh magazine.   Edinburgh, William Blackwood, 1828.   v. 23, p. 597–601)

Signed: A modern Pythagorean.

Adapted from The stout gentleman.

* — The man with the nose. (*In* Blackwood's Edinburgh magazine. Edinburgh, William Blackwood, 1826. v. 20, p. 159–163)

Signed: A modern Pythagorean.

Adapted from The stout gentleman.

* Mitchell, D. G. Dream life, a fable of the seasons. By Ik Marvel. New York, C. Scribner, 1851.

Dedicated to Irving.

Contains a letter from Irving.

All editions after 1863 have Irving's preface.

* [Myers, P. H.] The first of the Knickerbockers: a tale of 1673. New-York, Wiley and Putnam [etc.] 1848.

Dedicated to Irving.

— — New-York, G. P. Putnam [etc.] 1849.

Dedicated to Irving.

* Napione, G. G. Lettera di S. E. il sig. conte e cav. gran-croce Gian-francesco Galeani Napione di Cocconato al chiarissimo sig. Washington Irving, autore della Storia della vita e viaggi di Cristoforo Colombo, traduzione in lingua francese dall' originale inglese, Parigi, 1828. Torino, P. G. Pic, 1829.

[A poem inspired by Annette Delarbre.] (*In* New York American. New York, 1828, Dec. 10)

Signed: Caspar.

* Reflections on Irving's Pride of the village. (*In* New York American. New York, 1820. April 8)

Poem, signed: R. N. E.

* Shakespeare's home; visited and described by Washington Irving and F. W. Fairholt; with a letter from Stratford by J. F. Sabin; and the complete prose works of Shakespeare. With etchings by J. F. and W. W. Sabin. New York, J. Sabin & sons, 1877.

Based on Stratford-on-Avon.

— — New York, 1877.

Large paper edition.

Strass, K. F. H. Der Goldmacher nach W. Irving. (*In* Erzählungen. 1. Bdchn. Leipzig, Schurmann, 1830)

* Tarrytown-on-Hudson, New York. St. Mark's church. Appeal for funds for the completion of St. Mark's church, memorial of Washington Irving, Tarrytown-on-Hudson, N. Y. [n.p., n.d.]

Contains A reminiscence of Sleepy Hollow. By the Rev. Edmund Guilbert, M.A. Mr. Irving as a Christian; reprinted, by permission, from Harper's new monthly magazine.

* Taylor, Bayard. The lands of the Saracen; or, Picture of Palestine, Asia Minor, Sicily and Spain. New York, G. P. Putnam & co., 1855.

Dedicated to Irving.

* Thomas, E. M.   On Irving's Life of Columbus.   (*In* The Critic. New York, 1883.   v. 3, no. 65, p. 143)
  Poem.
* Thornbury, G. W.   Lays and legends; or, Ballads of the New World. London, Saunders and Otley, 1851.
  Dedicated to Irving.
  Vásquez, J. A.   In memory of Washington Irving.   (*In* The Santa Cruz quarterly.   Seville, 1925)
  Williams, J. L.   The land of Sleepy Hollow and the home of Washington Irving.   *See* VI.   Individual works.   The sketch book.

XI. CRITICISM OF IRVING

* Adams, Charles. Memoir of Washington Irving with selections from his works, and criticisms . . . New York, Carlton & Lanahan, 1870.
* Adkins, N. F. Fitz-Greene Halleck: an early Knickerbocker wit and poet. New Haven, Yale university press, 1930.
  See Index.
* Allibone, S. A. [Biographical sketch, bibliography, extracts from letters, reviews, etc.] (*In his* A critical dictionary of English literature, and British and American authors . . . Philadelphia, J. B. Lippincott & co., 1859. v. 1, p. 935-945)
* Álvarez Aguilar, M., *ed.* Washington Irving. Apuntes literarios. Madrid, Compañía ibero-americana de publicaciones [1930] (*In* Las Cien mejores obras de la literatura universal, traducción y prólogo de Miguel Álvarez Aguilar. v. 6, p. 7-12)
* Apetz, P. Washington Irvings Aufenthalt in Dresden. Dresden, 1914. (*In* XL. Jahresbericht des Königlichen Gymnasiums zu Dresden-Neustadt. p. 1-11)
* Arens, E. Washington Irving im Rheinland (1822). Ein Beitrag zur Geschichte der Rhein-Romantik. (*In* Eichendorff-Kalender, 1927/28. Ein romantisches Jahrbuch. Begründet und hrsg. von Wilhelm Kosch. 18. Folge . . . Aichach, L. Schütte, 1927, p. 93-120)
* Axson, Stockton. Washington Irving and the Knickerbocker group. (*In* Rice institute pamphlet. [Houston, Texas] 1933. v. 20, p. 178-195)
* Banks, L. A. Religion of Irving. (*In his* The religious life of famous Americans. Boston and New York [etc.] American tract society [1904] p. 137-147)
* Barnes, H. F. Charles Fenno Hoffman. New York, Columbia university press, 1930.
  See Index.
* Beers, H. A. An outline sketch of American literature. New York, Chautauqua press, 1887. p. 93-101.
* Benson, A. B. Scandinavians in the works of Washington Irving. (*In* Scandinavian studies and notes. Editor: A. M. Sturtevant. Lawrence, Kansas, 1927. v. 9, p. 207-223)
* [Benson, Egbert] Brief remarks on the "Wife" of Washington Irving. New-York, Grattan and Banks, 1819.

* Blackburn, P. C.   Irving's Biography of James Lawrence — and a new discovery.   (*In* Bulletin of the New York public library. New York, 1932.   v. 36, p. 742-743)
* Bowen, E. W.   Washington Irving's place in American literature. (*In* Sewanee review.   Sewanee, Tenn., University press, 1906. v. 14, p. 171-183)
* Boynton, H. W.   Washington Irving . . .   Boston and New York, Houghton Mifflin and co., 1901.
* — — "Irving."   (*In* American writers on American literature, by thirty-seven contemporary writers, edited by John Macy.   New York, Horace Liveright [c 1931] p. 58-71)
* Brainard, C. H.   John Howard Payne, a biographical sketch of the author of "Home sweet home" . . .   Washington, D. C., G. A. Coolidge, 1885.
* Bremer, Fredrika.   The homes of the New World; impressions of America; translated by Mary Howitt.   New York, Harper & brothers, 1853.   v. 1, p. 57-58; 60-61.
* Bruce, Wallace.   Along the Hudson with Washington Irving . . . Poughkeepsie, New York, Press of the A. V. Haight co. [1913?]
* Bryant, W. C.   A discourse on the life, character and genius of Washington Irving, delivered before the New York historical society, at the Academy of music in New York, on the 3d of April, 1860.   New York, Putnam, 1860.
* Burton, Richard.   Literary leaders of America.   A class-book on American literature.   Boston, Lothrop publishing co., 1904.   p. 12-41.
* — Washington Irving's services to American history.   (*In* New England magazine.   Boston, Mass., W. F. Kellogg, 1897.   New series, v. 10, p. 641-653)
* Canby, H. S.   Classic Americans.   A study of eminent American writers from Irving to Whitman.   New York, Harcourt, Brace & co. [1931]
* — Irving the federalist.   (*In* Saturday review of literature.   New York, Time inc., 1926.   v. 3, p. 461-463)
* — The short story in English.   New York, Henry Holt and co. [1909] p. 218-226.
* Cairns, W. B.   British criticisms of American writings, 1815-1833. Madison, Wisconsin, 1922.   (University of Wisconsin studies in language and literature.   No. 14)
* Clark, L. G., *ed.*   The literary remains of the late Willis Gaylord Clark.   New-York, Burgess, Stringer & co., 1844.   p. 278.
* — Memorial of Washington Irving.   Reminiscences of the late Washington Irving.   (*In* Knickerbocker magazine.   New York, John A. Gray, 1860.   v. 55, p. 113-128)
* — Recollections of Washington Irving.   (*In* Lippincott's monthly magazine.   Philadelphia, 1869.   v. 3, p. 552-560)

* Coad, O. S. The Gothic element in American literature before 1835. (*In* Journal of English and Germanic philology. Urbana, Illinois, 1925. v. 24, p. 72–93)

Cody, Sherwin. The story of Washington Irving. (*In his* Four famous American writers. New York, American book co., 1899. p. 10–70)

* Cook, Clarence. A glimpse of Washington Irving at home. (*In* The Century magazine. New York, 1887. v. 34, p. [53]–58)

— Irving at Sunnyside in 1858. (*In* Hours at home. New-York, Charles Scribner & co., 1865. v. 1, p. 507–512)

* Cooke, J. E. A morning at Sunnyside with Washington Irving. (*In* Southern magazine. Baltimore, Southern historical society, 1873. p. 710–716)

* Creighton, William. Sermons on the occasion of the death of the late Washington Irving, preached in Christ Church, Tarrytown, by the Rev. William Creighton, D.D., rector, and the Rev. J. Selden Spencer . . . New-York, Pudney & Russell, 1859.

* Cross, W. L. The development of the English novel. New York, London, The Macmillan co., 1911.
See Index.

* Curtis, G. W. Irving's "Knickerbocker." (*In* The Critic. New York, 1883. v. 3, p. 139–140)

* — Washington Irving. A sketch. New-York, The Grolier club, 1891.

* Dana, R. H. Sketch book. (*In* North American review. Boston, Gray and Bowen, 1819. v. 9, p. 322–356)
A review.

* DeVries, T. Dutch history, art and literature for Americans; lectures given in the University of Chicago . . . Grand Rapids [Michigan] Eerdmans-Sevensma co. [1912] p. [153]–210.

* — Holland's influence on English language and literature. Chicago, C. Grentzebach, 1916. p. 386–387.

* Dunlap, William. Diary of William Dunlap (1766–1839). The memoirs of a dramatist, theatrical manager, painter, critic, novelist, and historian. New York, 1930. 3 v.
Printed for the New York historical society.
See Index.

* Duyckinck, E. A., *ed.* Salmagundi . . . New York, G. P. Putnam, 1860.
See Preface.

* — Washington Irving. (*In his* National portrait gallery of eminent Americans. New York, Johnson, Fry & co. [1862] v. 2, p. 99–109)

* — and Duyckinck, G. L. Washington Irving. (*In their* Cyclopædia of American literature . . . New York, Charles Scribner, 1855. v. 2, p. 47–59)

* Everett, A. H.   Alhambra.   (*In* North American review.   Boston, Gray and Bowen, 1832.   v. 35, p. 265–282)
  A review.
* — A history of the life and voyages of Christopher Columbus.   (*In* North American review.   Boston, Gray and Bowen, 1829.   v. 28, p. 103–134)
  A review.
* Everett, Edward.   Astoria.   (*In* North American review.   Boston, Gray and Bowen, 1837.   v. 44, p. 200–237)
  A review.
* — Bracebridge Hall.   (*In* North American review.   Boston, Gray and Bowen, 1822.   v. 15, p. 204–224)
  A review.
* — "Remarks of Mr. Everett."   (*In* Proceedings of the Massachusetts historical society, 1858–1860.   Boston, Printed for the Society, 1860.   1859, p. 395–403)
* — Sketch book.   (*In* North American review.   Boston, Gray and Bowen, 1819.   v. 9, p. 322–356)
  A review.
* — Tour on the prairies.   (*In* North American review.   Boston, Gray and Bowen, 1835.   v. 41, p. 1–28)
  A review.
* Felton, C. C.   "Remarks of Professor Felton."   (*In* Proceedings of the Massachusetts historical society, 1858–1860.   Boston, Printed for the Society, 1860.   1859, p. 408–418)
* Ferguson, J. de L.   American literature in Spain.   New York, Columbia university press, 1916.   p. 8–31.
* Fetterolf, A. H.   Washington Irving.   Philadelphia, J. B. Lippincott co., 1897.
  Gaedertz, K. T.   "Zu Washington Irvings Skizzenbuch," zur Kenntnis der altenglischen Bühne.   Bremen, 1888.
* Gay, S. H.   Irving the historian.   (*In* The Critic.   New York, 1883.   v. 3, p. 141–142)
* Goggio, Emilio.   Washington Irving and Italy.   (*In* Romanic review.   New York, Columbia university press, 1930.   v. 21, p. 26–33)
* — Washington Irving's works in Italy.   (*In* Romanic review.   New York, Columbia university press, 1931.   v. 22, p. 301–303)
* Goodrich, S. G.   Recollections of a lifetime . . .   New York and Auburn, Miller, Orton and Mulligan, 1857.   v. 2, p. 442.
* Gosse, E. W.   Irving's "Sketch-book."   (*In* The Critic.   New York, 1883.   v. 3, p. 140–141)
* Greene, G. W.   Biographical studies.   New York, G. P. Putnam, 1860.   p. 155–222.
* Greenlaw, Edwin.   Washington Irving's comedy of politics.   (*In* Texas review.   Austin, Texas, University of Texas, 1916.   v. 1, p. 291–306)

* — *ed.* Knickerbocker's History of New York (Books III–VII). Edited, with notes and an introduction by Edwin Greenlaw. New York, Macmillan co., 1919.
* Griswold, R. W. The prose writers of America . . . Philadelphia, Carey and Hart, 1847. p. 201–222.
* Grosskunz, R. Die Natur in den Werken und Briefen des amerikanischen Schriftstellers Washington Irving. Leipzig, 1902.
* Guerra, Angel. Literatos extranjeros, impresiones críticas. Valencia, F. Sempere y cᵃ editores [1903?] p. [61]–67.
* Gwathmey, E. M. John Pendleton Kennedy. New York, Thomas Nelson and sons, 1931. p. 91–92.
* Hastings, G. E. John Bull and his American descendants. (*In* American literature. Durham, N. C., Duke university press, 1929. v. 1, p. 40–68)
* Haweis, H. R. American humorists. New York, Funk and Wagnalls [1882?] p. 7–36.
* [Hazlitt, William] "Elia and Geoffrey Crayon." (*In his* The spirit of the age: or, Contemporary portraits. London, Henry Colburn, 1825. p. 395–407)
* Hellman, G. S. Irving's Washington and an episode in courtesy. (*In* The Colophon, a book collectors' quarterly. New York, 1930. Pt. 1, p. 53–60)
* — Journal of Washington Irving, 1823–1824. Edited by Stanley Williams. (*In* Modern language notes. Baltimore, Johns Hopkins press, 1932. v. 47, p. 326–328)
  A review.
* — Washington Irving esquire, ambassador at large from the New World to the Old. New York, A. A. Knopf, 1925.
* Hemstreet, Charles. Literary New York, its landmarks and associations. New York, G. P. Putnam's sons, 1903. p. 87–105.
* Herold, A. L. James Kirke Paulding, versatile American. New York, Columbia university press, 1926.
  See Index.
* Hill, D. J. Washington Irving. New York, Sheldon and co., 1879. (American authors [v. 1])
* Hodgkins, L. M. A guide to the study of nineteenth century authors. Boston, New York, and Chicago, D. C. Heath & co., 1889. Section "American authors," p. 1–6.
* Holmes, O. W. "Dr. Holmes's remarks." (*In* Proceedings of the Massachusetts historical society, 1858–1860. Boston, Printed for the Society, 1860. 1859, p. 418, 422)
* — Irving's power of idealization. (*In* The Critic. New York, 1883. v. 3, p. 138–139)
* Homes of American authors; comprising anecdotical, personal and descriptive sketches, by various writers . . . New-York, G. P. Putnam and co., 1853. p. 35–61.

* Hone, Philip. The diary of Philip Hone, 1828–1851. Editor: Allan
    Nevins. New York, Dodd, Mead and co., 1927.
    See Index.
* Howe, M. A. DeW. The life and letters of George Bancroft. New
    York, Charles Scribner's sons, 1908. v. 1, p. 101, 106–108, 109, 148;
    v. 2, p. 105.
* Howells, W. D. My literary passions. New York, Harper & brothers,
    1895. p. 28–33.
* Ingraham, C. A. Washington Irving, and other essays, biographical,
    historical and philosophical. Cambridge, New York, Published
    by the author, 1922.
* Irving, P. M. The life and letters of Washington Irving. New York,
    Putnam, 1862–64. 4 v.
* Irving memorial.
    Scrap-book, 366 p.
* Irvingiana: a memorial of Washington Irving . . . New York,
    C. B. Richardson, 1860.
    Compiled by E. A. Duyckinck.
* Jameson, J. F. The history of historical writing in America. Boston
    and New York, Houghton Mifflin and co., 1891. p. 97–98.
* Jeffrey, F. Bracebridge Hall. (*In* Edinburgh review. Edinburgh,
    A. Constable; New York, L. Scott, 1822. v. 37, p. 337–350)
    A review.
* — History of the life and voyages of Christopher Columbus. (*In*
    Edinburgh review. Edinburgh, A. Constable; New York, L. Scott,
    1828. v. 48, p. 1–32)
    A review.
* — Sketch book. (*In* Edinburgh review. Edinburgh, A. Constable;
    New York, L. Scott, 1820. v. 34, p. 160–176)
    A review.
* Knortz, Karl. Geschichte der nordamerikanischen Literatur. Berlin,
    Verlag von Hans Lüstenöder, 1891. v. 1, p. 146–167.
* — Washington Irving in Tarrytown. Ein Beitrag zur Geschichte
    der nordamerikanischen Literatur. Nürnberg, C. J. Koch, 1909.
* Künzig, Ferdinand. Washington Irving und seine Beziehungen
    zur englischen Literatur des 18. Jahrhunderts . . . Heidelberg,
    1911.
* Langfeld, W. R. Washington Irving. A bibliography compiled by
    William R. Langfeld, with the bibliographic assistance of Philip C.
    Blackburn. New York, The New York public library, 1933.
* Lanman, Charles. Haphazard personalities; chiefly of noted Amer-
    icans. Boston, Lea & Shepard; New York, Charles T. Dillingham,
    1886. p. 75–91.
* Lathrop, G. P. "Poe, Irving, Hawthorne." (*In* Scribner's monthly.
    An illustrated magazine for the public. New York, 1876. v. 11,
    p. 799–808)

* Laun, Adolf. Washington Irwing [*sic*]. Ein Lebens- und Charakter-bild . . . Berlin, R. Oppenheim, 1870. 2 v.
* Leslie, C. R. Autobiographical recollections . . . Boston, Ticknor and Fields, 1860.
* Lewisohn, Ludwig. Expression in America. New York and London, Harper & brothers, 1932. p. 32–48.
* . . . The Literature of American history, a bibliographical guide . . . Edited for the American library association by J. N. Larned. Boston, Published for the American library association by Hough-ton Mifflin & co., 1902.
   See Index.
* Livingston, L. S. The first books of some American authors. III. — Irving, Poe and Whitman. (*In* The Bookman. New York, Dodd, Mead and co., 1898. v. 8, p. 230–235)
* [Lockhart, J. G.] Memoirs of the life of Sir Walter Scott, bart. Edinburgh, Robert Cadell; London, John Murray and Whittaker and co., 1837. v. 4, p. 87–95.
* — On the writings of Charles Brockden Brown and Washington Irving. (*In* Blackwood's Edinburgh magazine. Edinburgh, William Blackwood, 1820. v. 6, p. 554–561)
* Long, S. V. Irving. (*In* Cambridge history of American literature. New York, G. P. Putnam's sons [1917] v. [1] p. 510–517)
   A bibliography.
* Longfellow, H. W. "Remarks of Mr. Longfellow." (*In* Proceedings of the Massachusetts historical society, 1858–1860. Boston, Printed for the Society, 1860. 1859, p. 393–395)
* López Núñez, Juan. Románticos y bohemios. Un hispanófilo ilustre. Madrid, Editorial ibero-americana, 1929. p. 121–124.
* Lowell, J. R. A fable for critics . . . New York, G. P. Putnam, 1848. p. 65.
* Mabie, H. W. The writers of Knickerbocker New York. [New York] The Grolier club, 1912.
* McDowell, G. T. General James Wilkinson in the Knickerbocker History of New York. (*In* Modern language notes. Baltimore, Johns Hopkins press, 1926. v. 41, p. 353–359)
* McGee, S. L. La littérature américaine dans La Revue des deux mondes (1831–1900). Montpellier, 1927. p. 11–13, and *passim*.
* Macy, John. The spirit of American literature. New York, Double-day, Page and co., 1913. p. 18–34.
* Mantz, H. E. French criticism of American literature before 1850. New York, Columbia university press, 1917.
   See Index.
* Mapes, E. S. Where Irving worked and wandered. (*In* The Critic. New York, 1902. v. 41, p. 329–332)
* Menéndez y Pelayo, Marcelino. De los historiadores de Colón. Es-tudios de crítica literaria, segunda serie. Madrid, 1895. p. 201–204.

* Miller, H. E.   In the Sleepy Hollow country.   (*In* New England magazine.   Boston, Mass., W. F. Kellogg, 1900.   New series, v. 23, p. 449–469)
* Mitchell, D. G.   American lands and letters, the Mayflower to Rip-Van-Winkle.   New York, C. Scribner's sons, 1897.   p. 300–330.
* — Bound together: a sheaf of papers.   New York, C. Scribner's sons, 1884.   p. 3–16.
* — Dream life: a fable of the seasons.   New York, C. Scribner's sons [1863]   A new preface, p. v–xiii.
* — [Washington Irving.]   (*In* Atlantic monthly.   Boston, Phillips, Sampson and co., 1864.   v. 13, p. 694–701)
* Moore, Thomas.   Memoirs, journal and correspondence of Thomas Moore.   Edited by Lord John Russell.   New York, 1857.   2 v. *See* Index.
* Morris, G. D.   Washington Irving's fiction in the light of French criticism . . .   (Indiana university studies.   Bloomington, Ind., Indiana university, 1916.   v. 3.   Study no. 30)
* [Neal, John]   [Criticism of Irving.]   (*In* Blackwood's Edinburgh magazine.   Edinburgh, William Blackwood, 1825.   v. 17, p. 58–67) American writers, no. 4.
* — Randolph, a novel.   [n.p., 1823]   v. 1, p. 137–138.
* New York public library.   The Hellman collection of Irvingiana.   A catalogue of manuscripts and other material by or about Washington Irving given to the New York public library by Mr. George S. Hellman, by R. W. G. Vail.   New York, 1929. "Reprinted from the Bulletin of the New York public library of April, 1929."
* — The Seligman collection of Irvingiana.   A catalogue of manuscripts and other material by or about Washington Irving given to the New York public library by Mrs. Isaac N. Seligman and Mr. George S. Hellman.   New York, 1926. "Reprinted from the Bulletin of the New York public library of February, 1926."
* — The Washington Irving collection formed by Isaac N. Seligman.   By George S. Hellman.   (*In* Bulletin of the New York public library.   New York, 1920.   v. 24, p. 275–279)
* Parrington, V. L.   The romantic revolution in America 1800–1860.   (*In his* Main currents in American thought.   New York, Harcourt, Brace and co., 1927.   v. 2, p. 203–221)
* Pattee, F. L.   The development of the American short story, an historical survey.   New York, Harper and brothers, 1923.   p. 1–26.
* Payne, W. M.   Leading American essayists . . .   New York, Henry Holt and co., 1910.   p. 43–104.   (Biographies of leading Americans)
* Pemberton, T. E.   Washington Irving in England.   (*In* Munsey's magazine.   New York, F. A. Munsey co., 1904.   v. 30, p. 552–558)
* Plath, Otto.   Washington Irvings Einfluss auf Wilhelm Hauff.   (*In*

Euphorion, Zeitschrift für Literaturgeschichte hrsg. von J. Nadler und August Sauer. Leipzig und Wien, C. Fromme, 1913. Bd. 20, p. 459–471)

* Pochmann, H. A. Irving's German sources in The sketch book. (*In* Studies in philology. Chapel Hill, North Carolina, University of North Carolina press, 1930. v. 27, p. 477–507)

* — Irving's German tour and its influence on his tales. (*In* Publications of the Modern language association of America. Menasha, Wisconsin, 1930. v. 45, p. 1150–1187)

* — *ed.* Representative selections . . . with introduction, bibliography, and notes . . . New York, American book co., 1934.

* — — New York [etc.] American book co. [c 1934]

* Poe, E. A. Astoria. (*In* Southern literary messenger. Richmond, T. W. White, 1837. v. 3, p. 59–68)
A review.

* — Biography and poetical remains of Margaret Miller Davidson. (*In* Graham's magazine. Philadelphia, G. R. Graham, 1841. v. 19, p. 93–94)
A review.

* Prescott, W. H. Biographical and critical miscellanies. New edition. Boston, Phillips, Sampson and co., 1855. p. 88–122.

* — A chronicle of the conquest of Granada. By Fray Antonio Agapida. (*In* North American review. Boston, Gray and Bowen, 1829. v. 29, p. 293–314)
A review.

* Preston, W. C. The reminiscences of William C. Preston, edited by M. C. Yarborough. Chapel Hill, University of North Carolina press, 1933.

* Pröhle, Heinrich. Heinrich Heine und der Harz. Harzburg, Eigentum und Verlag von C. R. Stolle's Hofbuchhandlung, 1888.

* Putnam, G. H. Irving. (*In* The Cambridge history of American literature. New York, G. P. Putnam's sons, 1927. v. [1] p. 245–259)

* Putnam, G. P. Memories of distinguished authors. Washington Irving. (*In* Harper's weekly. Supplement. New York, 1871. v. 15, p. 492–496)

* — Recollections of Irving. By his publisher. (*In* Atlantic monthly. Boston, Phillips, Sampson and co., 1860. v. 6, p. 601–612)

* Quérard, J. M. La France littéraire; ou, Dictionnaire bibliographique . . . Paris, 1830. v. 4, p. 182.

* Randolph, A. D. F. Leaves from the journal of Frederick S. Cozzens. (*In* Lippincott's monthly magazine. Philadelphia, 1890. v. 45, p. 739–748)

* Reichart, W. A. Washington Irving, the Fosters, and the Forsters. (*In* Modern language notes. Baltimore, Johns Hopkins press, 1935. v. 14, p. 35–39)

* [Richards, T. A.] Sunnyside, the home of Washington Irving. (*In* Harper's monthly magazine. New York, 1856. v. 14, p. 1–21)

* [Ripley, G.] Washington Irving. (*In* Harper's monthly magazine. New York, 1851. v. 2, p. 577–580)

* Russell, J. A. Irving: recorder of Indian life. (*In* Journal of American history. New York, National historical society, 1932. v. 25, p. 185–195)

* Sanford, O. M. "An Irving centennial fifty years ago." (*In* Americana. New York, National Americana society, 1933. v. 27, p. 456–461)

* Saunders, Frederick. Character studies, with some personal recollections . . . New York, T. Whittaker, 1894. p. [63]–110.

* Schalck de la Faverie, A. Les premiers interprètes de la pensée américaine. Essai d'histoire et de littérature sur l'évolution du puritanisme aux États-Unis. Paris, 1909. p. 201–218.

* [Sedgwick, A. G.] Washington Irving. (*In* The Nation. New York, Evening post publishing co., 1883. v. 36, p. 291–292)

* Small, M. R. A possible ancestor of Diedrich Knickerbocker. (*In* American literature. Durham, N. C., Duke university press, 1930. v. 2, p. 21–24)

* Spiller, R. E. The American in England during the first half century of independence. New York, Henry Holt and co. [c 1926] *See* Index.

Sprenger, R. Über die Quelle von Washington Irvings Rip Van Winkle. Northeim, 1901.

* Stoddard, R. H. The life of Washington Irving. New York, J. B. Alden, 1883.

* Taylor, J. F. Washington Irving's Mexico; a lost fragment. (*In* The Bookman. New York, Dodd, Mead and co., 1915. v. 41, p. 665–669)

* Thackeray, W. M. Nil nisi bonum. (*In his* Roundabout papers. London, Smith, Elder and co., 1863. p. 339–352. Reprinted from The Cornhill magazine.

* Thoburn, J. B. Centennial of the Tour on the prairies by Washington Irving (1832–1932). (*In* Chronicles of Oklahoma. Oklahoma city, Oklahoma historical society, 1932. v. 10, p. [426]–437)

* Thompson, J. B. The genesis of the Rip Van Winkle legend. (*In* Harper's monthly magazine. New York, 1883. v. 67, p. 617–622)

* Tilton, Theodore. Half an hour at Sunnyside. A visit to Washington Irving. (*In* The Independent. New York, Independent corporation, 1859. v. 11, p. 1)

* Trent, W. P., *ed*. Notes and journal of travel in Europe 1804–1805 . . . New York, The Grolier club, 1921. 3 v. *See* Introduction.

* Tuckerman, H. T. Washington Irving. (*In* Hubbard, E. Little journeys to the homes of American authors. New York and London, G. P. Putnam's sons, 1896. p. [263]–296)

Underwood, F. H. Washington Irving. Philadelphia, J. B. Lippincott co., 1890.

* Vail, E. A. De la littérature et des hommes de lettres des États-Unis d'Amérique. Paris, Librairie de Charles Gosselin, 1841.
  See Table des matières.

* Vincent, L. H. Life, character and work of Washington Irving. (*In* American literary masters. Boston and New York, Houghton Mifflin and co., 1906)

* Wadepuhl, Walter. Amerika, du hast es besser. (*In* Germanic review. New York city, Columbia university press, 1932. v. 7, p. 186–191)

* Waldron, W. W. Washington Irving and cotemporaries, in thirty life sketches, edited by William Watson Waldron . . . Introduction by Rev. Theodore Irving, LL.D., nephew of Irving . . . New York, W. H. Kelley & co. [1867]

* Wallace, H. B. Literary criticisms and other papers. Philadelphia, Parry and McMillan, 1856. p. 67–91.

* Warner, C. D. Irving's humor. (*In* The Critic. New York, 1883. v. 3, p. 139)

* — Washington Irving. (*In* Atlantic monthly. Boston, Phillips, Sampson and co., 1880. v. 45, p. 396–408)

* — Washington Irving. Boston, Houghton Mifflin and co., 1881.

* — Washington Irving. (*In* The Critic. New York, 1893. v. 22, p. 220–221)

* Webster, C. M. Irving's expurgation of the 1809 History of New York. (*In* American literature. Durham, N. C., Duke university press, 1932. v. 4, p. 293–295)

* Wendell, B. A literary history of America. New York, Charles Scribner's sons, 1900. p. 169–180.

* Whipple, E. P. American literature and other papers, with introductory note by John Greenleaf Whittier. Boston, Ticknor and co., 1887. p. 42–45.

* Williams, S. T. Authorship in Irving's day. (*In* Saturday review of literature. New York, Time inc., 1934. v. 11, p. 400)

* — and McDowell, Tremaine, *eds.* Diedrich Knickerbocker's A history of New York . . . New York, Harcourt, Brace and co. [1927]
  See Introduction and Select reading list.

* — The first version of the writings of Washington Irving in Spanish. (*In* Modern philology. Chicago, University of Chicago press, 1930. v. 28, p. 185–201)

* — *ed.* Notes while preparing Sketch book, &c. 1817 . . . New Haven, Yale university press, 1927.
  See Introduction.

* — Peter Irving. (*In* Dictionary of American biography. New York, Charles Scribner's sons, 1932. v. 9, p. 503–504)

* — and E. E. Leisy, *eds.* Polly Holman's wedding. Notes by Wash-

ington Irving. (*In* Southwest review. Dallas, Texas, Southern Methodist university, 1934. v. 19, p. 449–454)
See Introduction.

* — and Hespelt, E. H. Two unpublished anecdotes by Fernán Caballero preserved by Washington Irving. (*In* Modern language notes. Baltimore, Johns Hopkins press, 1934. v. 49, p. 25–31)

* — Washington Irving. (*In* Dictionary of American biography. New York, Charles Scribner's sons, 1932. v. 9, p. 505–511)

* — Washington Irving: a bibliography. (*In* American literature. Durham, North Carolina, Duke university press, 1934. v. 6, p. 361–364)
A review.

* — Washington Irving and Fernán Caballero. (*In* Journal of English and Germanic philology. Urbana, Illinois, 1930. v. 29, p. 352–366)

* — Washington Irving and Matilda Hoffman . . . [Baltimore, 1926] "Reprinted from American speech, v. 1, 1926," p. 463–469.

* — Washington Irving, Matilda Hoffman, and Emily Foster. (*In* Modern language notes. Baltimore, Johns Hopkins press, 1933. v. 48, p. 182–186)

* — Washington Irving's first stay in Paris. (*In* American literature. Durham, N. C., Duke university press, 1930. v. 2, p. [15]–20)

* — and Hespelt, E. H. Washington Irving's notes on Fernán Caballero's stories. (*In* Publications of the Modern language association of America. Menasha, Wisconsin, 1934. v. 49, p. 1129–1139)

* — Washington Irving's religion. (*In* Yale review. New Haven, Conn., Yale university press, 1926. v. 15, p. 414–416)

* — *ed.* Tour in Scotland, 1817, and other manuscript notes . . . New Haven, Yale university press, 1927.
See Introduction.

* — William Irving. (*In* Dictionary of American biography. New York, Charles Scribner's sons, 1932. v. 9, p. 511–512)

* Wilson, J. G. The life and letters of Fitz-Greene Halleck . . . New York, D. Appleton and co., 1869.
See Index.

* Wise, Daniel. Washington Irving. New York, Phillips & Hunt, 1883. (Home college series, no. 8)

* Zeydel, E. H. Washington Irving and Ludwig Tieck. (*In* Publications of the Modern language association of America. Menasha, Wisconsin, 1931. v. 46, p. 946–947)

TITLE INDEX

of Irving's Works

DATE D